All Our Own Work

All Our Own Work

**The co-operative pioneers
of Hebden Bridge
and their mill**

ANDREW BIBBY

MERLIN PRESS

Published in 2015 by
The Merlin Press Ltd
99b Wallis Road
London
E9 5LN

www.merlinpress.co.uk

© Andrew Bibby, 2015

ISBN. 978-0-85036-710-2

Front cover illustration courtesy of Hebden Bridge Alternative Technology Centre/Mike Barrett

Catalogue in publication data is available from the British Library

The right of Andrew Bibby to be identified as author of this work has been asserted in accordance with the Copyright, Designs and Patents Act 1988.

All rights reserved. No part of this publication may be reproduced, stored in a retrieval system, or transmitted, in any form or by any means, electronic, mechanical, photocopying, recording or otherwise, without the prior permission of the publisher.

Printed in the UK by Imprint Digital, Exeter

CONTENTS

Introduction: A coming of age	1
Chapter 1: Origins	11
Chapter 2: Building the business	26
Chapter 3: Sharing the profits	34
Chapter 4: Governance	48
Chapter 5: Local and national	59
Chapter 6: The women at the Nutclough	73
Chapter 7: Oxford University	83
Chapter 8: Co-partnership	101
Chapter 9: Capital and labour	118
Chapter 10: International co-operation	128
Chapter 11: Working lives	137
Chapter 12: Into the twentieth century	150
Chapter 13: A time of change	166
Chapter 14: Takeover	179
Chapter 15: Conclusions	188
Author's afterword	197
Bibliography and sources	200
Notes	212
Index	232

INTRODUCTION: A COMING OF AGE

It was, according to the local paper, the most keenly awaited event in Hebden Bridge for years. Considerable efforts had been taken to ensure that the twenty-first birthday – the coming of age – of one of the town's most significant businesses would be celebrated in style. The event, held on Saturday 26 September 1891 in the recently extended Co-operative Hall in the centre of Hebden Bridge, commenced in fine fashion with a banquet for about eighty guests who tucked in to, among other things, roast beef, roast lamb, ham and tongue, chickens (boiled or roasted), roast ducks, pigeon pies, grouse, partridge and lobster salad. The sweets included damson and apple tarts, wine jelly and 'pineapple cream', and there was cheese to round things off. Victorians knew how to celebrate anniversaries.[1]

The local business whose continuing success would be formally toasted at the end of the meal was by 1891 employing 280 local people in the weaving and dyeing of fustian cloth and the making up of that cloth into ready-made clothing: the firm advertised a range of corduroy, moleskin, velveteen and twill clothes in a wide variety of colours which it sold across Britain. Hebden Bridge by the late nineteenth century was the centre of fustian trade, the town affectionately known by some as 'fustianopolis'. Fustian, a hard-wearing material made from cotton, was much in demand for day-to-day wear and, particularly, for workwear. Miners in south Wales, shipyard workers on the Clyde and agricultural labourers across Britain were among those who would go to work with clothes manufactured in this small Pennine mill town in the upper Calder valley, eight miles or so west of Halifax. Fustian was at that time what denim would become during the twentieth century.

The business had overcome early difficulties to become a stable and profitable concern. By its twenty-first year of operation it had built up an annual turnover of around £40,000, with net profits each year representing about 9 per cent or 10 per cent of sales: the profit in 1891 was a little over £3,700. Its manager Joseph Greenwood, the man who more than anyone else had been responsible for its development, could afford to look back on a successful venture: despite a number of difficult years, the business had been profitable every single year it had traded, had been able to reward its investors with a good return on their investment and had also built up a significant reserve fund.[2]

But these were, for Joseph Greenwood, not really the main reasons for satisfaction. The business he led, the Hebden Bridge Fustian Manufacturing Co-operative Society Ltd, was an attempt to demonstrate that working people could unite to make their own work and could successfully run their own enterprise. Central to Greenwood's approach was his belief that, by working co-operatively, workers could enjoy the fruits of their own labour, in doing so improving their living standards and conditions. He called it 'self-employment'. A fundamental part of his approach was the principle that at least some of the profit generated by the business should go back to the workers themselves. By 1891 the Fustian Society's male and female employees had already benefited considerably from this so-called 'bonus to labour'.[3]

'This must be one of the happiest moments in your life,' one of the guests had whispered to Greenwood during the evening meeting which rounded off the day's celebrations (the banquet itself had been just the start; there had also been a conference of around 400 co-operative movement representatives during the afternoon). Greenwood admitted that it was, but he went out of his way when he addressed the gathering a short time later to credit the success of the co-operative to 'united efforts all round'. He believed, he went on, that 'they were as a light set upon a hill, a light which would shine and have its influence on men who were now down in the gutter'. To those who wanted to rise to a higher social life the co-operative would be a means of encouragement. The aim was simple: 'to lift them to that higher standard which they were trying to accomplish for each and every one of them'.

They did not want life to be full of drudgery and ceaseless toil with perhaps nothing but the prospect of the workhouse in front of them, he added. No, they were determined 'to lay hold of these industrial operations and use them for themselves, that the whole of the social and higher walks of life might be theirs as well as those who had been in more fortunate positions'. This was what they were working for, he said – and this was an object, he concluded with passion, that they would accomplish.[4]

He was right to suggest that the fustian co-operative in Hebden Bridge had become a beacon for others. After more than twenty years of operation, it had become very well-known nationally in co-operative circles as an exemplar of co-operatively-run manufacturing – in fact, as *the* example generally referred to first when co-operative production was being discussed. 'For a co-operator not to know Hebden Bridge is to argue himself unknown,' had said one contributor a few years earlier in the movement's weekly newspaper *Co-operative News*.[5]

As a consequence, a string of guests had over the years begun to find their way to the co-operative's Nutclough Mill in Hebden Bridge, where Joseph Greenwood would lay on a tour of the works whilst taking time to expound his philosophy of co-operative production. Some of the visitors to the mill had been eminent. They included Thomas Hughes, best remembered today as the author of *Tom Brown's Schooldays* but throughout his life an active supporter of the co-operative movement. The future Archbishop of Canterbury Cosmo Gordon Lang had been to Hebden Bridge too (he was to reminisce later of his happy visits to 'the heroic little company which was for so many years a witness to all that was truest and best in co-operation'[6]). Beatrice Potter the future Fabian had also made the trip to Hebden Bridge shortly before her marriage to Sidney Webb, and there were many others like her who wanted to see the Nutclough works for themselves. Later there would be international visitors too, including a whole trainload of delegates from the International Co-operative Alliance congress in Manchester in 1902.

The role which the Hebden Bridge fustian co-operative played within the wider co-operative movement was reflected in the guest list for the coming-of-age celebration, which included many of the key figures of that period. George Jacob Holyoake, by then in his mid-seventies, had made the journey from his home in Brighton to West Yorkshire. Holyoake, who had once claimed to have been advocating co-operation for as long as Queen Victoria had been monarch (her reign had started 54 years earlier, in 1837), was by this stage of his life increasingly taking on the mantle of the 'grand old man' of the movement. Born in Birmingham the second child of a printer and a button maker, he had begun his working life in a foundry but in his twenties had become a lecturer and propagandist for the early Owenite co-operative movement. The last person in Britain to be imprisoned for blasphemy (sentenced in 1842 for six months following a flippant remark about religion he had made at a public meeting in Cheltenham), he later was to promote his views in favour of secularism through his influential magazine *The Reasoner*. His significant contribution to the co-operative cause was remembered after his death in 1906 by his name being given to the new headquarters building for the Co-operative Union, opened in Manchester in 1911; Holyoake House remains today the central offices of the Co-operative Union's successor organisation, Co-operatives UK.

George Jacob Holyoake began his speech in Hebden Bridge that day by expressing his delight at being there with those he called the 'Nutclough Pioneers'. It was a compliment which his audience would have well understood. The Rochdale Equitable Pioneers, who had started their small co-operative grocery shop in Toad Lane in Rochdale in 1844, had taken on an almost legendary status in co-operative circles, a status they still hold today both in Britain and worldwide. The reputation of the Rochdale Pioneers had been established partly by their signal achievement in developing a very successful co-operatively run venture but also to a considerable extent thanks to Holyoake himself, whose 1857 popular account of the Rochdale story *Self-help by the People* had gone through several editions and into several languages. Now here was Holyoake himself, standing up in the Hebden Bridge Co-operative Hall and suggesting that the town's fustian co-operative had a similar pioneering status in relation to co-operative manufacturing as Rochdale had for retail distribution.[7]

Another major figure in the nineteenth century co-operative movement, Edward Vansittart Neale, was there that day too. Neale, born seven years before Holyoake in 1810, had committed much of his adult life to labouring for the co-operative cause. His social background was very different from Holyoake's. He came from a privileged background, having been born in the Royal Crescent in Bath. A nephew of William Wilberforce, he had studied classics at Oxford and then become a barrister at Lincoln's Inn. He was profoundly influenced by the progressive Christian message of social reform preached by Rev F.D. Maurice in the 1838 book *The Kingdom of Christ* and with Maurice, Charles Kingsley (the author of *The Water Babies, Alton Locke*, and other novels with a strong social reforming theme) and others became an active member of the Christian Socialist movement. Thomas Hughes was an active member, too. A world away in class terms from the Rochdale Pioneers and separated geographically too by the distance between London and Lancashire, the Christian Socialists nevertheless played a distinctive role in the founding of modern British co-operation.

The Christian Socialists were particularly influenced by the co-operative workshops which had sprung up in Paris immediately after the 1848 revolution, and by founding the Society for Promoting Working Men's Associations they tried in the few short years from 1848 to about 1854 to replicate the idea in Britain. Co-operative production, they felt, was a more enlightened alternative to the degradation of the conventional factory system. It could bring harmony to a society riven by class strife.

Neale was particularly inspired by the possibility which co-operation could offer and used his personal wealth both to launch a Central Co-operative Agency, an attempt at an ambitious wholesaling centre for the whole country, and to invest in workmen's co-operative societies. Tens of thousands of pounds of his money at that time went with enthusiastic if reckless abandon into top-down attempts to create new artisan co-operative ventures, none of which succeeded.

Neale had not been disheartened, however, and his major contribution to co-operation had still been to come. From 1873 he had been the tireless servant of the British co-operative movement as the Co-operative Union's General Secretary. Just ten days before the Hebden Bridge celebrations, aged 81, he had finally given up this post, to be followed as the Co-operative Union's General Secretary by J.C. (Jesse) Gray, a former employee of the Nutclough co-operative (and as such most definitely on the guest list for the coming-of-age celebrations). Neale was finally able to leave his Manchester lodging house behind and live full time in the exquisite Bisham Abbey estate on the Thames which he had inherited six years earlier. Neale's death was to come a year later. Although it was Holyoake whose name was to be enshrined in a national co-operative building, Neale has his own legacy in Hebden Bridge: the town still has, in Neale Street, the street of houses erected shortly afterwards by the local co-operative store and named in his memory.[8]

George Robinson, the Marquess of Ripon, was at the Co-operative Hall as well. Ripon could easily trump Neale's place of birth: he had the highly unusual distinction of having been born in 10 Downing Street, during the time his father Viscount Goderich had briefly held the post of prime minister. He was another perhaps unlikely supporter of co-operation, having witnessed at first hand as a young man the *associations ouvrières* set up by workmen in Paris. He too had been associated with the Christian Socialists. A radically minded cabinet minister under Palmerston, Russell and Gladstone, he had first been invited to Hebden Bridge four years earlier to take the role in the naming of the Nutclough Mill's new engine. At that time he was back in Britain after returning from a five year stint as Viceroy of India.

'I think our gathering today is full of hope,' Ripon told his audience at the coming-of-age event. He added that the Hebden Bridge fustian society's success was particularly welcome, because – in contrast to co-operative distribution of the form epitomised by the Rochdale Pioneers – co-operative manufacturing had not proved quite such a straightforward proposition. 'We all know that there have been in the past history of co-operative production in this country too many examples of associations established under apparently fortunate circumstances and surrounded by great hopes, which have one by one, from one cause or another, been doomed to failure,' he said.[9]

Not all the guests that day were from the political elite. There were representatives of other manufacturing co-operatives, fellow strivers with Joseph Greenwood in the task of building a successful movement of productive co-operatives. Charles Shufflebotham, from the Coventry Watchmakers' Co-operative society, had made the journey to Hebden Bridge, for example. Then there was George Thomson, across from Huddersfield. Thomson was something different again. He had taken over his family's textile business at Woodhouse Mills in the town and, inspired by the writings of John Ruskin, had decided to convert his company into an employee-owned business. (It might be added that this was more than forty years before John Spedan Lewis was to do something similar with his London department store.)

There was also a leading member of the Rochdale Equitable Pioneers co-operative present. Abraham Greenwood had joined the society in 1846 two years after its start and had therefore just missed out on being one of the original 'pioneers'. He had nevertheless gone on to play an extremely important role in the wider co-operative movement, particularly in relation to the development of the Co-operative Wholesale Society (CWS) which he chaired from its founding in 1863 until 1870. He then became directly engaged in the CWS's banking operations (later to develop into the Co-operative Bank), and was also instrumental in the founding of the Co-operative Insurance Company. Abraham did not only share a surname with Joseph Greenwood, he also shared a long history of practical engagement in co-operative endeavour in the north of England. He knew Joseph Greenwood well, not just from the annual Co-operative Congresses and the round of regional events they had both attended, but also from their joint membership for many years of the Central Board of the Co-operative Union, the committee which was elected each year to oversee the movement.

Despite his considerable achievements, Abraham Greenwood was known by fellow co-operators to be somewhat retiring and not a particularly powerful speaker.[10] Perhaps that is why his speech at the Nutclough celebrations was short and – if the contemporary report is to be believed – not quite as lavish in its praises as many of the others.[11] There could however have been another reason. The problem was that, just as Joseph Greenwood had become well-known for representing the productive side of the co-operative movement so Abraham Greenwood had become equally associated with what the CWS had achieved. As such, therefore, they found themselves representing opposite sides of what, by the 1890s, had developed into a major fracture in the British co-operative movement.

Much the most dominant part of the movement comprised the distributive co-operative societies, the locally based retail stores, of which by 1891 there were over 1,300 with between them over a million members. The other arm of the movement, the grouping of productive co-operative societies exemplified by the Hebden Bridge Fustian Society, was by comparison a very much smaller affair. The whole idea of co-operative production was more problematic, too, as the Marquess of Ripon had suggested: whilst it had proved relatively easy to establish commercially successful distributive societies, there was a long list of unsuccessful forays into productive ventures which had gone under, carrying with them both high hopes and co-operative societies' investment capital.

This division into two distinct arms had not been the original intention. Co-operative societies formed at around the same period as the Rochdale society as well as those formed earlier (for, contrary to popular opinion, Rochdale was by no means the first co-operative venture in Britain) had generally much broader ambitions than just running grocery shops. In Rochdale itself, the aims set down in the 1844 rules included not only 'the establishment of a Store for the sale of provisions, clothing &c' but also 'the manufacture of such articles as the Society may determine upon, for the employment of such members as may be without employment'. It might be added that house building was a further aim, and there was also the expressed hope of eventually being able to 'establish a self-supporting home colony of united interests'.[12]

But early dreams of broader co-operative communities of this type rapidly faded, particularly after the working-class political activity associated with the Chartist movement ebbed away after 1848. Much to the chagrin of more committed co-operators, the reality by the later nineteenth century was that many members of local co-operative stores were signing up simply to benefit from the dividend. Neale had talked of 'the unbounded reverence' felt by the members of each society for 'the goddess Divi' when he had railed against this tendency in a speech at a Co-operative Congress a few years earlier.[13]

Neale, Holyoake and Joseph Greenwood were among those who felt that productive co-operatives were helping to keep alive the original idealism of the movement. J.C. Gray, the Co-operative Union's new General Secretary, had expressed this same view, too. Ten years earlier, when still working at the Nutclough Mill in Hebden Bridge, he had written: 'In our opinion co-operation has other ends in view, and the means gained by distribution ought to be used as a stepping-stone to something higher and nobler; that is the raising of the masses of the people from a state of low, grovelling dependence on the capitalist, by showing them that there is a power within themselves, that of labour, without which power no capital could earn any dividend... The aim of all co-operators ought not to be simply the accumulation of dividend, but it should go still further and enable the workers to become their own employers.'[14]

J.C. Gray's views were not shared by all. By 1891 there were two quite distinct ways that manufacturing was being carried out co-operatively, mirroring the two arms of the movement. On the one hand, there were small independent productive co-operatives, like the venture in Hebden Bridge. But there were also factories turning out biscuits, and soap, and boots and shoes, and chocolate confectionery and other necessities of everyday life, and these were being run by the Co-operative Wholesale Society and its Scottish sister organisation. (To be accurate, we should add that there was a third way that production was being carried out by co-operatives: a number of independent distributive societies, particularly the larger ones, undertook productive activities directly).

The CWS (the 'Wholesale') was the great commercial achievement of the English co-operative movement. Created in 1863 initially as a wholesale supplier of stock for independent societies predominantly in Lancashire and Yorkshire, it began its move into manufacturing in the early 1870s. It developed a banking operation at the same time and rapidly built up what became a great business empire, one of the most important in Victorian Britain. By 1891 its net sales were £7.42m. It had in place by then a worldwide supply chain network with offices in, among other places, New York, Copenhagen and Hamburg. It ran its own steamships. It was a highly successful version of what today would be called a multinational enterprise.

The CWS was a federal creation of the distributive co-operative sector, co-owned by independent co-operative societies who held its shares and who shared the profit dividend it paid. The CWS was in this sense rooted at the heart of the movement. The CWS chose, however, to run its own factories on conventional lines. It did not (at least not after very short early experimentation) give its own employees any share of the profits it generated, over and above their wages. Unlike the Hebden Bridge fustian society, it did not pay a 'bonus to labour'.

The arguments about profit-sharing and bonus to labour rumbled around the British co-operative movement for years like a thunderstorm which refused to go away. The issues were already well-aired when the Hebden Bridge fustian co-operative started in 1870 and as we shall see they were still being argued back and forth at the start of the twentieth century. On one side were those who saw profit-sharing as a touchstone for genuine co-operative principles – a representation of the ideals that those early pioneers had had to struggle so hard to try to bring about. Leading the attack from the other side were several of the key figures in the CWS, intent with getting on with the job of building a successful co-operative business which would share profits not with a few fortunate employees but with all its member societies. Both sides had cases to make and arguments to put forward. By the early 1890s, however, the tone of the debate had became increasingly bitter, even on occasions vitriolic. The Hebden Bridge Fustian Manufacturing Co-operative Society, as a high-profile successful productive co-operative which most definitely did pay a bonus to labour, found itself, like it or not, at the very vortex of all this turbulence.

This study will follow the story of the Hebden Bridge fustian society from its start-up in 1870 through to 1918. It is perhaps remarkable to have to make the point that this is the first significant history looking at the British productive co-operative movement to appear for more than a century. For much of the twentieth century, the story of the co-operative movement in Britain became effectively the story only of the retail and wholesale co-operative societies. Productive co-operatives continued to exist, employ people and make profits, but almost completely out of sight.

So why is a history of a business which manufactured fustian, a cloth whose name these days may well cause people to have to consult their dictionaries, of any interest today? In purely local terms, the story of the mill run by its workers is clearly of direct relevance in the development of Hebden Bridge. Hebden Bridge has in recent decades transformed itself from the mill town it once was into a singular place with a strong sense of community coloured by something of an alternative streak, described by one recent commentator as 'an active, creative, argumentative place'.[15] Its co-operative history remains there as a half-remembered story from the past, though often this story is told wrongly. Two recent local books, for example, both state that the fustian co-operative failed after the First World War and was rescued from liquidation by the CWS.[16] The story, as we shall see, is different: the co-operative made profits (during the First World War almost embarrassingly large profits) right through to 1918 when it did indeed pass – controversially – into the ownership of the CWS. However this was not a failed business: the price paid by the CWS for the acquisition meant that the fustian society's member-shareholders enjoyed a very healthy return for each pound share they held. Thereafter, the CWS continued with production in the town until the late 1960s. One way or another, co-operative production was an important element in Hebden Bridge's local economy for almost exactly a hundred years.

But this book will argue that there is a wider case for recounting the history of the fustian co-operative. Firstly, the Nutclough Mill contributed a number of key figures to the English co-operative movement. Joseph

Greenwood took an active role in the Co-operative Union, the Co-operative Productive Federation and also, in its early years, the International Co-operative Alliance, now the global voice for the whole worldwide co-operative movement. J.C. Gray, as already mentioned, learned his co-operative principles in Hebden Bridge before taking up the leadership of the national movement. And there are other figures we shall meet in this story who have a place in national, rather than simply local, history: Robert Halstead, for example, was the four-loom weaver at the Nutclough Mill who went on to become a powerful advocate of working-class university education and who played an important role in the establishment of the Workers' Educational Association.

Hebden Bridge also has its place in broader co-operative history as the town with the first branch of the Women's Co-operative Guild, the branch having been set up in 1883 almost as soon as the Guild was established nationally. The fact that this was a town with a strong productive co-operative mill which employed many local women is not coincidental.

The terminology has changed – what Joseph Greenwood and his colleagues knew as productive co-operatives are today more generally described as workers' co-operatives (or, particularly abroad, as worker co-operatives). But at a time today when the British co-operative movement is exploring its future role and relevance it is valuable to be reminded of those early experiments in co-operative business which did not follow the usual route of the locally based grocery store.

More broadly, the debates today about whether business models can be found to provide an alternative to rampant shareholder capitalism echo many of those held in the nineteenth century. The dilemmas and uncertainties which these debates throw up are exactly those which were wrestled with by Joseph Greenwood and his fellow workers in Hebden Bridge. How do you build a business with different business ethics which can nevertheless survive in a hostile competitive world? How do you find the capital you need, and what is a fair reward for investors? What compromises must be made to be profitable? What responsibilities do businesses have to their communities? Is employee participation simply a sop?

And perhaps a more general question: how can work lives be made more enriched and fulfilling for all?

Joseph Greenwood and those who built the Hebden Bridge Fustian Manufacturing Co-operative Society did not necessarily have better answers to these questions than we might have today. But their experiences did mean they had to confront the issues. This is why their history is worth telling.

CHAPTER 1

ORIGINS

The story of the creation of the Hebden Bridge Fustian Manufacturing Co-operative Society begins with a death.

This is how Joseph Greenwood himself told the story later:

> At the particular factory where we were working it was the custom for each to carry his own piece of cloth, 80 to 100 lbs weight, from one part of the works to another, about a quarter of a mile away. One of the cutters was an old man, not well able to carry his piece of cloth, and we had usually done this for him; but, on this occasion, a difference took place between two persons as to who was to do this, and, during the dispute the old man went off for his load of work. After he had brought it in, he sat down, overcome by fatigue, and died of exhaustion.
>
> Death at all times has its terrors, but when it is brought about through want and the necessity to work for daily bread at an advanced age, as in this case, it is a hard fate. It is a disgrace to society when the old and infirm cannot have means to live in comfort after a life spent in toil.[17]

Although he was not named by Greenwood, the 'old man' who died was an Irishman called Daniel Killeen.[18] His death occurred at the Midgehole mill complex, just to the north of Hebden Bridge, where cotton dyeing and finishing was undertaken by the firm of Worrals, and the date of his death was Tuesday 21 June 1870.[19]

As Greenwood went on to explain in his accounts of the story, the man had a wife but no children, and there was the funeral to consider: 'We were under the necessity of making a subscription to pay the funeral expenses, and after the funeral was over we began to talk about forming a sort of friendly society to meet circumstances of this kind'. But from this start, under Greenwood's prompting, the thinking quickly developed: perhaps the burial society could be turned instead into a co-operative society, one which actually employed the members? 'There is one advantage of adversity

– it brings its sufferers closer together; and to us workmen the opportunity seemed admirably fitted to determine us to stick better together for a start in co-operative work,' Greenwood explained.[20]

The story of the elderly Irishman's death is a moving one and Greenwood recognised its power. He regularly retold the tale when he was asked later on to describe how the fustian society had come about. He recounted it, for example, to the members of the Royal Commission on Labour, in Westminster Hall in October 1892, when he was called to give evidence before them on behalf of the co-operative movement.[21] We know that he certainly used the same story when visitors were being shown round the Nutclough Mill.[22] Greenwood believed Killeen to be over seventy (in reality he was probably in his early or mid-sixties, perhaps 64)[23] and Greenwood also offers the intriguing suggestion that Killeen had been a eye-witness at the Peterloo massacre in St Peter's Fields, Manchester in 1819, something which certainly adds to the attractiveness of the story but which has to be considered improbable.

But this is beside the point. Greenwood described Daniel Killeen's death at work not just because it was a convenient starting point for an account of the co-operative's development but because it was for him a symbol of everything that was cruel and inhuman about the way that work had been organised – everything that he hoped a co-operative enterprise could overturn.

Joseph Greenwood himself was 36 years old in the summer of 1870, and it would not be surprising if he had felt that he had little in the way of real achievement to show for his life so far. He appeared to be caught in a tedious daily existence, working at a repetitive and physically demanding job as a fustian cutter in exchange for relatively low wages. Future events would show him to be a man of energy and drive, but his past efforts to change his lot in life and to make a difference in his home town seemed, looked at objectively, to have accomplished very little. He was no longer a young man: he was married, already with four of the six sons who, together with his wife Sarah, would make up his family. He was broadly speaking half way through the number of years he could expect to live.

Joseph Greenwood was born on 28 December 1833, the eldest child of William and Maria Greenwood. They were living in Stephenson House, on a hillside to the north of Hebden Bridge's neighbouring town of Mytholmroyd. Walk up there today through the woods and fields, and Stephenson House and the properties nearby speak of a comfortable lifestyle in beautiful surroundings. From the hill there are fine views south towards the Pennine hills.

It was not quite such an idyllic picture in the early nineteenth century. Joseph Greenwood had to contend with two factors related to his birth, neither of which would be wished for. The first was that he was born to parents who worked as hand loom weavers; the second was the time when he was born. Together these two facts meant that Joseph faced a very difficult start in life.

The plight of the hand loom weavers in the first decades of the nineteenth century has been well documented. E.P. Thompson, who devotes a chapter in *The Making of the English Working Class* to the weavers, reminds us that this was the period when 'the great majority of weavers were living on the edge – and sometimes beyond the edge – of the borders of starvation'. He goes on to point out that weaving communities in the Pennines, some with 300 or 400 years of continuous existence, 'were literally being extinguished'.[24]

A detailed account of the state of hand loom weavers in the Hebden Bridge area at around this time was written by a sympathetic doctor Robert Howard. Howard described the situation in the hamlet of Heptonstall Slack, a hilltop settlement above the Calder valley which had suffered a 'typhus' outbreak (more probably a typhoid epidemic caused by appalling sanitation) in the winter of 1843-4. Howard writes:

> The clothing of the handloom weaver may be stated as follows: a fustian cotton suit which serves for years and at the present time is so covered with patchwork that the whole puts on the appearance of real thrift and an attempt to resist the outrages of time. The stockings also are so much mended that it would not be easy in many instances to point to the original fabric...
>
> Respecting their diet, it may fairly be said that oatmeal and potatoes are well nigh what they contrive to exist upon... The dinner consists of small pieces of suet fried with addition of water and salt, a quantity of boiled potatoes is now added and the whole is blended into a partial pulp. This with a portion of oaten bread constitutes the dinner. Occasionally however extravagance is committed by introducing a very small portion of market bacon... The tea and supper are so united as to form one meal that is ordinarily oatmeal porridge, old milk and oaten bread... It may be stated, as an unquestionable fact, that they have no means sufficient of it to satisfy the cravings of nature and it is evident that in this part of the country the inhabitants are undergoing a rapid deterioration.[25]

The hand loom weavers' plight in the 1830s and 1840s was made more shocking because, not so many years previously, hand loom weaving had provided an independent lifestyle of some (relative) comfort. The history of the weavers at the time of Greenwood's birth was, in E.P. Thompson's words, 'haunted by the legend of better days'.[26] The wages paid to hand loom weavers had been driven down, and driven down again, from the time of the Napoleonic wars. William Cobbett reported in 1832 that thousands of weavers in the Halifax district who had previously been able to earn twenty to thirty shillings a week* were now living on four or five shillings a week 'or even less'.[27]

The parlous condition of the hand loom weavers was such that, a year after Joseph Greenwood's birth, a parliamentary select committee investigated the situation. Three years later, in 1837, Parliament chose to establish a Royal Commission on Hand-Loom Weavers and commissioners were appointed to travel the country to obtain first-hand evidence. In practice, these interventions achieved nothing. The one remedy which Parliament could have delivered and which would perhaps have helped was the imposition of a legal minimum wage – a demand that the hand loom weavers themselves had made in 1808. Such a move was proposed in a parliamentary bill in 1835 at the prompting of John Fielden, the radical MP from neighbouring Todmorden, but the bill was roundly defeated. The hand loom weavers were basically on their own.

Joseph Greenwood recalled this period of hardship himself when, in his seventies, he wrote a set of memoirs. His description closely echoes Robert Howard's account of Heptonstall Slack. His father, he said, had had no other opening than to work at the hand loom: 'The work was irregular and poorly paid, 12s per week was as much as could be earned and he was not now in the position to rent a farm as well. My mother had also to work at the loom, to help to keep up the house, and to do all the housework besides. The times were hard and all the fare was bare. We had oatmeal porridge and skim-milk for food with rarely a change during the week.'[28]

Joseph's family had certainly known better times. His father and his father's older brothers had received what, for the time, was a good education. They had been taught at a local school run by a Cambridge educated scholar and William had been able to continue his education until he was seventeen. One of Joseph's uncles had himself become a schoolmaster. But Joseph Greenwood had no such opportunity for education: the money was not there to pay school fees, and from a very young age he was needed by his parents to contribute to the household's work, by bobbin-winding. His formal education was effectively limited, he recalled, to nine months'

---

* Before decimalisation in 1971, there were twenty shillings (s) to the pound and twelve pence (d) to the shilling.

attendance at 'a very indifferent children's school'. It was his father who taught him to read and write, and who also taught him arithmetic. Joseph seems to have had a particular affinity with the latter.[29]

Hand loom weaving hung on longer than might be imagined in the hilltop communities of Lancashire and Yorkshire, being undertaken perhaps for want of anything better by older people who struggled to find alternative employment. Gradually, however, the cottages emptied: 'The same windows which used to be lighted after dark from within were now in darkness,' Joseph Greenwood wrote elegiacally, describing the countryside around Hebden Bridge. 'The sound of song and the shuttle is departed.'[30]

William Greenwood would have been concerned that his son had a trade in life which was not hand loom weaving, and an opportunity for Joseph to learn the craft of fustian cutting arose (so Joseph's memoirs recount) when he was nine, when a newly-married couple moved in to the house next door. The man made clogs; his wife and the young Joseph worked at the fustian frames.

Fustian cutting involves wielding a specialist knife, perhaps best visualised as having about the length as a rolled umbrella but the thinness of an old-fashioned paper knife. Fustian itself, as a coarse cotton cloth, comes off the loom with raised ribs of thread running the length of the piece, which are made of tiny loops of cotton put in by the weft. To make material with a ribbed pile such as corduroy these loops have to be cut.

Fustian cutting is at the same time skilled work – make a tiny wrong move, and the cloth itself will be damaged – and numbingly repetitive. Joseph Greenwood wrote in his memoirs:

> It would be a tiresome description to go into the details of fustian cutting, for it is a tedious and arduous work and like all handwork unless one keeps going nothing gets done. The children and young persons employed have to be raised on stages, beside the frame on which the cloth is strung, with a rapier-like knife in the right hand. The knife is made with a fine, thin, guide fixed on the point so that it will slide under the floats of weft and cut open the pile of the cloth. The left hand holds on to the frame rail and slides along the side; the frame is about two yards long.

Because of the repetitive strain of the work, Greenwood added that many children and young people grew up deformed, with one shoulder higher than the other and the right leg bent inwards.[31] Fustian cutting by young children was eventually to be outlawed by legislation in 1864.

The basis of the local economy of Hebden Bridge changed several times during the nineteenth century. Traditionally the weavers of the Hebden Bridge area had primarily woven worsted cloth for the Halifax market. However from the start of the nineteenth century Hebden Bridge increasingly turned from wool and worsted to cotton. The economic focus, in other words, shifted away from the West Riding of Yorkshire towards Manchester. Cotton spinning began in the upper Calder valley before 1800 and became the bedrock of the local economy as the nineteenth century developed, before going into a decline as the century ended. Small mills erected beside streams, driven initially by water power, were extended and steam engines installed.

The fustian industry also developed. The first mention of fustian weaving in the area appears to be in the 1790s in relation to a mill at Mytholm, just west of Hebden Bridge. By 1818 there were, according to one study, 52 fustian manufacturers from Hebden Bridge, Heptonstall and the neighbouring town of Todmorden whose names could be found in a trade directory of the time. Todmorden subsequently developed its economy away from fustian, but by the middle of the century Hebden Bridge's industrial base was effectively focused on cotton spinning and on fustian. The water from the streams in the vicinity were found to be very good for dyeing the fustian cloth, which meant that as well as fustian weaving a significant business in dyeing and finishing was built up. Hebden Bridge's later economic development can be explained partly because there was local expertise in more than simply weaving the basic cloth 'in the grey'.[32]

The 1840s, which became known as the 'hungry forties', were if anything an even more difficult decade than the 1830s but they were also the years of the Chartist movement. Chartism has been described as the first major working-class political intervention in British history. Its strongholds included the industrial towns of Yorkshire and Lancashire; Hebden Bridge, Todmorden and the communities in the upper Calder valley were also caught up in the fervour. Chartist leaders such as Feargus O'Connor and Ernest Jones addressed mass rallies, including those on the moorland outcrop of Blackstone Edge a few miles away. The arrival in the valley of copies of the weekly Chartist newspaper *The Northern Star*, edited at the time in Leeds by O'Connor and his collaborators, was keenly awaited.[33]

Joseph Greenwood recalled watching the demonstrators pass through Hebden Bridge towards Halifax in August 1842 during the period of Chartist agitation known as the Plug Riots (in order to enforce a general withdrawal of labour, the strikers put the steam boilers in the mills out of action by removing their plugs). Greenwood also remembered the political debates and discussions of the time: 'At home with my grandfather and uncles I heard more about Fergus (sic) O'Connor. He was the idol of the north. On Sunday mornings a small company would gather together and sit in a circle around the hearth to hear the *Northern Star* read, and to discuss the progress of the agitation; the places on the moors for the next meeting; the New Land scheme and its prospects (amongst those present being subscribers like my grandfather and uncle); the petitions to Parliament to be sent out by delegation for signatures &c.' As Greenwood put it on another occasion, the Chartist years were 'thrilling times'.[34]

The story of co-operation in Yorkshire and Lancashire from the 1840s onwards has to be understood in the context of Chartism. Several of the men who came together to launch the Rochdale Pioneers society in 1844 were active Chartists and indeed Rochdale's Abraham Greenwood was secretary of the local Chartist Association when he was eighteen. In Hebden Bridge, too, the first established co-operative society came out of the local Chartist movement. It was set up four years after Rochdale, in 1848.

One of those instrumental in its launch was John Hartley, twelve years older than Joseph Greenwood and therefore in his twenties during the heyday of Chartism. Hartley requires a proper introduction. He was born in the settlement of New Bridge north of Hebden Bridge (today the entrance to the National Trust's Hardcastle Crags woodlands) in October 1821 and started work young as a piecer in one of the town's two silk mills in the Colden valley. These silk mills, according to Greenwood, had a reputation as being the centres of radicalism locally: the silk workers were the elite of the working class, radicals in advance of their time, he said.[35]

Hartley had had little formal education but became an avid reader, including of course the *Northern Star*. He joined up with other like-minded young men in what they called the American Society. The idea was to make weekly subscriptions which would enable them to make the move to America, where they intended to live together in a co-operative community. It may not have been a particularly practical idea, but it was a sign of the lure of the New World for those living through difficult times.[36]

Perhaps fortunately for Hebden Bridge, Hartley and almost all the other American Society members never made it across the Atlantic but instead made their mark in their home town. The news of the Rochdale Pioneers society filtered through to Hebden Bridge through another member of the Society, Thomas Mitchell, who had moved to Bacup where he was instrumental in establishing a co-operative in 1846. The possibilities were, according to Hartley, discussed on Sundays at meetings at the Chartist Room, at Dulesgate on the road out of Todmorden towards Bacup. Todmorden established a co-operative society in 1846, and two years later it was Hebden Bridge's turn.

'On a Monday morning after one of our meetings James Mann [another member of the American Society] brought a book to the silk mill where he worked, entering his own name and the amount he was prepared to subscribe towards the new stores. Mine was also put down and then we set to canvass the silk mills, Whitley's Mills in Rawtenstall Wood, Bankfoot Mill and other neighbours,' John Hartley recalled. The embryonic society managed to recruit seventy members and attract seventy pounds; it operated for the first year or so only in the evenings, using unpaid labour. Hartley was one of the regular volunteers.

The new society was not the first attempt at co-operation in the town: there had been perhaps four previous attempts, including an informal flour-buying group around 1841-2 where the flour was distributed at a local Chartist room. It was the first in Hebden Bridge, however, to adopt the approach also being used at Rochdale, of paying profit dividends according to purchases rather than according to investment. It was to blossom quickly into the highly successful Hebden Bridge Industrial Co-operative Society.[37]

The working men who became involved in the co-operative movement locally tended to be associated with one of the non-conformist chapels. John Hartley himself was a member of the Wesleyan chapel in Heptonstall; Joseph Greenwood would be connected throughout his life with the Birchcliffe Baptist chapel in Hebden Bridge.

A significant influence in Greenwood's life at this time was the temperance movement, a feature of progressive working-class life in the mid-nineteenth century which may not today always receive the attention it deserves. The growth of temperance in the north of England is associated particularly with Joseph Livesey, a cheese merchant from Preston who launched the first teetotal publication, and with Thomas Whittaker also from Preston who after some youthful escapades brought on by excessive drinking became in his twenties a full-time temperance missionary. He was one of a number of temperance lecturers to visit Hebden Bridge at this time, where they did not always receive a peaceful welcome. Greenwood recalls one lecturer being attacked by a near neighbour of his, a former hand loom weaver, 'a rough, wild looking man with shirt sleeves rolled up' who had just left a local pub (the man ended the evening in the Heptonstall lock-up). Greenwood signed the abstinence pledge and joined the Order of the Rechabites, the friendly society linked to the temperance movement whose name was taken from an Old Testament tribe who refused to drink wine.[38]

In 1849 Greenwood, now fifteen, was working at Machpelah close to the centre of Hebden Bridge, cutting corduroy for a small fustian master John

Moss. In the intervening years since he had first started fustian cutting, Greenwood had spent a short time working as a farm boy at an isolated cottage called Nelmires, just on the edge of the open moorland above Mytholmroyd (Nelmires today is a desolate, roofless ruin). He had also briefly accompanied his father to undertake work building the new railway north of Keighley, a period of outdoor work he clearly relished. Less happy had been the time in 1848 spent on Churnet Valley railway construction work near Rudyard, Staffordshire. The railway contractors had put in a very low tender for the work and probably cut corners.[39] Greenwood appears to have suffered two accidents when working there, including a potentially serious leg fracture. Recovery clearly took some time.

John Moss, Greenwood's master, was a strong temperance advocate and temperance lecturers frequently visited the Machpelah workshop where Greenwood worked. It was one lecturer, George Lomax from Manchester, who in criticising the town's young men for not having their own Mechanics' Institute was indirectly responsible for Greenwood's first venture into what could be called local civic life.[40]

The launch of the Mechanics' Institute in Hebden Bridge in late 1854 is of relevance to the later story of the Hebden Bridge Fustian Society partly because Greenwood's role in both is a similar one but partly also because as we shall see there is direct connection between the focus on self-help in education at the Mechanics' Institute and the co-operative's later strong commitment to working-class educational initiatives.

The original minute book of the Mechanics' Institute survives, and this includes the report sent by Hebden Bridge to the Yorkshire Association of Mechanics' Institutes in May 1856. This stated that the Institute

> owes its origin entirely to the efforts made by three young men, who at the commencement of the month of December 1854 canvassed the neighbourhood in the hopes of being enabled to establish a society for mutual improvement. Their efforts at first met with but scanty success, a dwelling house was, however, taken, and the first meeting was held on Saturday the 16th of December, when they numbered 12 members who agreed to pay 1/6 on entrance and 3d per week, which sum was subsequently reduced to twopence.[41]

Greenwood himself, one of the three young men, adds some detail to this story:

We took an empty cottage in the best street of the village. We had no furniture of any sort, simply the bare whitewashed stone walls, but we met and stood in a circle, one holding the candle while we deliberated, and another wrote out the resolutions on loose paper … Our first thought was what were we to strive for. Mutual instruction in elementary subjects of education we felt should be our first aim, and a reading room the next.[42]

At a meeting on 20 December, the members agreed to accept Joseph Greenwood's offer of the loan of a desk (it had previously been his father's), as well as to begin writing and arithmetic classes; Greenwood, with two others, undertook to lead the class in arithmetic. In January they resolved that 'such members as have books in their possession be requested to lend them to the institution till the committee can command funds sufficient to replace them with new books' and in March decided that 'a superintendant (sic) or principle (sic) be chosen, whose office shall be to govern and regulate the institution during hours of business'. Joseph Greenwood was appointed as the Institute's first occupant of this new position.

He continued to play an active role as the Mechanics' Institute became established, taking on different roles: secretary in 1856, secretary and librarian in 1857 (in charge of the 230 volumes now in the library), secretary again in 1858. In 1856 the Institute had grown to the point where it could move to bigger premises. However the old rooms appear to have been kept on and it is these which the committee minute in January 1857 probably referred to. The minute read that it was agreed that 'Joseph Greenwood reside on the premises and keep order and at the year end be presented with 50s'.[43]

Joseph Greenwood did not occupy the place alone. For at the start of December 1855 Joseph had married Sarah, a local girl four years younger than him, whom he had met through his Sunday School. Her father was a stone-mason and hand loom weaver and it would have been no surprise to anyone living in Hebden Bridge at the time to know that his name was also Greenwood: Greenwood was at the time such a common surname in the town that many Greenwoods were given by-names (nicknames).*

Sarah Greenwood, née Greenwood, had like her new husband not been able to have much of an education, and indeed she signed the marriage certificate with a mark. She took on the role of cleaning the Mechanics' Institute. However in the summer of 1859 the committee agreed to allow

---

* There is an abiding anecdote still told in the town today that one local man became so used to his by-name that he failed to recognise his own official name.

her to have the assistance of another woman in this task.[44] The reason may have been because she was pregnant. Joseph and Sarah's second son, William, was born the following April. Their first-born, Virgil, had been born in May 1858.

The American Civil War broke out in the Spring of 1861. The Lancashire cotton industry was dependent on cotton from the southern states and the Union blockade imposed on the Confederate ports that year very quickly had a devastating effect on the quantity of cotton imported into Britain. The Cotton Famine became a time of great suffering in the cotton manufacturing centres, including Hebden Bridge. By the autumn of 1862 the local press was reporting that, of the 1,800 or so local people engaged in cotton manufacture, 942 were wholly unemployed and a further 570 only working part-time. The same paper in November suggested that the average weekly income per head was now averaging no more than two shillings. A relief committee was eventually established.[45]

With two small children in their family, this was probably an extremely difficult time for Joseph and Sarah and it may have contributed to a rupture with the Mechanics' Institute. In December 1861 the committee awarded Joseph Greenwood 10s for his work for the Institute. However the following month Greenwood asked for a further 1s 6d weekly allowance, which the committee declined. 'The committee do not desire the removal of J Greenwood from his situation but unless he can remain on his present terms the committee feel bound to offer the same to public competition,' the minute reads.

Greenwood stayed on, but thereafter things appear to have become difficult. In July 1863, for example, the committee complained of the untidy state of the Institute and threatened Greenwood with three months' notice to quit. A year later they were peremptorily telling him to use less gas.[46]

To add to the family difficulties, it may well have been around this time that Joseph became engaged in a dispute with his employer John Moss for whom he had been working for almost two decades. Greenwood respected Moss as a fellow temperance advocate but, having been in touch with fustian cutters in Manchester and with their attempts at trade union organisation, he felt that the terms of employment at Machpelah left much to be desired. 'Things were bad, our representations were unheeded, and although our shop comrades did not all agree with us in our trade union views, things were drifting more and more towards a strike.' Greenwood took a leadership role: 'In any difference between employer and employed some one of the latter has to stand out and speak for his shopmates; it was then, and has been my misfortune since under similar circumstances, to take that post,' he recounts in his memoirs. The date of the dispute is not given but was likely to have been around 1863.[47]

There was a sequel to this dispute, however: a first attempt by Greenwood and some of his fellow workers to establish a co-operative workshop. It was, in his words, a false start: at that stage 'we had only a vague idea of Co-operation and mutual help,' he recalled later. Money was a problem; with the exception of one person no-one could find the capital needed, even the relatively small amounts needed by fustian cutters. Five would-be co-operators crowded with their cutting frames into a dimly-lit room in a cottage, but 'the requisite enthusiasm was wanting and we were without experience'. The idea of a co-operative was allowed to drop. 'The shop drifted into the old rut of employer and employed.'[48]

Already in his thirties, Joseph Greenwood and his family took the decision to leave Hebden Bridge. They moved across the hills to Huddersfield where they lived for a number of years. Greenwood says nothing of this period in his memoirs, and life may well have been difficult. The Greenwoods' third and fourth sons, Harry and Fred, were born in Huddersfield, respectively in March 1865 and April 1867.

By the end of the 1860s, however, the family had returned to Hebden Bridge and Joseph was working, still cutting fustian, at the Midgehole mills run by Worrals. He had also got involved in the Hebden Bridge co-operative society. In the time since its founding in 1848, the society had grown significantly. It had moved from its original small store to better premises in Bridge Lanes, Hebden Bridge, and then again from there to the centre of the town in 1869. Two branch stores had also been opened serving outlying communities, in 1867 and 1868. By the end of the decade the society was able to offer its customers not only grocery but also drapery, millinery, hardware, furnishing, and the provision of boots, shoes and clogs. It had 1,040 members in 1872, by which stage annual sales were well over £30,000.[49]

John Hartley continued to be active in the society's life and had also been involved in another venture. The Hebden Bridge Cotton and Commercial Company was established as a cotton spinning concern around the time of the start of the American Civil War. This was Hebden Bridge's most prominent attempt at what are usually described as working-class joint-stocks, an idea particularly associated with the town of Oldham where local people were to pour enormous sums of money into a series of cotton mills and to enjoy, initially, great returns before, later, the bubble burst. As the name suggests, these firms were registered under joint stock company law (as opposed to being incorporated under the Industrial and Provident Societies Act, the legislation for co-operative societies first introduced in 1852), but with many of their shares held by working people. In the days when most mills were run by individual owners, these companies represented an alternative form of more collective ownership of manufacturing enterprises.

Working-class joint-stocks in the early days were often considered to be within the family of co-operatives, or at least to be closely linked to the co-operative movement, and this seems to have been the case in Hebden Bridge during at least the 1860s. John Hartley left his silk mill and took a job as an overlooker at the Cotton Company's Calder Mill. It would seem that he tried to persuade the company's shareholders to make some of the profit available to employees by paying 'bonus to labour', a move which apparently did not find favour with management.[50]

Although there were some who continued to argue that the working-class joint-stocks were within the co-operative fold, in practice as shares were sold on to other investors the early principles, such as they were, were quickly lost sight of. The Hebden Bridge Cotton and Commercial Company had a chequered commercial history but continued trading for many years; in 1874 it was enmeshed in a messy and expensive legal dispute with the Hebden Bridge co-operative society over land access rights.[51] The Hebden Bridge area had a second venture, the Colden Cotton Company, which could also be described as a working-class joint-stock.

It was under the auspices of the Hebden Bridge Cotton Company that the Owenite co-operative lecturer and activist J.C. Farn gave a lecture in Hebden Bridge at the end of April 1870 on the theme of Manufacturing Co-operation. 'Have you ever asked yourselves how it is that the working classes, who create all the wealth, should only have enough of it to keep the wolf from the door?' he asked his listeners. 'Have you ever asked yourselves why the immense increase in your trade, which has built up so many fortunes for others, has not built up any fortunes for you?' He called on local people to 'make further experiments' in manufacturing co-operation and concluded his lecture, 'In this Manufacturing Co-operation alone is to be found a solution to those difficulties arising from the conflicts of Labour and Capital'.[52]

The decision of Joseph Greenwood and his fellow fustian cutters and dyers in 1870 to try to establish a worker-run co-operative society did not come out of nowhere, therefore. We do not know if Greenwood heard Farn's lecture but he was certainly a delegate at the conference of Lancashire and Yorkshire co-operative societies held on Good Friday in Bury. He was also at the Manchester national Co-operative Congress, held a few weeks later at the beginning of June; John Hartley was there too, as another of

Hebden Bridge's three delegates. 'The papers read there, and the discussions on them, made a deep impression upon our minds – especially those which were directed towards productive co-operation,' Greenwood wrote later.[53] He claimed that it was at the Manchester Congress that he first got the idea of beginning a co-operative productive society in Hebden Bridge.

The Manchester Congress was the second such event in what became thereafter an annual tradition. The Congress held in London a year before effectively began the process of creating a formal structure for the British co-operative movement: although the Co-operative Union name was not initially used, the 1869 event is taken as the organisation's launch date. This was the first attempt at a national event to have taken place since the small number of Christian Socialist conferences in the early 1850s (there had also been a number of congresses during the Owenite period of the co-operative movement, in the years from 1831-1835). The London Congress in 1869 was promoted strongly by some of the old guard from Christian Socialism days, with Neale very much to the fore. Charles Kingsley and John Ruskin were among those supporting the initiative. Delegate numbers from the north of England, the heartland of actual co-operation, were limited.

For the 1870 Congress in Manchester, however, Lancashire and Yorkshire co-operators turned out in significant numbers, having agreed at their own regular regional conference to support this new national initiative. Greenwood and Hartley would have heard Neale on the last day of the conference reminding his listeners of the Rochdale Pioneers' original aims of including co-operative manufacturing along with store-keeping. Greenwood seems to have been particularly inspired, however, by some remarks made by the radical churchman Rev W. Nassau Molesworth, the vicar of Spotland near Rochdale, who was to become known to some as the 'co-operative parson' and who argued for workers to subscribe capital to be used for their own employment.[54]

If Greenwood returned on the train from Manchester mulling over this possibility, the opportunity to put the idea in practice came quicker than he might have expected. Daniel Killeen's death was only a fortnight later. Thereafter Greenwood seems to have moved fast. It seems unlikely that the temperance and suffrage campaigner Jessie Craigen, who gave a lecture in Hebden Bridge in mid-July on productive co-operation, was in the town entirely by chance (Joseph Greenwood's hand in the arrangements is suggested by the fact that he was elected to the chair for the evening). Jessie Craigen's message was exactly what he would have wanted to hear said: 'The working men must stir themselves up, and learn to thoroughly understand the machinery and when they had got sufficient capital they must produce manufactures for themselves,' she told her audience.[55]

It would appear that Greenwood's new co-operative began informally trading in July. A few weeks later, on 1 September 1870, the Hebden Bridge Fustian Manufacturing Co-operative Society Ltd was formally incorporated.

CHAPTER 2

BUILDING THE BUSINESS

For any new business, the first few months – in fact the first few weeks – can be crucial. Greenwood and his fellow workers faced two particular challenges: finding the capital they needed, and finding customers. Neither task was straightforward.

The idea was to be a co-operative of fustian cutters and fustian dyers. 'No-one was to be a member unless actually engaged in the trade,' Greenwood later made clear.[56] Setting up the cutting side of the operation was relatively straightforward: a fustian cutter at that time required no more than about thirty shillings to two pounds to be able to start work. The dyeing side of the business was going to be more of a challenge, and Greenwood estimated that £1,000 in capital would be needed to start a dyeing plant.[57] Given that the weekly subscription was set at 3d per person and that initially about thirty fellow cutters and dyers joined Greenwood in the endeavour, the dyeing operation would clearly not be an immediate possibility. Greenwood realised that they would have to engage in trade to get there.

The original business model therefore, if that term does not sound too grand for what Greenwood himself said were the 'puny' origins of the co-operative, was to use what capital they managed to acquire to purchase fustian pieces direct from the looms. These would be sent out, in turn, to those members of the society who were cutters who would cut the pieces in their own homes. The pieces would next be sent to local commercial dyers. The final pieces, cut and dyed, would then be sold. Greenwood had identified the local co-operative stores as the target market.[58]

The work undertaken in the fustian cutting was to be rewarded during this early period not in cash but by crediting members' share accounts in the co-operative with an equivalent amount. Everything else at that stage was voluntary: 'All the office, warehouse or other work of any kind except the cutting was 'done for love',' Greenwood later said.[59]

This included the task of persuading the local co-operatives to take the finished goods, and here the reception they met was not as enthusiastic as they had expected. For stores within walking distance, members of the co-operative went in the evening after work to meet the store committees or their managers (the assumption has to be that it was Greenwood himself who often undertook this task). 'The reception we met with, and do yet meet with, in some instances is more than sufficient to damp the zeal and enthusiastic fervour of ordinary individuals. Some of us were innocent enough to think that we had only to present our goods to get orders, especially as fustian is an article in which co-operative stores deal largely,' Greenwood said in a paper for the 1872 Co-operative Congress. Indeed, being a co-operative turned out to be something of an actual disadvantage, arousing suspicions that their goods were inferior to those from conventional manufacturers.[60]

'We have found it hard work to go from store to store during the week, after a day's work at the mill or frame,' Joseph Greenwood added. For stores further away, samples were dispatched by post. The Hebden Bridge, Mytholmroyd and Bacup societies were the first customers. Over Darwen store near Blackburn was the first to respond positively to the society's postal soliciting.[61]

Despite the challenges, the fustian society rented its first premises, a single room ten foot by ten foot, in Crown St, Hebden Bridge. 'Our spare time was given to fitting up the small fixtures we could afford, buying the boards and making the shelves ourselves, which served to hold our small stock. We bought a second-hand chair and table, and with two forms we were completely furnished for a meeting-room. A minute book, account books, and a little stationery also we bought. We canvassed, and had meetings again and again, trudging back to our homes at eleven every night in the week,' Greenwood wrote.[62] This cannot have been easy for Sarah Greenwood, who was pregnant during the autumn of 1870 with their fifth son, Crossley, born at the start of the 1871 new year.

As well as the problems of finding customers, a further difficulty emerged in that the pieces sent out to members for cutting were not being returned promptly. Furthermore there were some who lost faith in the endeavour. Three of the original 32 members quickly withdrew from the society, one because of fear that his existing employer would take offence, two simply because they did not believe the co-operative would succeed.[63]

In reality, the business would not have succeeded in the way it was originally conceived. What made the difference between failure and success was that the members, with Greenwood as their leader, understood that they needed to change their plans. Very quickly, within a matter of weeks (probably at a general meeting held on 7 October),[64] the co-operative took two very significant decisions. These decisions were to affect very profoundly the future development of the co-operative. Both involved significant compromises to the original vision of a worker-run co-operative.

Indeed many of the difficulties and disputes which the society later had to overcome were direct consequences of the decision. But on the other hand the changes put the Hebden Bridge fustian society on the path to success.

The first decision was to extend the products being offered to customers. The message which had come back from several of the co-operative stores was that they were more interested in selling ready-made fustian clothes than they were in taking the fustian pieces. The co-operative therefore decided to purchase a sewing machine and employ a cutter and finishers, to work initially in their own homes. These new workers were taken into membership of the society.

The work of using the Singer sewing machines and making up garments was considered at that time exclusively women's work. The Hebden Bridge fustian society's decision to produce ready-made clothes, therefore, had additional significance in that many of the co-operative's future members and employees would be women. From this point on, women made up a large proportion of the co-operative's workforce.

The second decision was equally important. It was to allow external investors to put money into the business. Greenwood had been discussing the way forward with John Hartley who, since he worked in cotton spinning, had not been directly involved as a member of the co-operative. Hartley seems to have been instrumental in recommending the new approach, offering to buy shares with his own money.[65] He also agreed to become president of the young society, taking over from one of the founder members early in 1871. It was a highly welcome development.

Both Hebden Bridge's Industrial Co-operative Society (the store) and the Cotton and Commercial Company had managed to attract considerable local capital: by the start of the 1870s both ventures had each approximately £15,000 in investment capital.[66] But the Cotton Company had recently been encountering some turbulent trading times whilst two years earlier the co-operative store had suffered an unexplained theft of £600 from a locked safe.[67] Added to that a working-class joint-stock in neighbouring Todmorden had just recently gone into liquidation.[68] As a consequence, local investors were cautious and the money did not initially flood in to the fustian society.[69] Nevertheless, by the end of December 1870 share capital had climbed to £82 18s 3d, the co-operative had 95 members – some workers, some investors – and was able to announce a turnover since launch of £55. There was also a profit made: it was precisely £3 1s 8d.[70]

Despite the difficulties, the early days of the Hebden Bridge fustian society were a time of enthusiasm and satisfaction. Here is Joseph Greenwood's account of this period:

The Society lived and prospered; it formed part of our lives. No day was too sacred to work for it and to devise plans and to seek the association of men and confer with them on our and similar undertakings. It may shock some to know that we often met on Sundays to talk about our obstacles and our progress ... Friends came to see us, and we went to see them. The fields and the lanes, the wild flowers, and the ferns just opening their young fronds, and the bright green tufts of the tender leaves of spring were made more beautiful. The purple moorlands, and nut brown shades of October, had charms all the sweeter and mellower. The streams from the hills, the glistening sunlight on the white roads, the moss and fern, the banks and the footpaths by the river, were more and more delightful. We felt we were doing God's work, and in that faith and communion we were content.[71]

By the end of 1871, the society had over £500 in share capital, and had made a profit of £31. It had 112 members, seventeen of whom were categorised as being workers.[72]

Another early change had been to abolish the system of having fustian cutting done by members in turn in their homes and to concentrate cutting and making up in its own premises, undertaken by paid employees. During the summer of 1871 the society moved from its original single room, rented at 2s 6d per week, to a set of three rooms costing £13 a year.[73]

Lloyd Jones, a veteran co-operative advocate who lectured in the town in the summer of that year, helped ensure that the co-operative could sell its goods more widely. Lloyd Jones was, like Greenwood, a fustian cutter by trade. Originally from the textile town of Bandon, County Cork, he had moved to Manchester in his mid-teens in 1827 and had become active in the co-operative society then operating in Salford, running for a time its associated free school. He became a co-operative lecturer and missionary in the years between 1838 and 1844, and also had the experience of visiting Paris in 1848. He became involved thereafter with Neale and the Christian Socialists and had much to do with enabling links to develop between the northern co-operative movement and London.[74] A prolific journalist, he was in Hebden Bridge in August 1871 as part of a fact-finding lecture tour of northern towns.

Lloyd Jones had played a prominent role at both the 1869 and 1870 Co-operative Congresses and in Manchester had railed against co-operative societies for becoming nothing more than individuals in search of a dividend. He was critical of some of the 'apathy as to the true and complete meaning of the idea' of co-operation he found during his 1871 northern tour too, but clearly was impressed by the fustian society – perhaps helped by the gift of a souvenir fustian knife given him for old time's sake by an Irish member of the co-operative and by the pleasure of being invited for a Sunday afternoon stroll on the hills.[75] It was through Lloyd Jones's support and contacts that the Co-operative Wholesale Society agreed to become agents for the co-operative's products; shortly afterwards the separate Scottish Co-operative Wholesale Society also signed up as agents.

All this helped to mean that 1872 was a year of rapid growth: annual turnover was £4,637, five times the previous year's figure. External investors had rushed to get involved in the action; at the year end the society had 207 members, including 23 workers and 12 co-operative societies. Total share capital was now over £1,800, primarily from individual investors. Co-operative societies (led by the Halifax) had put in approximately £500. There was a profit on the year of £275.[76]

The Hebden Bridge Fustian Manufacturing Society was past its start-up phase. Nevertheless, the co-operative had still not achieved its original ambition of operating a dyeing plant, and therefore of offering work to some of its early members. This was to be remedied in 1873, when the society took its most ambitious step yet. On 23 September, in exchange for a consideration of £5,650, it became the owner of the Nutclough estate in Hebden Bridge, acquiring an empty mill equipped with an engine, boiler and water wheel, a mill-owner's house, and just up the hillside two reservoirs holding the water needed for the mill.

'Nutclough is pronounced 'Nutcluff',' George Jacob Holyoake once explained to readers of *Co-operative News*. 'Clough means a rill running between mountains. There are many cloughs near and about Hebden Bridge, but Nutclough is the prettiest name of all, for nuts once grew plentifully on the rill side. Now they grow co-operators there – not only an equally interesting, but more profitable fruit.'[77] Holyoake went on to praise the natural beauty of the surroundings which, somewhat curiously, he compared to the Catskills in New York state. Later visitors were also to wax eloquent about the co-operative's estate; one was to praise its picturesque beauty, 'with its rocks and trees, and the cascades from which the mill receives the soft, pure water'.[78] Today Nutclough is still an attractive place, just away from Hebden Bridge's town centre. The path through the woods is used by walkers and the upper reservoir, though silted up, is often a home for ducks.

The decision to acquire the Nutclough Mill was taken at a special meeting of the co-operative's members held on 24 May 1873 (ten days after the birth of Joseph and Sarah Greenwood's sixth and last son Lloyd). It meant that the co-operative could now be run from its own freehold property rather than relying on rented space. It also meant a step-change in the co-operative's operations, including the employment for the first time of dyers. The average number of workers almost doubled between June 1873 and June 1874, from 27 to 50. By the end of 1874 54 were employed. According to Greenwood, 36 were women machinists and finishers and 18 were male cutters and dyers.[79]

On top of the £5,650 purchase cost for the Nutclough estate, the co-operative also spent a little over £2,500 on alterations and machinery for the mill. The expenditure was possible only because of a £5,000 loan from the Co-operative Wholesale Society and a further £2,000 lent by local co-operative societies. Whatever the tensions between Joseph Greenwood and the CWS in later years in the debate over profit bonuses to labour, the CWS was able to play an invaluable role at this point in the fustian society's development. The CWS was in the early stages of developing what was to become its banking operation, having created a year earlier what it called its 'deposit and loan department'. Although legally the CWS was unable to operate a banking department until a change in the Industrial and Provident Societies Act in 1876, in practice this was what it had begun to do in the early 1870s. Money was pouring in from local co-operative societies looking for a home for their excess capital and the CWS was in turn lending it out again. By August 1872 the CWS already had made advances of £11,200.[80] Both the CWS loan and the other borrowings taken out for the Nutclough purchase were repaid in early 1877, made possible through an increase in the fustian society's share capital.

The introduction of dyeing meant a change to the co-operative's business in other ways. Although some of the dyed fustian pieces were retained to be made into clothing, around four-fifths of the dyeing was undertaken for the private trade. It meant, as Joseph Greenwood explained later to the members of the Royal Commission on Labour, that he had had to go out to find these new customers — though he added drily that this had turned out to be rather easier than the original task of persuading co-operative stores to take their goods.[81]

Until the expansion into the Nutclough Mill, Greenwood had effectively been undertaking all aspects of the management of the co-operative himself, acting as both manager and secretary. This was not sustainable and a few months into the new working arrangements, almost certainly during the second half of 1874, the two roles were separated.

Joseph Greenwood recruited a local young man, Jesse Clement Gray, to join him at the Nutclough. Gray was born in July 1854 and therefore had probably just turned twenty at the time of his appointment. He was the son of the Baptist minister William Gray who had moved from Ripley in Derbyshire to take up the pastoral leadership of Hebden Bridge's Birchcliffe chapel in 1860, so Jesse had spent most of his childhood in the town. He had attended a local grammar school, leaving when he was thirteen. He was working for the Lancashire and Yorkshire Railway company as an audit clerk when he was offered the post at the Nutclough Mill.[82]

Greenwood would have known exactly who he was appointing as his new right-hand man: as a member of William Gray's Baptist congregation, he would have seen the young Jesse growing up and starting work. Jesse, who initially seems to have been given the title of Assistant Secretary, was quickly promoted to be the co-operative's Secretary. He was to remain at the Nutclough until the end of 1883 when he was to take the experience he had gained in Hebden Bridge out to the national co-operative movement. First as Assistant General Secretary and then as General Secretary of the Co-operative Union, Gray was to make a considerable contribution to the development of British and, later, international co-operation. It is a story surprisingly little known, and one which will be returned to later in this book.

Greenwood remained as the co-operative's manager. As well as being what would today be described as the chief executive, he was directly responsible for overseeing all the aspects of the operation and production work of the factory. The secretary's task was primarily administrative. His brief, as defined by the co-operative's 1870 rule book, was to 'keep minutes of all proceedings of the committee and of general meetings, and ... make all returns and ... do all other things necessary to keep the Society in compliance with the acts of Parliament'. One of the secretary's tasks was to keep the share register and membership records up to date.[83]

The expansion of the business as a result of the Nutclough purchase also led to a third post being created in what we might begin to describe, using modern terminology, as the senior management team. This was the position of Traveller, the travelling sales representative whose task was to keep in touch with the cooperative's customers, particularly its co-operative store customers, and ensure that their shops were adequately stocked with the products being turned out by the Nutclough Mill. The post of Traveller was given in 1874 to John Hartley, an appointment which must have given Greenwood considerable satisfaction. Hartley, who stepped down as president of the management committee when he became an employee, was to remain the society's Traveller until his death in 1903.[84]

Together, Greenwood and Hartley became familiar figures at co-operative events, where no opportunity was lost to display the Nutclough's products and to solicit custom. Gradually a tradition developed at the annual Co-operative Congresses of staging at the same time an exhibition of co-operative goods. At the 1873 Congress in Newcastle the Hebden Bridge fustian society was one of only about three or four societies with small displays in the entrance lobby; by 1876, in Glasgow, the exhibition had required its own room and three years later the Corn Exchange in Gloucester had to be booked.[85] Regional co-operative events also provided a sales opportunity: at a conference in Accrington in 1876, one of the leading figures of the host society attributed their large trade with the Nutclough to the latter's 'persistent efforts' in pushing its goods. (This business could not be taken for granted, however: five years later an Accrington delegate was reporting that they had changed to buying more of their fustian stock from another – non-co-operative – supplier.)[86] Meetings of the Calderdale Co-operative Association, originally established in 1871 as a meeting point for societies in the Calderdale area, also proved a good occasion to remind local stores of the Nutclough's products; Greenwood was secretary of the local association for many years.

Commercially speaking, everything was going well. 'The starting of a productive society was very much like a ship crossing a dangerous bar in going out to sea,' Greenwood was to remark some years later,[87] and by the end of 1875 the Hebden Bridge Fustian Manufacturing Society was sailing out into open waters. The 1874 calendar year, the first full year at the Nutclough, saw the co-operative's sales climb from £6,864 to £12,626 and a year later turnover had increased to almost £17,500. Profit in 1875 was over a thousand pounds for the first time and the co-operative had approaching £300 in reserves.[88]

Nevertheless, extremely choppy waters were close at hand.

CHAPTER 3

SHARING THE PROFITS

It was the special general meeting of the fustian society called for 8 January 1876 which was, for Joseph Greenwood, a make-or-break moment. In fact, as he was to make clear on several subsequent occasions, it was *the* most significant event in the whole life of the co-operative. The society's management committee had set up a rules revision sub-committee the previous autumn and proposals for change were now being presented to the members for their endorsement. There was one major change proposed: that in future the workers at Nutclough Mill should no longer receive a share of the profits.

This move represented a very significant shift away from the co-operative's roots. The majority of the members of the management committee was endorsing the change, but it was certainly not a proposal which the society's manager was prepared to support. Effectively the Hebden Bridge Fustian Manufacturing Society, despite its demonstrable commercial success, had reached an existential crisis.

The meeting was held on Saturday afternoon, after work in the mills had finished, and the hall was packed.

The first proposal on the table was that the word 'Co-operative' should be removed from the society's name. It is not clear whether this came from the committee or was a deliberately provocative bit of mischief, but in any case the proposal was defeated. But then came the debate on the 'bonus to labour'.

It is worth quoting Greenwood's account of this part of the meeting:

The delegates from the societies sat mixed with the individuals in the meeting, but the women workers sat mostly together. Minor alterations were agreed to, but the signs of strife were upon the countenances of the chief persons who were about to take part in the main struggle. The Chairman seemed to be in a nervous state. The Society's representative, who above all others should have been in favour of the worker, led the way and moved the adoption of the altered rules. This was seconded.

There was one member who was in at the foundation of the Society who sat gloomy, drawing his breath very quick, but feeling intensely moved. He was not gifted with the power of speech, but he felt the duty lay upon him, and he got up and clearly stated the purpose for which the Society was started, going from point to point, and charging the promoters of the alterations with breaking an obligation and doing a great wrong to the men who were the founders and who had made the Society a success. He moved the rejection of the altered rules. This was seconded by a former President, and one who had done great service to the Society. He could not let go the principle for which as Co-operators they had striven so much, and felt bound to support it.

The former president in this account is John Hartley. The principal speaker against the rule change, though Greenwood puts the account into the third person, must surely be Greenwood himself.

The main speaker in favour of the abolition of the labour share of profit was a delegate from the Co-operative Wholesale Society, Henry Jackson from Halifax. He described the bonus to labour as a 'mere sentiment, a sham and a delusion'. As a principle for dividing profits, it was utterly impracticable, he said. He went on to criticise those who advocated it (and he mentioned among others Hughes, Neale and Lloyd Jones), challenging them to come up with a single example of where it had been successful.

There then followed what *Co-operative News* politely described as a 'long and animated discussion' and what Greenwood called 'a most inextricable confusion, when a delegate from a large society in a Yorkshire town got up in the midst of the hubbub whistling a popular tune'. Eventually order was restored and the vote taken: 60 against the proposed rule change, 50 in favour.[89]

It was a close-run thing. It is difficult to see how Greenwood would have been able to retain his position as manager had the voting gone the other way. And it is difficult to imagine that posterity would have been very interested in the story of the Hebden Bridge Fustian Manufacturing Society either.

The row continued in the correspondence columns of *Co-operative News*. Henry Jackson for the CWS attacked the workers (and 'over thirty of these were women and children') whom he said 'to all appearances had been drilled previous to the meeting as to how they should vote'. The employees had too much voting power, he added, given the interests of investors and customers. 'On this occasion this power has been used against those who supply the great bulk of capital and trade,' he argued.[90]

Greenwood himself responded a week later. There were, he said, 135 members present, with workers comprising only a third of the number. There was also only one fourteen year old, he continued, all the other workers being men and women. 'It cannot be said, then, that the workers decided the question,' he wrote. 'The argument that voting power should be in proportion to capital is, to my mind, erroneous and dangerous.' Nevertheless, Greenwood then went on to point out the reality of the situation at the Nutclough Mill: 'During the history of this society there never has been any danger to apprehend from the labourers, their voting power has always been far below the proportion of capital; and, if it were different, it is unlikely they will ever attempt to swamp capital, because capital will always be a necessity for them as will also trade.'[91]

To understand how the co-operative had arrived at the January 1876 show-down, we need to retrace our steps a little. After the initial caution shown by investors in the fledgling business – once the business had demonstrated that it was there to stay – the money started to come in much more quickly. Greenwood's original target of £1,000 in capital was reached during 1872, more than two-thirds of it coming from individual investors. By the end of 1875, two years after the Nutclough purchase, capital from individuals had reached almost £4,000 (Table 1).

Table 1
Share capital, Hebden Bridge Fustian Manufacturing Society 1870-1875[92]

Half year ending	Share capital (individuals)	Total share capital (individuals, co-op societies, workers)	Loans
Dec 1870	83	83	3
June 1871	111	111	35
Dec 1871	410	523	95
June 1872	1160	1513	-
Dec 1872	1281	1806	-
June 1873	1302	2331	-
Dec 1873	1648	3194	7000
June 1874	1882	5298	7000
Dec 1874	2305	6421	7000
June 1875	3233	8158	6000
Dec 1875	3953	9060	6000

There was good reason for investors' enthusiasm. Shareholders received a 10 per cent dividend on their investment in the first half of 1871, and 12½ per cent for the remainder of 1871 and the whole of 1872. This was generous: long-term government bond yields were averaging around 3.2-3.3 per cent during this period and while the bank base rate fluctuated quite markedly in the early 1870s it was generally in the 2.5-3.5 per cent range.[93] A start-up co-operative business was necessarily much more risky than government bonds but by this stage the business was well established.

Things were in danger of getting out of hand. Indeed, the Hebden Bridge fustian society was beginning to show signs of becoming a co-operative equivalent of just another working-class joint-stock, run with the aim of producing returns for investors. Some individuals had put their money into the business out of support for what Greenwood and his fellow co-operators were trying to achieve: the two old Christian Socialists Neale and Thomas Hughes had both become shareholders, for example.[94] But many others were undoubtedly less interested in principles. Numerically, too, the individual investors were now outnumbering workers very considerably and, as shareholders in the co-operative, all had a vote and a voice.

The issue of interest was resolved, for the time being, at general meetings held on January 25 and February 22 1873 which agreed to fix the dividend for shareholders in future at 7½ per cent. Not everyone was very happy. *Co-operative News* was to report eight years later John Hartley's recollection of the occasion: 'They canvassed the individual shareholders, offered to pay out any that were dissatisfied, and had to give an assurance they would not be parties to reducing the interest to less than the 7½ per cent. By these promises they succeeded in carrying the resolution mainly by the eloquence of individual shareholders.'[95] One of the eloquent shareholders could well have been Neale, who frequently attended general meetings in Hebden Bridge.

Arguably, 7½ per cent remained generous: the CWS would charge the fustian society 5 per cent on its £5000 loan, for example.[96]

But if profits were being made, what about the workers? Already, in July 1871, Hartley and Greenwood had managed – with a certain amount of difficulty – to institute the principle that at least some profit should be go to labour. A modest £7 profit had been made by the society in the first half of 1871: £5 of this had been distributed to investors and £2 retained. The second half year saw £24 profit generated, of which investors between them received £17 with a further £2 being split between the workers in proportion to their wages.[97] Greenwood later recalled, 'There was rather a stiff opposition from some of the friends whom we had taken into membership, and who were not with us when we started. This idea of dividend to labour created some excitement, too, among the outside public and although a small part only was recommended, it was regarded as a new-fangled notion, and one that could not be just to the shareholder'.[98]

Greenwood was up against the difficulty that at this stage there were really only two widely recognised models for co-operative, or quasi- co-operative, businesses. One was the model followed by the rapidly expanding number of distributive co-operatives (grocery stores), where in general only limited capital was needed. The other form of business which had taken off in communities such as Hebden Bridge was that of the working-class joint-stock. The idea of worker 'self-employment', although it had been discussed by the Christian Socialists twenty years earlier, was indeed something of a novelty. And if the workers were unable to fund their business themselves – such was the argument which would have been used against Greenwood – by what right should they enjoy a top-up of their wages at the expense of those who put in the capital?

During 1872 and early 1873 a series of general meeting decisions, including two major revisions of the co-operative's original rules for which Neale's assistance had been solicited, had helped to establish a way forward. Firstly, it was agreed that co-operative societies would also be admitted to membership. It is likely that this was seen at this stage as a way of helping to redress the power of the individual external investors; it also had the welcome benefit of encouraging more societies to start buying products from the fustian society. As Table 2 shows, societies quickly took advantage of this: 52 were signed up by the end of 1873 and 99 by the end of 1875. (The three societies enrolled before 1872 had probably done so through individual members acting as trustees).

Table 2
Membership, Hebden Bridge Fustian Manufacturing Society 1870-1875[99]

Half year ending	Worker members	Co-op society members	Individual (non-employee) members
Dec 1870	-	-	95
June 1871	-	-	96
Dec 1871	17	3	112
June 1872	23	9	158
Dec 1872	23	12	172
June 1873	24	43	178
Dec 1873	34	52	170

June 1874	50	63	164
Dec 1874	54	70	170
June 1875	59	91	172
Dec 1875	71	99	167

It was also agreed to introduce a new rule which firmed up exactly what should happen to the trading profits. After allowance for depreciation and reserves, profit (so the 1873 rule-book read) 'shall be applied, in the first place, to the payment of a dividend on capital paid up on shares at the rate of 7½ per cent per annum (should the profits permit) and the remainder shall be divided at an equal rate per £ between labour and purchase'. The dividends to labour and to societies on their purchases were to be added to their share account until at least £20 was reached. Co-operative societies who were not members of the Hebden Bridge Fustian Manufacturing Society received half dividends; customers outside the co-operative movement received no dividend.[100]

What had happened in effect was that the Hebden Bridge fustian society had restructured itself to become what in today's parlance would be known as a multi-stakeholder co-operative. All three groups of stakeholders – the workers, the investors, and the co-operative store customers – had a common interest in the continued success of the business and were now sharing the profits. Of course, in other respects there could be diverging interests.

When put into force, the new rule meant that investors (increasingly including co-operative societies as well as individuals) continued to claim their 7½ per cent. 'Labour' and 'purchase' received 2½ per cent dividends for five of the seven half-years from July 1872 to December 1875 and 3¾ per cent for the two half-years when profits were somewhat higher. Thereafter dividends varied between 0 per cent (in very bad years) and 3¾ per cent (in the good years) until the early 1890s.

Giving the co-operative societies a profit share on purchases, as well as being the standard way of doing things in the distributive co-operatives, also copied the way that the CWS operated. There was an implication for labour, of course, in that its own share of the profits was diluted. There would be no return to the 5 per cent bonus to labour which had been paid between July 1871 and June 1872 for another two decades.[101]

These changes gave the fustian society the ability to find the capital for the Nutclough Mill purchase but inevitably represented something of a compromise between the stakeholders. It was this compromise that the 1876 special general meeting threatened to overturn.

It is impossible to understand the full significance of the 1876 meeting in Hebden Bridge without having a broader sense of the issues around capital and labour which were actively being debated in the co-operative movement at that time. Bonus to labour, as mentioned in the Introduction, became a enormously significant and deeply divisive issue. Why?

Some of those at the stormy Hebden Bridge meeting would have been aware of what had happened a number of years earlier across the Pennines in Rochdale. In 1854, ten years after opening their Toad Lane store, the Rochdale Equitable Pioneers had been able to meet a second of their original aims, that of manufacturing, with the establishment of a cotton mill. The Rochdale Co-operative Manufacturing Society was created as an independent legal entity but with strong support from stalwarts from the Rochdale Pioneers, including Abraham Greenwood. J.T.W. Mitchell, who was to lead the CWS for 21 years during its most entrepreneurial period, was another member of the Pioneers closely engaged with the Manufacturing Society.

The Rochdale Co-operative Manufacturing Society had started by giving its workers as of right a share in the profits: in fact, initially the workforce received a 4s in the pound (20 per cent) bonus on their wages, while investors were paid 10 per cent. But the shareholders were discontented and in due course the rules were changed. It was agreed that capital would receive a 5 per cent dividend as a first call on profits, and that profits thereafter would be split equally between investors and workers. In 1860 however the investors returned to the fray, proposing the removal of any profit share to labour. They won the vote, although not at that stage by the necessary two-thirds majority; this was achieved two years later, at the height of the Cotton Famine.

'Thus ended the great Rochdale experiment in Producers' Co-operation,' wrote a later historian of the movement, G.D.H. Cole.[102] The abolition of a labour share of profits was indeed at the time a controversial move among Rochdale co-operators. William Cooper, one of the original leaders of the Pioneers society, railed against 'the rapacity of certain working men in Rochdale, who, on becoming employers of labour, took the bounty off their work-people at the so-called co-operative mill'.[103]

Other productive co-operatives had similar tales to tell. During his time living in Huddersfield Joseph Greenwood may well have been in contact with the Huddersfield and District Spinning and Manufacturing Society which had commenced trading in the early 1860s. This society also provided a bonus to labour, in this case split half and half with capital but only after 7½ per cent had already been paid to investors. As at Rochdale, the arrangement only lasted a short time, however. 'Things went on well for about four years, and I remember that one year the profits made was over 20 per cent, and the workman's bonus was something handsome. After three or four years the envy of those members who did not work for the society, and consequently did not participate in the bonus, began to find vent in action,' one of the co-operative's leaders later recalled. The bonus was abolished.[104]

Unwelcome precedents for arrangements at Hebden Bridge had been set, therefore – including at Rochdale, the recognised cradle of modern co-operation. Far more significant in terms of the debate on bonus to labour, however, were recent decisions taken by the CWS in relation to its manufacturing operations. The 'Wholesale' had been established in 1863 through the efforts of northern co-operators (again with the Rochdale Pioneers to the fore), and had originally acted as a conventional wholesale operation, buying in bulk to supply the independent co-operative societies.

In 1872 the CWS decided to begin manufacturing biscuits, opening what was to become a celebrated factory at Crumpsall north of Manchester a year later. A short time after it also entered the boot and shoe business, opening a factory at Leicester, and in late 1874 a soap works was purchased in Durham. These forays into production immediately brought the question of bonus to labour into the heart of the co-operative movement – should it be paid, and if so how? Some senior figures were determined to ensure that labour did receive a fair share of the fruits of its labour. Neale raised the question at the May quarterly meeting of the CWS. Six months later, at the November 1873 quarterly meeting, it was raised again, this time by Edward Owen Greening.[105]

Greening, three years younger than Joseph Greenwood, was to go on to become a significant figure in the co-operative movement, and to be an active protagonist in the disputes on bonus to labour and profit-sharing. Educated at a Quaker school in Manchester, he joined the temperance movement as a young man and was also active at the time of the American Civil War in Manchester's Anti-Slavery Society. He began lecturing in support of the Union states; he gave a lecture at the village of Portsmouth near Todmorden in 1863 during the Cotton Famine, for example.[106] In 1868 he stood unsuccessfully as an MP for Halifax.

His own attempt to turn the family business which made wire products into a joint-stock company paying a profit share to labour failed when the business folded during the second half of the 1860s. However he moved south to London to take over the management of the newly established Agricultural and Horticultural Association, a co-operative society set up in

1868 to provide seeds, fertilisers and other agricultural inputs to farmers. This, and the associated monthly newspaper *Agricultural Economist*, gave him a platform within the co-operative movement until well into the twentieth century. He visited the Nutclough Mill on several occasions and became a close associate of Greenwood. He was on the guest list for the 1891 coming-of-age banquet but had to send a telegram at the last minute giving his apologies (the excuse was that he was busy trying to get the next issue of *Agricultural Economist* out in time).[107]

Greening and Neale raised the issue of the workers' role at the CWS productive works again at the first CWS meeting in 1874. What they wanted, Greening said, was to make the CWS's employees 'co-partners instead of mere hired workmen'.[108]

The CWS agreed to introduce a profit-sharing arrangement at its works, but only on a pilot basis. The scheme introduced was also a complicated one, linked both to profits and to sales. A CWS members' meeting at the end of 1874 agreed grudgingly to keep the scheme going a little longer but at the meeting the following June the committee recommended its abolition, and this was carried by a two-thirds majority.

The arguments at that meeting suggest that the CWS had approached bonus to labour as a form of experiment in profit-related pay, rather than as a matter of co-operative principle. One speaker, Henry Whiley, described the pilot as a miserable failure 'so far as perceiving any effects in the management'. Rochdale's Abraham Greenwood said that while 'he had not yet lost faith in the bonus principle' he did not support the way the CWS had implemented it. 'At present they gave a man the maximum of wages, and then in addition to that they gave him bounty; now as a believer of bounty he would take less wages in the hope of making more profit.'[109]

As might be expected, the CWS decision not to continue the pilot did not please those who had been arguing strongly for profit-sharing with workers. Lloyd Jones, who gave two lectures in Hebden Bridge in March 1876 under the auspices of the Industrial Co-operative Society (the store), made his views plain. If he had been asleep for ten years, he said, and had woken at the end of that time to be told that co-operators had established a manufacturing operation where the worker was merely a worker for capital, he would not have believed his ears. He praised Hebden Bridge for having still 'some of the old spirit that had been so successful in the past'.[110]

Neale also tackled the issue in a paper presented a day later to a co-operative conference, this time in next-door Mytholmroyd. Always something of a theoretician, he came up with what today would be a classic stakeholder approach to the question, arguing in favour of a scheme which shared the benefits of co-operative production four ways: to meet 'the interest of the residents round any centre of manufacture, the interest of the workers engaged in it, the interest of those who own the capital employed, and the interest of those who consume the articles produced'.[111]

The arguments carried on at the 1876 Co-operative Congress, in Glasgow. Thomas Hughes thundered that any co-operative society which did not pay bonus to labour should not be allowed membership of the Co-operative Union. Greening praised the results of the Hebden Bridge decision in January: 'The men felt that they had an interest in the concern and encouraged by their wives they rallied round the manager and succeeded in avoiding a disgraceful blot upon the co-operative escutcheon'.[112]

And yet the fixation on the way that profit was to be distributed is somewhat curious. Firstly, the concept of profit in a co-operative is a difficult matter to pin down. Practically speaking, a co-operative store could choose to drop its prices and reduce the profits it made, or it could maintain prices and simply pass the equivalent savings back to its members when it came to be time for the dividend. In distributive co-operative societies at least, profit was really no more than that part of the net mark-up on goods which the society chose to pay across later rather than at the time of purchase. This was recognised by, among others, the tax authorities; indeed co-operative societies continue even today to be taxed differently from conventional businesses.

With productive co-operatives, the nature of profit was perhaps not so clear-cut. However, it was still potentially a flexible affair. For example, the Hebden Bridge fustian society could have chosen to reduce the size of the profits it made by paying higher wages to its workers, or by investing in better working conditions for them. It could also have reduced profit levels by reducing the prices it charged its co-operative society members for their purchases.

To what extent did this happen? We shall look at wage levels at the Nutclough in more detail in a later chapter (see pages 142-5), but at this point we can note that Greenwood did sometimes claim that the co-operative paid more in wages than equivalent firms. At the 1880 Co-operative Congress, for example, he stated that Nutclough workers 'received 25 to 30 per cent more wages' than those of other firms.[113] This does not mean necessarily that wage rates were higher (although as we shall see they probably were, to a limited extent); one of the features of the fustian industry in Hebden Bridge was the amount of time when workers were on short-time and instead of working were forced (using the local term) to play, unpaid. The summer season was notorious in particular among fustian cutters as a time when playing was endemic. One of the achievements Greenwood claimed for his society was that it had been able to keep its workers more regularly employed.

Any over-generous policy in relation to wage levels would have come in for scrutiny, however. To give one example, the CWS's John Shillito, a regular delegate at Hebden Bridge Fustian Manufacturing Society meetings, wanted to know at a 1884 general meeting why wages had increased when turnover hadn't. (The answer was that the workers had been transferred to doing improvement work around the mill, but Shillito's scrutiny of the accounts would have been noted).[114]

In relation to pricing policy we have much more direct evidence that profits were indeed lower than they might have been. The co-operative agreed shortly after 1876 (in 1878, according to E.O. Greening) to offer a 2½ per cent discount on invoices issued to co-operative stores. Greening, staunch advocate of the bonus to labour that he was, was not impressed, calling it 'a mere device to arrest and secure a large share of the profits and reduce the share due to labour'.[115] Whatever the motivation in introducing the discount, Greening was right in terms its practical effect.

The profits available for distribution were also kept lower than they might have been as a result of the Hebden Bridge fustian society's very prudent approach to depreciation – or in other words by the significant amounts it wrote off each accounting period for its machinery, buildings and other fixed assets. This approach, whilst it helped ensure the long-term sustainability of the business, particularly protected the investors' interests and could be seen as an implicit extra reward to capital.

In reality, therefore, this emphasis on the profit bonus to labour had an importance out of all proportion to its practical effect on workers' incomes. Indeed the sums paid to the workers in bonuses were miniscule when compared with the income they received from their regular wages (Table 3).

Table 3
Income from profit-share as percentage of total worker income (wage bill plus profit-share) for selected years, 1872-1892[116]

Half-year ending	Income from profit-share as per cent of total income
Dec 1872	2.4
Dec 1874	3.5
Dec 1876	2.3
Dec 1878	0.0

Dec 1880	2.3
Dec 1882	2.3
Dec 1884	2.3
Dec 1886	3.4
Dec 1888	3.5
Dec 1890	3.5
Dec 1892	4.6

The point also has to be made that the 1872 rules revision, by establishing that profits beyond that paid to capital would be shared at an equal rate between labour and 'purchase' on a per-£ basis, was in effect heavily weighted against the workers. There may have seemed an element of equality of treatment involved, but this was spurious: treating money spent on purchases with money earned in wages is not a like-with-like comparison.

The way that the profits were divided between the three stakeholder groups becomes all too clear if it is illustrated in graphical form (Figure 1).

Figure 1
Proportion of distributed profits going to investors, co-operative stores and workers for selected half-years 1872-1893 (excluding money retained in reserve funds)[117]

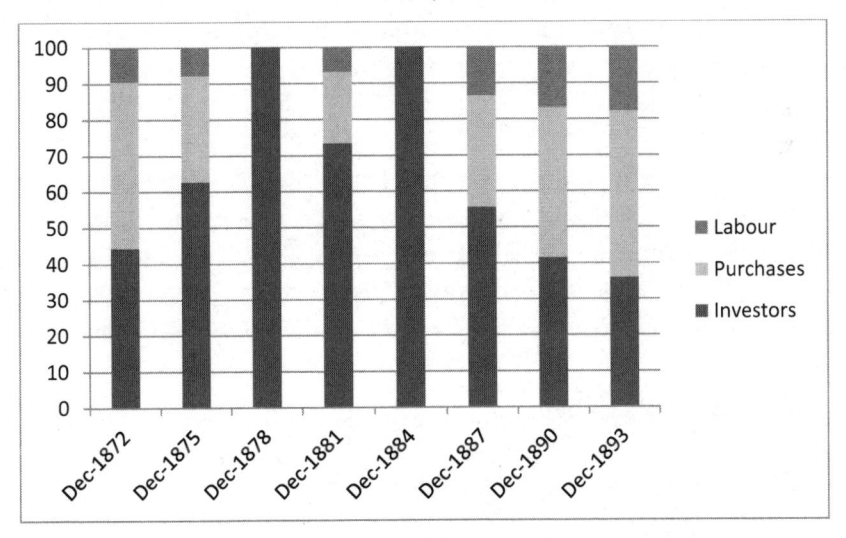

It would of course have been possible to have divided up the cake differently. Simply splitting the excess profit beyond the investor's share 50:50 between labour and 'purchase' would have immediately made a considerable difference.

This exact point had indeed been pointed out in a report presented to the 1874 Co-operative Congress which directly referred to the Hebden Bridge fustian society and suggested that such a 50:50 division of profits, while it would hardly be noticed by co-operative stores, would lead to a much higher bonus which would be 'felt very sensibly' by the workers. (We can detect Neale's hand in this paper.)[118]

Later on, at a time when productive co-operatives had increased in both number and confidence, other ways to divide profits were tried out elsewhere. In the Midlands, where several strong boot and shoe co-operatives grew deep roots, the standard approach was to pay 5 per cent to capital and then divide the remainder to each worker in proportion to his or her earnings. In some cases, it was reported, the bonus could be as high as 25 per cent of wages.[119] Later still a set of model rules produced for producer co-operatives by the Labour Association proposed a very precise formula: 10 per cent of profits for an employees' provident fund, 5 per cent to education, 3 per cent to special service, 1 per cent to each management committee member, 20 per cent to customers and the remainder (about 42 per cent) to labour.[120]

J.C. Gray himself pondered this question and came up with a theoretical approach in a paper written for the Co-operative Congress in 1886, when it was held at Plymouth. Gray's approach was based on trying to calculate the value added by labour and capital, as well as the contribution made by custom. He offered a worked example, which gives an insight into his thinking:

> A society pays £850 per year to capital, being interest at the rate of 5 per cent; it also pays £6,000 as wages to its workers, which amount we must take as the interest on the labour employed. The society does a trade, say, of £20,000 per annum, and the net profits, after paying the wages of capital and labour, are, say, £750. By this rule of proportion we obtain the following figures:
>
> | | |
> |---|---|
> | Value of money capital | £17,000 |
> | Value of labour capital | £120,000 |
> | Value of trade | £20,000 |
>
> Which gives a total of £157,000 having an interest in the profits which have been obtained (£750). If we divide this £750 into 157,000 parts it gives the following result, namely to capital £82; labour £573; and trade £95.[121]

This is an intriguing approach, but it is not one which would have had any chance of being implemented in the early days of a pioneering productive co-operative such as Hebden Bridge Fustian Manufacturing Society. There was no doubt that Joseph Greenwood was aware that the formula being followed in Hebden Bridge was not rewarding the workers as well as they might have been. He later described the £282 paid in profit bonuses to labour during the society's first seven years as 'ridiculously small' when compared to the amount paid to investors.[122] But, small though it might be, the continuation of bonus to labour at the Nutclough Mill was important to him: it represented the continuation of a fundamental principle. The Hebden Bridge Fustian Manufacturing Society was there not just to pay interest to investors or dividends to co-operative customers; it was also there to be run for the benefit of its workers.

CHAPTER 4

GOVERNANCE

There was one satisfactory outcome of the 1876 dispute over the bonus to labour and that was the arrival into the life of the fustian society of Joseph Craven. Craven was an active and committed co-operator, the chairman at the time of his local society in the village of Heptonstall just north of Hebden Bridge. He would go on to make a highly significant contribution to the development of the co-operative at the Nutclough, not as a worker there but as the long-serving President of the management committee. He would also later have a national role, as President of the Co-operative Productive Federation. With Joseph Greenwood and John Hartley he was to be one of the three key figures from their generation of co-operators to be associated with the Nutclough venture.

After 1874 when John Hartley had stood down from the post of President to join the Nutclough workforce, the fustian society's committee had shown itself to be much less in tune with Greenwood's original vision for the co-operative. It looks as if, in the aftermath of 8 January 1876, a little quiet work was now going on to try to remedy this situation. This, at least, is how we can interpret a local press report of Joseph Craven's recollection of how he came to be involved (the report is taken from an event in 1896 held to mark Craven's 21 years of service to the management committee):

> He was returning home from a distributive society's meeting of which he was then chairman; he was met on the road by one of their shareholders, and asked to go on the Board, and after considering the matter fully, for he was then living three miles away from the place – at least it was three up and two down (laughter) – and it took him quite an hour to go home from Hebden Bridge, he consented and was elected. When he undertook to do the work he wanted to put his whole heart and soul into it.[123]

Joseph Craven was born in 1833, the same year as Greenwood, so he too had to contend when growing up with the hard economic conditions of the 1830s and 1840s. His family situation was even more difficult than

Greenwood's. His mother had married a man with a serious alcohol problem, and it would appear that because of his abusive behaviour she had been forced to leave him when Joseph was a young child. (This man is described in one account as Joseph's step-father, so it is possible that his mother was previously widowed.) Joseph Craven and his mother fled from Cullingworth near Haworth to Heptonstall. When he was seven he was sent to work in the mill down the hill at New Bridge, where his mother was also working.

When he was slightly older, Joseph moved to take work in Rochdale, where he was in contact with the Pioneers society and came to know some of the leading members. The mill he was employed in was part of the family business of John Bright, the Quaker and radical statesman who, with Richard Cobden, was leading the fight against the Corn Laws. Craven, according to Greenwood writing later, carefully saved the extra money he was now earning to help support his mother who had remained at Heptonstall.

At his mother's request he returned to Heptonstall from Rochdale. He became actively involved in both the village co-operative and a nearby Methodist church and perhaps not surprisingly given his family background he also committed himself to the temperance movement. It was through temperance work and their shared membership of the local Rechabites' 'tent' (lodge) that he and Joseph Greenwood first really came across each other, although the two men only got to know each other well following Craven's involvement at the Nutclough. He was elected to the committee at the regular general meeting of the society held at the end of January 1876 following the resignation of another member and became the President in 1879. 'His frank and open disposition was accompanied by a strict truthfulness and a quiet cheerfulness which carried with them a conviction of his being actuated by sound moral motives,' Greenwood was later to write. He became Greenwood's 'dear friend'.[124]

Craven's engagement in the life of the fustian society was, of course, in his spare time. As the local press report quoted above made clear, he was living at some distance from Hebden Bridge at this time, in the hamlet of Edge Hey Green, Colden (about seven hundred feet above Hebden Bridge in the valley bottom below). This was close to his place of work, the isolated cotton mill which was operated by the working-class joint-stock, the Colden Cotton Co. Later he was for many years to be an employee of the highly successful Sowerby Bridge Flour Society, the largest co-operative corn mill in the country. This Flour Society, which had begun in 1854, had expanded from Sowerby Bridge in 1874 into Hebden Bridge with the acquisition of a second mill, Breck Mill at the western end of the town. Having work in the valley meant that at this point Craven and his family were able to move to the centre of Hebden Bridge. He was thereafter to become active in the Hebden Bridge distributive society as well as at the Nutclough.

Much later Joseph Greenwood was to write, in the obituary he contributed following Joseph Craven's death in 1909, that to have him on the management committee at the Nutclough 'was an acquisition on the side of the fundamental principles of the society'.[125] Another obituary notice added that Craven 'was always a workman himself, and he remained so in spirit as a director'.[126]

Nevertheless, Joseph Craven was joining the management committee at a difficult time. For the first time since the society's establishment the steady upward movement in sales and profits faltered. Sales were down in the second half of 1876 and in the 1877 calendar year had fallen to £18,765 compared to £19,602 the previous year. Worse was to follow. In 1878 sales fell again, to £17,614, and in 1879 reached an even lower point, £17,470. Profits fell too.[127]

For the first six-month period in 1877 no dividend was felt possible for workers or on purchases. A small (1¼ per cent) dividend was managed after the following six months, but the trading situation in 1878 then deteriorated so that the bonus to labour and purchase was again withdrawn for the whole year. 'Trade has, generally, been extremely bad and the trade of the society has experienced unusual depression,' the management committee reported to the general meeting on 3 August. Investors, whose normal 7½ per cent return had been maintained up to now, argued that money should be taken from reserves to keep up their rate of return. Significantly, however, they lost this fight: the meeting resolved that the investors would have to make do for six months with (the still generous) 6¼ per cent. This half-year was the only time in the co-operative's life that the investors found themselves obliged by trading conditions to accept a cut in their return.[128]

The Hebden Bridge Fustian Manufacturing Society had encountered for the first time the macroeconomic trade cycle and had had its first taste of a recession. The cotton trade generally was suffering significant difficulties during the latter years of the 1870s. The workers at the Hebden Bridge Cotton and Commercial Co, for example, were forced to agree to a 5 per cent cut in wages in November 1877 in an attempt to ensure the continuation of full-time working. In the summer of 1879 the mill closed altogether for a short time because of lack of trade.[129] Nationally, the recession was unusually deep, worsened by a significant bank failure in 1878.[130]

At the Nutclough Mill, there was a small decline in the number of employees in 1877-8 (down from an average of 83 to 79) and average wages also fell slightly, a sign of short-time working. In March 1879 the mill temporarily moved from a 5½ day to a four day working week.[131]

Not surprisingly, the downturn had its effect on the fustian society's management committee. The dyeing operation which had commenced with the purchase of the Nutclough estate a few years earlier and which was supported by Greenwood came under particular scrutiny, accused of not paying its way. Greenwood wrote later that 'a continuous undercurrent of dissatisfaction was prevalent. The Committee among themselves and some outside members were grievously at variance with those inside. The Committee often sat till late.' It meant a night-time hike up the hill to Edge Hey Green for Joseph Craven: 'He had to trudge down from his mountain home and up again at night in all weathers, leaving the Committee-room often at eleven o'clock,' Greenwood recalled.[132] Craven would then have to be up in time to start his own work at the mill in Colden, at six in the morning.

The role of the management committee requires some discussion. When they started out, Joseph Greenwood and his fellow workers not only had to build their business and find the customers they needed to make the sales, they also had to establish workable structures for decision-making. Who would be given the power to direct the business? Then, as now, there were particular issues in developing governance structures which functioned well but which were also in line with the essential democratic principles of co-operation.

What we today call corporate governance was known to Joseph Greenwood and his colleagues as 'government'. It was understood to be an important aspect of a successful business but it was also a challenge. Hebden Bridge Fustian Manufacturing Society was not completely starting from scratch: it had the model of the now well-established distributive cooperative societies to follow. Nevertheless, the Industrial and Provident Societies Act under which it was incorporated was only eighteen years old in 1870 and there was almost no experience within the UK co-operative movement at that time of tailoring IPSA rules for the specific requirements of productive co-operative enterprises.

When starting out Greenwood simply adopted a set of model rules prepared by the Registrar of that time Edward William Brabrook, designed primarily for co-operatives running grocery stores.[133] As was standard, the rules established that the fustian society was to be governed by an elected Committee. This was to be ten-strong, made up of the President (subject to annual re-election) and nine members, three of the nine retiring in rotation every six months.

One highly significant aspect of the way the committee was structured at the Hebden Bridge Fustian Manufacturing Society has yet to be mentioned and it raises in some ways the most profound and difficult question relating to the co-operative, at least for those of us who are approaching the story from the perspective of a modern understanding of the workers' co-operative movement. Clause 22 of the 1870 rules adopted by Greenwood and his fellow-workers for incorporation included the following nine words: 'No paid Servant can be appointed on the Committee'.[134] The same wording was carried forward into the 1872 rules and to each of the subsequent revisions.

What this sentence meant, of course, was that whilst the employees of the fustian society, in their role as shareholders, could participate at general meetings they were unable to put themselves up as candidates when the committee elections took place. All the committee must be made up of other individuals, who (whilst they might very well have family members working at the Nutclough Mill) were not themselves employees.

This is completely at variance with current ideas of governance in workers' co-operatives, and it would also at first sight appear to run against the frequently expressed desire by Joseph Greenwood for the fustian society to be a demonstration of worker self-employment.

Beatrice Potter, better known to history by her married name Beatrice Webb, was later to seize on this issue in her highly polemical book *The Co-operative Movement in Great Britain*. Those shareholders at Hebden Bridge who were also employees were practically disenfranchised by the disqualification to act on the committee of management, she pronounced. Workers were deposed from their sovereign place, as directors of their own labour. Employees of the Hebden Bridge fustian works and other productive co-operatives with the same rule, she went on, were 'in no better position than the porters on an ordinary railway'.[135]

Greenwood would have strongly argued against these assertions. But the question of why this rule was introduced in 1870 and then repeatedly maintained through several rule revisions needs considering. It was a question which the eminent economist and university professor Alfred Marshall was to ask Joseph Greenwood, when Greenwood gave evidence before the Royal Commission on Labour in 1892.

'You have not found it well to have a number employed in the works on your committee?' Marshall, one of the Commissioners, asked. 'No,' replied Greenwood, adding by way of explanation 'That arose because, in the beginning of the Society's history, it was thought not advisable to have workers on the Committee.'

Another Royal Commissioner, the senior Conservative politician and

Leeds MP Gerald Balfour, immediately followed this up with further questioning. Their exchange went as follows:

> *Greenwood*: I think it is more in regard to custom than to anything else. It is not a very sore point with the workers. I believe if it was a sore point and they asked and agitated for its removal among the members they would obtain it, but it was the custom at the beginning of our society and it was regarded, and has been so throughout the district in connexion with co-operative works in such a way that servants should not be on the Committee.
> *Q*: Then from what class is your Committee drawn?
> *Greenwood*: Our Committee is drawn from workers in the same kind of work in the locality who may be shareholders and from representatives of the stores; about half of each class.
> *Q*: This rule seems to be a serious infringement of your principle that the workers should themselves govern the concern?
> *Greenwood*: Yes, that is so, and I think if it was to be considered now they would be recognised and duly represented on the management committee[136]

Greenwood's views had changed by 1892. Earlier, in a paper presented to the 1877 Co-operative Congress he had written that 'It would be well that the actual workers should not sit on the board of management but that these should be composed of other men, who would be removed from a suspicion of wrong-doing'.[137]

There is a clue here perhaps as to Greenwood's original caution. Co-operatives had faced and found ways to overcome a host of practical problems in the development of the movement from the 1840s onwards. One issue was how to guard against individual self-interest and indeed outright fraud, given the sums of cash which could be passing through even a moderately sized co-operative store during an average working week. In this respect, restricting the rights of employees could be seen as an appropriate safeguard.

Co-operative managers were regularly described as the 'servants' of the membership. Offering them the possibility of participating in their societies' strategic management could give them power to pursue their own interests. It could turn them into masters.

In this context, we can note that concerns remain today in co-operative activist circles that societies can be run by senior employees in their own interests rather than in the interests of the membership. Some of the less satisfactory examples of corporate governance in recent decades in British co-operative societies can be directly attributed to precisely this tendency towards 'management capture'. It may also be relevant to remind ourselves that, for similar reasons, it is still a principle of British law that those who are employees of charities cannot normally also be trustees.

Concerns such as these in part explain Greenwood's original attitude. There was another related concern, perhaps, which was the fear of a potential degeneration of original co-operative idealism into a business which was effectively run by a cabal of workmen in positions of authority. Beatrice Potter herself identified this risk: 'So-called associations of workers are constantly resolving themselves into associations of small masters – into an industrial organization which is perilously near, if it not be actually included within, the domain of the sweating system.'[138] Greenwood himself had the experience of seeing an earlier attempt to establish a co-operative of workmen in Hebden Bridge quickly turn itself into a one-person business (Chapter 1).

There was also, of course, a possible downside to employee representation in productive co-operatives as another of the Royal Commissioners, the Sheffield MP A.J. Mundella, suggested during the 1892 hearing. Could there be problems of discipline if employees were given powers of responsibility over their supervisors, he asked? Greenwood responded that he had heard that there had been 'serious friction' of this kind in certain other individual productive co-operatives but he added, 'As I am the manager and have the control of these works I do not think I should have any very serious difficulty with the men who work in it and who might be on the Committee in their representative character'.

Mundella pressed the point: so the rule at Hebden Bridge preventing workers on the committee, he asked, might be safely relaxed? 'I think it might in our case,' Greenwood responded.[139]

By the 1890s when the Royal Commission on Labour was sitting, and certainly by the first two decades of the twentieth century, the Hebden Bridge Fustian Manufacturing Society was increasingly out of step with other more recently established productive co-operatives, where employees were represented on management committees (indeed some co-operatives had their committees entirely composed of employees). The Board of Trade, which regularly surveyed this aspect of co-operative business, reported that in 1899 there were 88 trading productive co-operatives in Britain which between them had 334 employees serving on their management committees. On average, employees made up slightly more than 40 per cent of committee membership.[140] By 1918 only 17 societies (out of 67) remained with similar structures to the fustian society, without employee representation of any kind.[141]

The Hebden Bridge Fustian Manufacturing Society never did make the change Mundella had discussed with Greenwood and the 1870 rule remained unrevoked. The issue did however get raised at the January 1894 general meeting, a little more than a year after Greenwood's hearing at Westminster. After a debate the meeting voted, just, in favour of employees on the management committee: 45 in favour and 43 against. This was not the two-thirds majority needed for a rule change (and it is not clear in any case whether the meeting had been formally constituted for a rule change discussion). There was talk of the issue being debated again later, but nothing appears to have been done.[142] With the benefit of hindsight, this could be considered a missed opportunity.

How in practice did the fustian society's management committee work, and how did it relate to Joseph Greenwood as manager? Today, the role of a board of directors is understood to be strategic rather than operational. Directors' tasks are to set the overall strategy to be followed by a business, and to perform a scrutiny function over the work of the executive officers as they attempt to implement that strategy. The practice in co-operative societies in the second half of the nineteenth century, however, was for committees to be very much hands-on in the work they did. Local co-operative society committees met weekly or even (as with the society in Mytholmroyd)[143] twice-weekly when detailed operational decisions, including stock ordering and invoice paying, would feature as key items on their meeting agendas. The Hebden Bridge Fustian Manufacturing Society followed this convention, its committee meetings taking place every week. The tradition quickly became established that these took place on Tuesday evenings, starting at 6.30 pm.

Members of the fustian society's committee took on these responsibilities in their leisure time, having probably already worked from 6am to 6pm at their own paid employment. It was conventional in co-operative societies for committee members to be paid for their labours, and again the fustian society followed usual practice. The 1870 rules, carried forward into later versions of the rules, stated that 'the Society in general meeting shall from time to time fix their remuneration which shall be divided among them in proportion to the number of their attendances on the business of the Society'. Initially this would have amounted to no more than pennies (one local society was paying its committee members 3d per meeting in the late 1870s).[144] By 1892, the Fustian Manufacturing Society was allocating £25 per half-year for committee members' 'salaries', which suggests about two shillings per head per meeting.[145] By 1918 the committee members' remuneration had reached £22 per head per year, or around nine shillings for each meeting attended. The President was given £26 per year.[146]

Despite the lack of detailed wording in the rules, the convention quickly developed, as Greenwood implied in his reply to Gerald Balfour at the Royal Commission hearing, that the committee would comprise both representatives of individual investors and of co-operative stores. It is not always clear from the documentary evidence which category individual committee members fell into (and in some instances individual investors may also have had strong co-operative links) but in general in the early decades of the society the split appears to have been broadly half-and-half.

Some local co-operative societies were regularly represented. As might be expected, the Hebden Bridge Industrial Co-operative Society, the society John Hartley had helped found in 1848, had a close relationship with the fustian society just up the road. It had grown steadily and at the start of 1879 had just under 1,400 members and an annual turnover of £43,000. In 1876 it had opened a major new store in Crown Street in the heart of the town, and it would go on to extend this in a further substantial extension opened in 1889. By then it would be able to boast, on the second floor of the main store, a main Co-operative Hall able to accommodate many hundreds of people, a smaller hall alongside capable of accommodating around two hundred, as well as a full catering kitchen for functions. These two Co-operative halls became the centre of local community life.

The largest store in the upper Calder valley was the one at Todmorden, centred on the Dale Street department store but with branches in almost every settlement and village nearby. In 1878 it had 2,330 members and turnover of £80,000, on which it paid a dividend of 2s 11d on purchases. Later, to celebrate its fiftieth birthday in 1896, it was to choose to donate its library of books, many thousand strong, to the people of Todmorden and to build a new public library building to house them. Todmorden also had a second separate co-operative society, Bridge End, focused on the Rochdale end of the town. Beyond Bridge End, just before the Lancashire county boundary, was another society in the village of Walsden.

There were a cluster of co-operative societies near Hebden Bridge, many established in a wave around 1860-1861. These included the society at Heptonstall (1860), at Cragg Vale (1861), Midgley (1861), Luddendenfoot (1860) and in Luddenden village (1865). The Mytholmroyd society, which was set up in 1861, served a larger community than these village societies. By 1879 it had about 500 members and a turnover of over £6,000. There were much smaller societies in the hilltop settlements of Pecket Well,

Blackshawhead and Wainstalls. Slightly further afield (but also participants in the Calderdale Co-operative Association) were the societies at Sowerby Bridge, Brighouse and Halifax.

Some members of the Fustian Manufacturing Society's committee stayed no more than a year or two, but there were some stalwarts who served for many years. A few names out of many can perhaps be mentioned. For example, the Todmorden society nominated John Speak, a committee member for eleven years up to his death in 1890, when John Toothill took his place for almost twenty years. The Mytholmroyd society's Adam Sutcliffe served for a number of years in the 1880s-1890s; Thomas Pickles who was on the committee from the late 1880s to the early twentieth century and Thomas Morgan (a committee member from 1901-1918) were also Mytholmroyd nominees. Arthur Ainley, who joined the Management Committee in 1894 and was to take over as President from Joseph Craven, was active in the Cragg Vale society. Midgley, Sowerby Bridge, Luddendenfoot, Heptonstall and Brighouse also contributed committee members at different times. Some of the independent members, the representatives of the individual investors, also served for long periods.

There was a tendency, once elected, for committee members to be re-elected when their terms of office expired. But elections, held at the half-yearly general meetings, were not necessarily formalities and places were contested. Members could lose their seats: John Bradbury, who served as the fustian society's President for a short time and was a senior figure at the Hebden Bridge distributive society, came bottom of the poll in February 1881, for example.[147]

Committee members took their responsibilities seriously and would have considered it a matter of principle not to miss meetings without very good reason. Attendance figures for each member were published in the half-yearly accounts, made available to members and submitted to the Registrar of Friendly Societies. Taking as an example one period for which records have survived (that from Jan-June 1892) we find that six of the committee of ten had attended every one of the 23 weekly meetings. Two other committee members missed just one meeting and the remaining two were present at all except two of the meetings. (An explanatory note adds that two of the absences were due to sickness.)[148]

Under the rules it was the committee who appointed the co-operative's manager and secretary, and also had the power to dismiss them. The second point is significant: working for a co-operative society at this time as a senior employee could be a precarious occupation, and it was not uncommon for societies' committees to summarily dismiss their managers. Indeed, one of the issues with co-operative democracy in some societies could be the capriciousness of members in relation to their employed staff.

Because of the risk of employee fraud in co-operative societies, it became accepted practice for societies to require sureties from their managers. The Fustian Manufacturing Society drew up legal agreements in 1877 for both Greenwood and J.C. Gray, under which £100 guarantees were pledged in the event that either should be found 'wasting embezzling losing misspending misapplying or unlawfully making away with any of the monies chattels wares merchandise or effects whatsoever ' of the co-operative. The pledge was offered in J.C. Gray's case by his father, the Baptist minister; Greenwood asked a local businessman William Hall to be his guarantor.

These surety deeds were filed away in the co-operative's records (and indeed are still to be found in a box of archive material) but fortunately neither was ever required to be executed.[149] But there were moments when relations between the management committee and Joseph Greenwood were strained: 'There have been times when we could not always agree, but it has never come to a severance' was how Greenwood put it at the Royal Commission on Labour hearing.[150]

The sense after 1879, when Joseph Craven took over as president, is that these sorts of difficulties receded. The economic situation helped: as the 1880s arrived, sales and profits once more started moving forwards. Things were looking up again.

CHAPTER 5

LOCAL AND NATIONAL

For Joseph Greenwood, the symbolic turning point when the previous 'desponding and depressing' period could be left behind was the Exhibition of goods produced in co-operatively run manufacturing works, which was staged in Hebden Bridge's Co-operative Hall for four days between 5 and 8 March 1879.[151]

The Exhibition had been Greenwood's idea. He had been to a similar exhibition which had been staged in 1878 in the north-east, at Chester-le-Street, and had floated the idea of doing something like this in the Lancashire and Yorkshire region at a meeting in September. By the end of the year the planning process was in full swing and by late February 1879 the final arrangements had been made.[152] As well as fustian from the Nutclough, there would be – among other things – quilts from a co-operative in Eccles, flannels from Littleborough, linen from Dunfermline, silk twist from Leek, hosiery from Leicester, shawls from Paisley, woollen cloth from Leeds, and cutlery from Sheffield. The Coventry watchmakers' cooperative would be exhibiting, as would Edward Owen Greening's Agricultural and Horticultural Association. The CWS was offering to show off biscuits from Crumpsall and shoes from Leicester. Most of the co-operatively run corn mills, including the local Sowerby Bridge society, would be there too. For sceptics in the co-operative movement who questioned the whole concept of co-operative production – and there were indeed some quite vocal sceptics around at this time – the Hebden Bridge Exhibition could demonstrate what had been achieved. In all, the products of around twenty-five co-operative works were to be on display.

Great efforts had been made to decorate the Co-operative Hall for the occasion. Appropriate mottos had been inscribed on banners (made of fustian) around the walls: one read 'Success to Local Societies', another 'Work is Worship', a third 'Self-help is true help'. There were others: 'Knowledge is Power'; 'A Penny Saved is a Penny Gained'; 'Co-operation is Mutual Help'.

The big innovation at the Exhibition was the use of electric light, produced by two machines brought in for the occasion. According to *Co-operative News*, the technology proved somewhat temperamental, although when the electric lights could be made to work the effect was apparently much admired. The rest of the time gas lighting had to suffice, as it did in the Nutclough Mill of course.

The Exhibition was open from noon on Wednesday to Saturday evening, free of charge during the days but with a 3d charge in the evenings. A conference for co-operative store buyers and managers was fixed for the Wednesday afternoon when 150 people showed up. Another well-attended conference was held on the Saturday.

E. O. Greening was up from London for the opening ceremony and Neale had made the journey across from the Co-operative Union office in Manchester. Greening, revealing that he like Neale was an investor in the Nutclough enterprise, praised the society's progress in glowing terms. The time would come he said when Hebden Bridge people should consider erecting a statue to Joseph Greenwood and those who had worked alongside him. 'Hebden Bridge is notable for having made a success both in co-operative distribution and co-operative production,' he told his audience. And indeed it was true: add in the effect of the Sowerby Bridge Flour Society's mill in Hebden Bridge and the overall size of the town's co-operative economy was beginning to become very significant. Hebden Bridge was increasingly a co-operative town.[153]

The Hebden Bridge Exhibition in March 1879 had been arranged under the auspices of the North-Western section of the Co-operative Union which had matched the fustian society's own initial grant funding of £25. The event happened in large part because Joseph Greenwood was by now a member of the Co-operative Union's Central Board, having been elected at the 1878 Co-operative Congress in Manchester. It was a sign that he had become a familiar and respected figure in northern co-operative circles, and that Hebden Bridge's Nutclough Mill was well on the co-operative map.

Greenwood's election in 1878 would help to cement the Fustian Manufacturing Society's reputation in the national co-operative movement. John Hartley had himself been elected to the Central Board at the 1873 and 1874 congresses, but had either stood down after these two years (perhaps as a consequence of no longer being President of the fustian society) or had failed to be re-elected.[154]

The role of the Co-operative Central Board which Greenwood joined needs clarifying. It was a large body which came together only occasionally, meeting regularly as a whole body usually once or twice a year. Members of the Central Board in each part of the country met very frequently (normally monthly) in their own sectional boards, however, and these had considerable autonomy in undertaking initiatives in their own area. So it was in the north-west that Greenwood's efforts as an elected member of the Central Board were primarily focused and it was to the North-Western sectional meeting of the Board that he took his suggestion for the Hebden Bridge exhibition.

This regional autonomy stemmed from the way that the Central Board was set up at the 1870 Congress. Originally Congress had operated with just two sections, one for the north (based on the Lancashire and Yorkshire heartlands) and one for London. This reflected the political reality behind the 1869 and 1870 Congresses which brought together the northern co-operative leadership with individuals based in London committed to the idea of co-operation. In 1873, this arrangement was refined to allow for five sections, respectively London and the South, the North-West (this included Yorkshire), the North (with Newcastle as its centre), the Midlands, and Scotland. After two more years a sixth, Western, region was created. (Later on, there were to be further changes, including a short-lived Irish section and one for the South-West.) The name Co-operative Union, to denote the whole federated structure, gradually gained parlance during the 1870s; the Union was legally incorporated under co-operative legislation in 1889.

The Central Board was too unwieldy to be an executive body, but each section appointed some of their number to a smaller United Board which met more regularly. The United Board began simply as a point of liaison but gradually developed more of an executive role, particularly once Neale had been appointed as General Secretary in 1873 and had as his Assistant a younger co-operator called Joseph Smith. (Eventually, the United Board was itself seen to be meeting too infrequently, and an office committee was created to handle more detailed administrative matters).

The North-Western section of the Central Board at this time tended to choose its United Board delegates each year by rotation, and Greenwood served in this second capacity for 1881-2, 1883-4 and 1892-3.[155] He was also regularly nominated by his section to serve on the national sub-committee of the Central Board which worked to encourage productive co-operation across the movement.

Once elected, Greenwood became a stalwart of the Central Board, re-elected year after year. His position became even more secure when the North-Western section restructured the way its Central Board members were elected so that Greenwood was able to represent the Calderdale (or sometimes West Calderdale) district of the section. Although some years challenged in elections, there were also many years when he was returned unopposed. He would serve continuously on the Central Board until the year 1920 by which time he was in his late eighties.

The Hebden Bridge Exhibition was, at least according to the *Co-operative News* reporter, 'in every sense a complete success'. Over 1,600 paid their threepence to attend on Wednesday, Thursday or Friday evenings, and a further 1,300 crowded in on Saturday, with reportedly hundreds more unable to get admission. And Greenwood would have been delighted at the coverage his own society received in the co-operative movement's weekly paper: 'Hebden Bridge Fustian Manufacturing Co-operative Society made perhaps the most important display, showing a vast variety of goods', the paper noted: ninety different varieties of cords, moleskins, velveteens and twills had been on display, in a large variety of colours. 'The Hebden Bridge Fustian Society, we need hardly say, stands in the forefront of co-operative productive societies and is a striking illustration of the success which may be achieved by a faithful and persevering adherence to its first principles,' the *Co-operative News* added.[156]

This position had indeed been built by perseverance, for the loyalty of co-operative stores could not always be taken for granted. The cold shoulder which Joseph Greenwood had sometimes encountered in the very earliest days from co-operative store buyers (Chapter 2) seems to have been a recurring experience. The society's Secretary J.C. Gray prepared a paper on the loyalty of co-operative stores – or sometimes, the lack of it – towards productive co-operatives for a conference in Hebden Bridge two years after the March Exhibition, in 1881. It was, he said, ironic that private buyers were happy to buy the goods from productive co-operatives when stores were reluctant: 'Many societies, instead of showing a desire to encourage co-operative production will do just the reverse, and will not even give them a trial, and it is not confined only to our smaller societies,' he wrote. And he also disclosed that even the CWS, the fustian society's own agents, was not always playing fair: 'We found that our trade in a certain district was not what it ought to be, or what it had been formerly. On inquiry we found that one of our agents had been supplying a lower class of fustian goods to the societies in that district, entirely unknown to us, and this while being agents for us and professing to sell our goods only. These low goods were obtained from a private firm.'[157] The Society intervened and arranged (somewhat against its will) to provide the poorer quality goods the CWS had been sourcing elsewhere.

Joseph Greenwood told a co-operative audience on another occasion that while he did not believe in 'the doctrine that productive societies ought to receive the support of the stores on the mere grounds of sympathy', he did believe that their goods could hold their own against any private competitor in the same line of goods, 'if fairly dealt with'. In his experience, he went on revealingly, 'he had found it much easier to do business with private individuals than with the store buyers'.[158] Greenwood regularly attended the Manchester cloth market to meet the private merchants and to obtain goods for dyeing and finishing.[159]

There would continue to be ups and downs in the trading performance of the Fustian Manufacturing Society as the years went by, but nevertheless in its second full decade of trading the signs were increasingly heartening. The business was growing by around 10 per cent a year and profits were keeping up too. In general, the profit to sales ratio had improved during the first ten years of trading, and was now usually between 8-10 per cent of turnover (Figure 2).

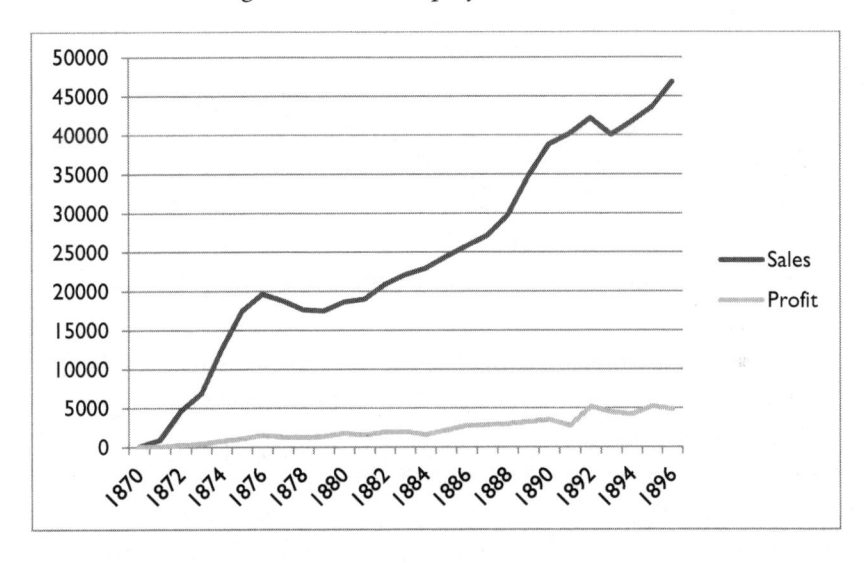

Figure 2: Sales and profits, 1870-1896[160]

The fustian society's business with co-operative stores, including goods sold through the CWS and the Scottish CWS acting as agents, was much the most important part of its trade: generally at least three-quarters, rising toward four-fifths of all sales in the 1890s, were to co-operatives.

Despite J.C. Gray's strictures about disloyalty, the number of co-operative societies choosing to become members of the fustian society steadily increased, from 112 at the end of 1880 to 227 in 1888, 266 in 1891 and 314 in 1896. There was, of course, a strong incentive for any co-operative buying the Nutclough's products to do so in that dividends on purchases were paid at double the rate paid to non-member co-operatives.

Throughout the 1880s and into the 1890s, society membership grew very much in line with membership in the society by workers (Figure 3). There was one difference between the two classes of membership, however: from the 1872-3 rules revision onwards, co-operative societies were given one vote and the right to one delegate at each general meeting for each £100 or part of £100 invested. The one member, one vote rule continued to apply for individuals.

Figure 3: Hebden Bridge Fustian Manufacturing Society membership, 1870-1896[161]

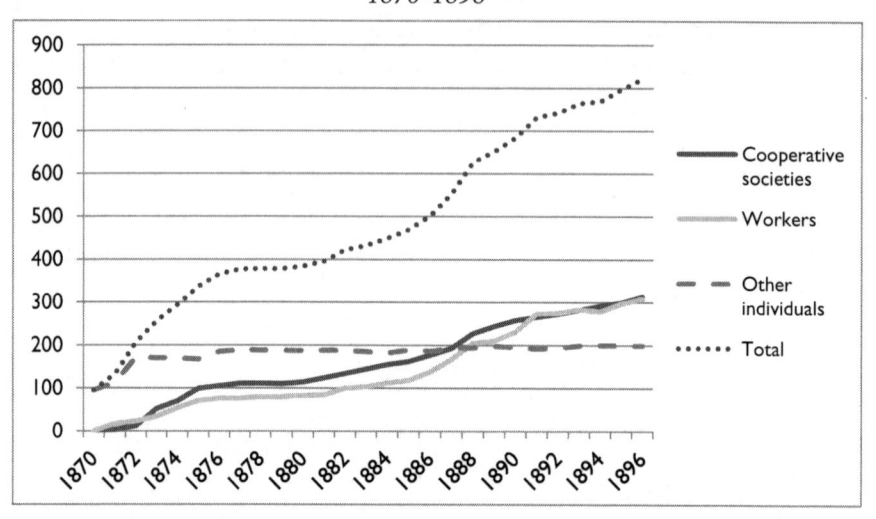

The growth of the business meant regular investment in the infrastructure. What had been a small mill at the time of the purchase in 1873 was extended, and then extended again, over the life of the co-operative. Plans to add a fifth storey to the mill were approved in 1878 and the works seem to have been finished by the following year. 'The little factory of four storeys had become too small, and did not afford enough accommodation. The workpeople and the machinery were crowded and the place was uncomfortable, especially in the cutting-room (which was in an attic) and in the sewing-room, which was greasy, and the floors much worn. The old high-peaked roof was therefore taken off, and another storey put on,' Greenwood recounted.[162] At the same time the co-operative built a new house and stables, Nutclough Mill House, across the road at the Nutclough woods side of the mill, and this became the home of Joseph Greenwood and his family.[163] The mill-owner's house next door, Nutclough House, which had been acquired in the 1873 purchase was perhaps considered inappropriately grand for a co-operatively run business's manager. It was rented out and brought in useful extra income: £40 a year in rent was the asking price in 1883.[164]

Further additions to the mill were authorised in 1884. The significant development at this time, however, was the construction of a new weaving shed, separate from the main mill itself, which opened in 1886.[165] The Fustian Manufacturing Society had taken a major decision: it was henceforth going to undertake its own fustian weaving work.

Greenwood had been hinting at this development for some time. At the July 1882 general meeting he had suggested that there was scope for further development into manufacturing,[166] and clearly Joseph Craven and the committee agreed with him. The benefits of this step towards vertical integration of the business, so that everything from weaving to final tailoring was undertaken, were considerable according to Greenwood: 'We could now buy the weft and twist of the kind suitable for our requirements and make goods just to the regulated weights and certain quality, which, in buying cloth from several makers, we could not obtain,' he wrote.[167] Some woven cloth was retained for the fustian society's own needs, some sold to private buyers. Separate business accounts were maintained for what was called the Winding, Doubling and Weaving Department, so that its contribution to the co-operative's profitability could be independently monitored.

The new weaving shed was built to hold 140 looms and was thrown open for a public launch event at the end of March 1886 when an estimated eight hundred people turned up, among them the fustian society's old friends Thomas Hughes and Edward Vansittart Neale.

Within four years, the Fustian Manufacturing Society was growing again. The weaving shed was substantially extended in 1890 in order to accommodate 244 looms and at the same time the mill itself was extended to the north to include at the far end a tower, still a distinctive landmark in the town. A year later in 1891 there were further architects' plans commissioned, this time for a terrace of twelve houses directly to the east of the mill, facing on to the main road to Keighley and across from Joseph Greenwood's Nutclough Mill House. Four similar terraced cottages had been built at the same time as the weaving shed, and ultimately the co-operative was to have a portfolio of eighteen houses which it rented out to Nutclough workers.[168]

No sooner had these building works been completed than there were further additions being planned. The committee's report to its members in June 1892 advised that 'We find we have not room enough in the dyehouse to do the ever-increasing trade in that department and to meet this we are building a new drying-store more removed from the main mill'.[169] The new drying store, a two storey building between the mill and the river Hebden, was on the opposite side of the complex to the weaving shed. Separating the drying store from the mill turned out to be a good move: in late January 1912 a serious fire was to take place in the small hours of the night when a cloth piece came into contact with a gas jet; the drying store itself was gutted but the main mill was saved.[170]

Despite all the progress being made, despite the expansion into weaving and the satisfyingly steady growth in sales and profits, there remained a significant issue which came to concern Joseph Greenwood and his management committee increasingly during the 1880s and which was not finally resolved until January 1890. This was the question of the reward being given to the investors in the co-operative.

As we have seen, John Hartley and his fellow co-operators had with some difficulty persuaded investors in 1873 to accept that the return on their share capital would be limited to 7½ per cent. As the years went by thereafter, however, 7½ per cent came itself to be seen as excessively generous. There was an early realisation of this in the mid 1870s: the fustian society had been prompt at repaying the CWS's £5,000 loan for the Nutclough purchase but to do so it had to pay 7½ per cent on share capital instead of 5 per cent to the CWS. The co-operative also found itself the subject of speculation by external investors who looked on the business simply as a place to make money.

The 1872 and 1873 rule changes had established that the maximum shareholding for individuals (though not for co-operative societies) would be fixed at £100. At some point around this time the management committee, concerned at the number of individual investors becoming co-operative members, also resolved to decline any further investments from outside investors. But because the shares were transferable there turned out to be a way round this. Joseph Greenwood described what happened as follows:

> During the years 1874 and 1875 there was growing up a great abuse of the labour rule. Employés having left the service of the Society and owning one or two shares, which that privilege had given them, were pestered and tempted to dispose of them at high premiums. The rules of the Society allowed at that time that all shareholders who had not taken the full – viz. 100 shares – could do so if they could become members, the share list being closed to outside investors. This was done so that the buyer could have ninety-nine shares (or as the case might be) at par, bearing interest at seven-and-a-half per cent.[171]

Greenwood elsewhere[172] stated that single shares had at one point been going for as much as £2 10s, the point of course being that an investor could top up their holding to the maximum of 100 shares permitted for a total outlay in this instance of just £101 10s.

The problem was discussed at length at the general meeting in July 1876 where Neale was present and offering advice, and the necessary rule change made in January and February 1877. This removed the right of individual shareholders to take up additional shares. It also introduced the principle that, while existing shares would remain transferable to third parties, in future shares issued to workers through the profit bonus would instead be withdrawable. Withdrawable shares, whilst they attracted interest, could be cashed in by workers only when they left the fustian society's employment, at par.

This may have solved one problem but it did not eliminate the unnecessarily high returns which were going to existing shareholders. The co-operative could access capital much more cheaply: in 1879 it was offering to take short-term loans from local co-operative societies for 4½ per cent, for example.[173]

A first effort was made to reduce the interest to 6 per cent in January 1881, with the Halifax society proposing the change. Perhaps unhelpfully Neale raised a possible legal obstacle, suggesting that the courts might rule that such a change was illegal as being unfair to one category of shareholder. The vote was lost by a large margin.[174] Nevertheless the issue of the interest rate continued to be discussed. Later that year one of the fustian society's management committee members George Smith argued that the time was coming when as a consequence the business would not be able to compete successfully with other firms. Greenwood himself made a similar comment a year later.[175]

A long-term solution of a kind was put in place in July 1884 when the co-operative created a new class of share. B Shares were to attract interest of 5 per cent, and would be the only shares available from then on for co-operative societies and workers. The change seems to have been brought in a year later. Nevertheless there was still almost £17,000 capital remaining as A Shares, earning the full 7½ per cent. £7,813 was held by co-operative societies in June 1885, £7,185 by individual investors and about £1,900 by workers.[176]

By 1888, the situation appeared to some members of the Fustian Manufacturing Society to have become intolerable. Local co-operative stores were now offering 4 per cent or 5 per cent on shares (the large Halifax society had dropped its rate to 3¾ per cent).[177] Why was the Nutclough still paying 7½ per cent on the bulk of its capital? The question was asked by John Dawson of the Todmorden society at the July 1888 general meeting, in proposing a reduction to 6 per cent. 'The bulk of the advocacy of the Nutclough works was that the worker was the chief concern; the practice had been that the capitalists got all the honey. It was time they either altered their practice or altered their preaching,' he said.

He was supported by, among others, Abraham Greenwood, Neale and J.C. Gray who reiterated what Dawson had said: 'The proportion of profits to labour at Nutclough had not been nearly so large as it should have been, according to their professions'. But these views were minority views among the members present. When Dawson rose to reply at the end of the debate he was met with a call of 'Socialist! I'll meet thee in Todm'den and tak' it out of thee!' The motion was lost, 52 votes to 42.[178]

A similar discussion was held at the following half-year meeting, in January 1889, when nearly 200 members turned up. This time the vote – for a 5 per cent interest rate – was won (114 to 76) but the cause was lost, since the necessary two-thirds majority was not reached. 'The individual shareholders in the Hebden Bridge Manufacturing Society are evidently under the mistaken impression that the co-operative motto is "Each for himself" instead of "Each for all", if we may judge from some of their utterances at the half-yearly meeting,' an editorial in the *Co-operative News* put it.[179]

And so, predictably, the debate resumed at the July 1889 general meeting. This time it was the Leeds society proposing the change. 'The day had gone when it was either wise or just to continue paying a dividend at the rate of 7½ per cent,' said their delegate. But individual shareholders put up a strong fight. One, a Mr J.S. Machin, revealed that he had been one of those who had purchased his shares at a premium. Now, he said, he was being asked to relinquish 'some portion of the dividend which he had been brought to consider was his rightful due'. The vote was taken: 137 in favour, 73 against. Not quite enough: the number of votes in favour which would have successfully achieved the two-thirds majority was 140.[180]

'The individual shareholders should surely have taken into consideration the great risk they were putting the Society to in face of the claims of the consumer. They ought reasonably to have allowed that during the years their investments were held they had been almost twice repaid and still had their shares. That some of them had bought at exceedingly high premiums it was true, but this was something with which the Society had nothing to do,' wrote Joseph Greenwood later.[181]

In fact, the individual shareholders chose to counter-attack. In December

1889 they arranged a private meeting, held in the White Lion Hotel in Hebden Bridge, which was attended by about a dozen investors. The strategy agreed at the meeting was to obtain a list of private shareholders from the society and canvass them 'to get up a strong opposition to the motion of the Leeds Society'.[182]

But their efforts failed. Finally, in January the following year, the two-thirds majority was obtained, and interest on Class A shares reduced to 5 per cent. The issue of how much power investors should have in co-operative businesses is a live one today as it was in the 1880s, but the conclusion has to be drawn that, in the case of the Hebden Bridge Fustian Manufacturing Society, the investors had abused their power.[183]

Meanwhile there had been changes in the Nutclough Mill's management. The national co-operative movement had been mourning early in 1883 the unexpected death of the Co-operative Union's Assistant General Secretary Joseph Smith who had died while still only in his early forties. Smith's death meant that an unanticipated job vacancy came up. The role of the Assistant General Secretary, which carried a salary of £150 a year, involved office hours (9.30am – 6pm, 1pm on Saturdays) rather than mill hours, even if it did include necessary attendance at weekend and evening meetings. The work, according to the job advertisement, 'is essentially of a propagandist nature; a readiness to promote the cause of co-operation by taking part in Public Meetings, Conferences, and Festivals is a qualification to which the committee attach much importance'.[184]

J.C. Gray, the society's Secretary, applied and in December 1883 heard that he had been the successful candidate. Greenwood, it seems likely, put in a good word on his behalf. Gray had married in 1879 and by 1883 he and his wife Mary had two small children, Ethel who was three and her brother Harold, who was one. It was probably a good time for a career move. The Gray family packed their household goods and made the move to Manchester. Gray began his new job in January.[185]

Neale, as General Secretary, was 72 years old at the start of 1884 and while he remained active in the movement throughout the decade there was clearly an opportunity for Gray, not quite yet thirty, to make his mark. Beatrice Webb later said that in 1889 Neale was too old to be a force any longer in the Co-operative Union's affairs and that Gray was effectively acting as General Secretary.[186]

His elevation to the General Secretaryship on Neale's eventual retirement in 1891 seems by that point to have been a foregone conclusion. But Gray turned out to be very well-suited for the responsibilities. He combined, as one writer put it, 'those practical qualities which go to make a capable administrator with an all-abiding faith in a principle and a whole-hearted devotion to a cause'.[187] Certainly his administrative skills were much admired. He demonstrated considerable tact and political judgment, particularly after 1891 when the much respected veteran Neale had gone and when there were real dangers of the movement fragmenting. There were egos to massage and difficult societies to placate. Gray once complained in a private letter that 'the Plymouth people are a most discontented lot and are never satisfied. They are always having a dig at The Co-operative Union in regard to some matter or other.'[188]

When the occasion was right, however, Gray also revealed himself to be a visionary. This was when his heritage as the son of a Baptist preacher perhaps came through in the passion of his words (this was also when he could sometimes surprise those in his audience who had come to see him simply as an efficient administrator). 'He is an idealist: looking at co-operation not as a huge organised consumers' interest, but as a true and equitable co-operation between capital and labour. He is not a self-seeker; he is a refined and modest-natured man,' wrote Beatrice Webb, adding that she thought he secretly harboured greater political ambitions. When she visited the Manchester office, she recounted, she and Gray shared both cigarettes and 'talks on philosophy, religion and politics' together.[189]

Gray's most notable speech was to be his Chairman's address at the Co-operative Congress in 1906 when he called for the hundreds of independent co-operative societies to merge together, to harness their collective resources and their capital, and to take the co-operative economy out of the margins and into the heart of the British economic system. This speech has gone down in co-operative history as the call for the one National Society. 'Then we may go forward towards the realisation of a true Co-operative State or Commonwealth, wherein justice and equity shall rule; where industry in all its forms shall receive its just reward; where homes shall be made healthy and happy; where all the comforts of life may be enjoyed by those who have earned them; and where the poor and oppressed may be uplifted and find rest, and misery and want be banished from our land,' Gray concluded his speech.[190]

His audience reacted ecstatically at the time, but the idea was too ambitious and the vested interests too great; it was quietly allowed to drop. If a major reorganisation of the structure of the co-operative movement had ever been possible, it certainly was not realistic in 1906 and at some level Gray, who knew the movement inside out, must have understood this. His 1906 speech is perhaps to be understood more as a cry from the heart from a man who would shortly become seriously ill, who sensed that something had gone awry with the co-operative dream.

We can add at this point as it were in parenthesis that the co-operative movement spent much of the later twentieth century struggling to find its way forward in changing times; when the one big national society foreseen by Gray did eventually emerge – partly by default – in the early twenty-first century in the form of the Co-operative Group, talk of the Co-operative Commonwealth was certainly no longer on anyone's agenda. Gray's biography has not been written and his significant contribution to the development of an effective organised co-operative movement, both in Britain and internationally, generally forgotten. There is one memento, however: a marble bust of Gray, located close to a similar one of George Jacob Holyoake, looks down on employees today in the offices in Manchester of Co-operatives UK.

Gray got a rousing send-off from Hebden Bridge at a special tea party held in his honour by the fustian society on 12 January 1884. Gray took the opportunity to thank Joseph Greenwood for initiating him into an understanding of co-operation. When he had started at the Nutclough, he said, 'he knew nothing of co-operation nor of what it was capable'. And he concluded by giving his parting blessing to his old co-operative: 'That Society has been a successful one, and they could make it still more prosperous in the future'.[191]

His place as Secretary at the Nutclough was taken by Leonard Stocks, then 21 years old. Stocks was born in Triangle, in the Ryburn valley between Sowerby Bridge and Ripponden, and after attending nearby Rishworth Grammar School had worked for a time in a solicitor's office in Halifax and then as a clerk at Sowerby Bridge station. He was to demonstrate great loyalty to his new employer and, as we shall see, his involvement with the Fustian Manufacturing Society was to be a life-long one.[192]

In a few years' time Stocks was to have an assistant, straight from school. Crossley Greenwood, born at the very beginning of 1871, was of all Joseph and Sarah Greenwood's six sons the one who shared with his father an obvious skill in accounting and bookkeeping. Joseph's oldest son, Virgil, had followed his father's trade and become a fustian cutter. He suffered a potentially serious fustian knife accident at the Nutclough when a youth in 1878;[193] later, after marriage, he moved away to the Burnley area. William, second born, became a cutter as well. Harry took up a trade as an iron moulder at the nearby foundry in Mytholmroyd. He also suffered a serious accident when a youth, when molten metal was spilled accidentally on to his hand.[194] Fred became a foreman fustian dyer. Lloyd, the youngest, became a fustian warehouseman.[195] Although the evidence is not conclusive, we can be pretty certain that all Joseph's sons except Harry were found work at the Nutclough. But it was Crossley who was marked out for the white-collar job, and whose story we shall return to.

What of their father? As well as his election to the Co-operative Union's Central Board, Joseph Greenwood had by the late 1870s felt able to play a more active role in the civic life of his home town. Hebden Bridge was just at the start of what were to be two decades of significant growth, the period in the town's history which established the town very much in the form that it remains today. In August 1879 Greenwood joined the town's Local Board, the main vehicle for local government in the town, and immediately got stuck in to the waterworks committee, sorting out the laying of water mains through the town.[196] Initially co-opted to fill a casual vacancy, he was thereafter to be elected and re-elected again and again, both to the Local Board and then, after the Local Government Act of 1894, to the successor body Hebden Bridge Urban District Council. Later he was to be particularly concerned with local schooling and, as an alderman, in 1908 he laid the foundation stone for the new secondary school for the town. He continued as a local councillor until 1912, when he was in his late seventies. A committee room at Hebden Bridge town hall was renamed in his memory in 2010.

CHAPTER 6

THE WOMEN AT THE NUTCLOUGH

The Nutclough Mill was the workplace for women as well as for men. From the very earliest days – as we saw in chapter 2, from the time in 1870 when the decision was taken to undertake the manufacture of ready-made clothing – the Hebden Bridge Fustian Manufacturing Society was as much a co-operative of working women as it was of working men.

Information about the respective employment figures for male and female workers over the years is scanty. In 1893, we know that there were 195 women members of the society at a time when 280 people were employed. In 1902, we are told that around 170 women were employed making garments when the total workforce was around 330.[197] It is likely, but not provable, that women made up a majority of the workforce throughout the life of the co-operative.

What is frustrating, if entirely predictable, is how difficult it is to get a sense of what women's experiences at the Nutclough were like. In the accounts and documents we have available today we generally get only glimpses of their lives. Women workers do appear from time to time but through the prism of other people's accounts. Here are the women machinists, for example, 'all full of happy interest in their work and all exchanging glances with the head of the establishment [Greenwood]' in one visitor's account of a tour of the works in 1898.[198] Here they are again, in considerable numbers at a general meeting of the society and giving 'an unusual charm to the proceedings', according to the local reporter.[199] These are women appearing in the shadows of some other story. Their own story is to a considerable extent, to use Sheila Rowbotham's celebrated phrase, one that is hidden from history.

But not entirely. Two observations can be made right at the start about the position which women occupied in the Hebden Bridge Fustian Manufacturing Society, one positive and one rather less so. The first point is that all workers, men and women alike, were admitted into full membership of the co-operative.

This needs to be stated because it might not necessarily have been the case. The fustian society began as a co-operative of fustian cutters and dyers, all of whom we can be sure were men. But there was no attempt made to restrict membership rights when the co-operative moved beyond fustian cutting into the new area of tailoring. Greenwood, it is true, did grumble at the time when shares were being snapped up speculatively at a premium at one of the implications of this policy: 'In the middle of the year 1873 we were employing twenty-four persons... Only four were of our own trade, i.e. of those who were members at the beginning. The remainder had just been made members by their dividend, under a new rule we had passed. The principle of creating dividend to labour was bringing into the Society men and women who had had nothing to do with its formation and thus they reaped where they had not sown.'[200]

Nevertheless there was certainly no attempt by the co-operative's founders to keep membership just for themselves, a practice which J.C. Gray later had to deal with in relation to some boot and shoe productive co-operatives in the Midlands. 'If the persons are fit subjects for employment they are also fit for membership. Directly a so-called co-operative society closes the doors of its membership against any of these employés so as to retain greater benefits for the more fortunate members it ceases to be co-operative,' was Gray's blunt verdict at that time.[201]

However, if they were given full membership rights it also has to be acknowledged that the women members of the Fustian Manufacturing Society were not given a formal role in its governance. Some sixty or so people served at one time or another on the management committee, and all of them were men.

This reflected practice in the co-operative movement generally. In 1890, across all the local co-operative societies the breadth of Britain there were no women to be found on any management committees. Slowly (but very slowly) women began to make some inroads. In 1892 there were six, in 1896 sixteen and by 1900 twenty-one women committee members. The numbers climbed to 49 in 1910 and 220 in 1920, still a tiny percentage given the large number of societies operating at this time. There were rather more women to be found on societies' education committees, though here too men continued to dominate.[202]

'There is certainly room for more women to share in the responsibility of guiding and directing our great movement,' wrote Catherine Webb in 1897.[203] Catherine Webb, a tireless proponent of co-operation and author of the standard textbook of the time on the subject, could speak from personal experience having been elected to the Co-operative Union's Central Board in 1895. Alongside her on the Central Board for some years in the 1890s was Mary Lawrenson, elected a year earlier in 1894. But both Webb and Lawrenson were members of the southern sectional board with its very different history to that of the northern movement. Despite several efforts by Sarah Reddish, a talented trade union and co-operative organiser from Bolton, the votes for the North-West's sectional board of the Central Board continued to be given to the male candidates. 'The remains of masculine prejudice against us are to be found more in the north than in the south,' sighed the Women's Co-operative Guild annual report for 1896-7.[204]

It was through the Women's Co-operative Guild, however, that the women of the movement were to become organised. If the creation of the CWS can be considered the great commercial success of the nineteenth century co-operative movement, the establishment and development of the Women's Co-operative Guild is arguably its greatest social achievement. From shallow roots in 1883 the Guild was to grow into a powerful tool for women's self-empowerment. The annual Guild conferences, held from 1892, were at that time a rare opportunity for socially-minded women to come together on a national basis to discuss, debate and socialise. As has been well documented, the Guild increasingly began to take up social and political issues. It campaigned early on for fair treatment and equal pay for women employees of co-operative stores, on children's health and maternity provisions, and on women's suffrage. Later, in 1914, its stand in support of divorce law reform led to a dispute with the Co-operative Union's Central Board and the temporary withdrawal of funding support. Later still, in the 1930s, the Guild debated the almost taboo subject of abortion.[205]

It was the women of Hebden Bridge who, in the autumn of 1873, could claim the plaudits for having established the first branch of the Women's Co-operative Guild. A first meeting was held in mid-September in the board room of the town centre store of Hebden Bridge Industrial Co-operative Society, when about forty people turned up. The necessary offices of President, Secretary and committee were elected and it was agreed to hold the first monthly meeting a fortnight later, on 3 October. 'A good beginning has been made and much interest is shown,' reported *Co-operative News*.[206]

The impetus behind the start of the newly created branch was very much due to Martha Helliwell, who took on the role of its first secretary. Mrs Helliwell, as she was always referred to in accounts of the time, was in her early thirties. Born Martha Ann Smith, she had married Shackleton Helliwell in 1871 and the couple were at this stage living in Heptonstall with three young children. Shackleton, working as a commercial clerk and later to become a mill manager, was one of the two lay auditors for Hebden Bridge Fustian Manufacturing Society, elected to scrutinise the books and the accounts of the society and to report back to the membership. In exchange for his services he and the second auditor were awarded a small honorarium.

The Co-operative Congress in 1883 was in Edinburgh. Joseph Greenwood, John Hartley and Joseph Craven were all booked in as delegates, as was John Speak from the Nutclough's management committee in his role as a delegate of the Todmorden society. For the first (and it would seem the last) time Shackleton Helliwell decided to attend the Co-operative Congress as well, and he took Martha with him.[207] It is tempting to speculate that there may have been another reason for taking a city break in Edinburgh, away from the Calder valley: had Martha been ill, or even perhaps suffered a miscarriage or loss of a child? There was a seven year gap between the birth of her third child Hetty, born in 1879, and her next child and a much later census record suggests she had suffered the death of at least one child.[208] Nevertheless, the evidence remains very inconclusive.

Martha Helliwell's participation at Edinburgh meant that she was present at the first national meeting of what was still being called the Women's League for the Spread of Co-operation, or sometimes the Women's Co-operative League. About fifty women were present at what was held as a side-event to the main Co-operative Congress.[209]

The story of the creation of the Women's Co-operative Guild has been told in the standard history *Caring and Sharing*, published for the centenary in 1983. The original impetus came from Alice Acland who late in 1882 began contributing a series of articles to *Co-operative News*. From the start of 1883 her contributions became a regular 'Women's Corner' in the newspaper and it was early in February that year that she was encouraged in a letter from Mary Lawrenson to consider establishing a 'Central Board' for women in the movement.[210] Acland endorsed the idea, proposing 'an association, or guild of women bound over to do all we could to help in the cause of co-operation'.[211] Acland was confirmed as the Guild's first organising secretary at the Edinburgh meeting, but ill health forced her to relinquish this role and Mary Lawrenson became the secretary from 1885 to 1889.[212] Lawrenson in turn was followed by Margaret Llewelyn Davies who exercised a powerful influence over the Guild's subsequent development as its general secretary until 1921.

Martha Helliwell may already have met Alice Acland in Hebden Bridge the previous winter. Alice had been with her husband, the Oxford don Arthur Acland (A.H.D. Acland), when he had given a set of three lectures in the Co-operative Hall. Indeed, Alice Acland did her bit to liven up the proceedings by contributing a number of songs during the lectures, accompanying herself on the piano.[213] The Aclands were friends of several of the Christian Socialists including Neale, who was present for at least one of the Hebden Bridge lectures, and Thomas Hughes. Arthur Acland himself was playing a significant role in the co-operative movement at this time and was a member of the Co-operative Union Central Board for the southern section.[214] Acland was later to be an MP and a member of Gladstone's government in the early 1890s.

Martha Helliwell came back from Edinburgh obviously inspired with the potential which this new women's organisation offered. She was the speaker at the first official monthly meeting of the new Hebden Bridge branch held on 3 October when she read a lengthy paper under the title *Co-operation: Its advantages and how we may improve it*. Her presentation was a homily encouraging her audience to be more loyal to their local co-operative store and more aware of the wider aims of the co-operative movement. The new League, she argued, could play its part: 'We have kept too much aloof from each other, but now an opportunity has occurred in the formation of a woman's league, by which we may get to know each other's feelings upon different matters'. But League members' primary role was in the home: 'how we may make that home comfortable with the least expenditure'.[215]

Following this initial meeting, the new Women's Co-operative Guild branch started promisingly. Members, including Martha Helliwell, were invited by Joseph Greenwood in his role as the secretary of the Calderdale Co-operative Association to join their male counterparts at the Association's quarterly meeting in early December; it happened to be Hebden Bridge's turn to host the meeting.[216]

By March 1884 *Co-operative News* was able to publish the following report from Hebden Bridge:

> The number on our books is 60. We have had five monthly meetings ... Two meetings were taken up in discussing Drapery and other things. Some of them alleged that the prices were exceedingly high, while others affirmed that, taking into account the quality, the prices were only reasonable. However, a good number were in favour of cheaper goods to meet the wants of the poorer classes, who were obliged to go elsewhere to get them. A deputation of three members was appointed to see the Drapery Committee, and suggest such alteration as might be necessary for doing a good trade.[217]

The branch had organised a first public tea and meeting – basically a celebratory party – in February, held naturally enough in the Co-operative

Hall. This was attended by men as well as women, and was a mélange of songs, recitations and speeches. John Hartley, Joseph Craven and Joseph Greenwood all attended and offered words of support for the women's new initiative.

By June 1884, six branches of the Guild were functioning, with membership figures given as follows:[218]

Hebden Bridge	60
Rochdale	42
Woolwich	43
Norwood	20
Chelsea	14
Coventry	16

Already in the summer of 1884, however, there were signs that the Hebden Bridge branch was encountering some problems. A letter in *Co-operative News* in July from another active member Marianne Sutcliffe reported that the League had already done good even if 'all has not gone on as we would wish'. She pointed out that it was hard to persuade people to come to meetings in the summer: 'People prefer more to walk abroad at this season of the year, when everything looks so beautiful'.[219]

Martha Helliwell wrote a week later: 'I have had to work very hard in my own neighbourhood in order to establish a branch of the league and now we have fairly started our drawback is the want of funds in order to form some class that may interest our members'.[220]

Martha Helliwell had been one of a small number of women who had been elected at Edinburgh to the first Central Committee of the Guild (others included Abraham Greenwood's daughter at Rochdale, and also Miss Shufflebotham, the daughter of Charles Shufflebotham of the Coventry Watchmakers co-operative society.) Helliwell appears to have been nominated again in 1884, but at some point shortly thereafter she stepped down. Her photograph appears in the centenary history of the Guild as a member of the original Central Committee, but effectively at this point she took herself out of the pages of the Women's Co-operative Guild national history.

What caused Martha Helliwell's departure? It may well have been very difficult for a mother of three young children to have the time or resources to engage in national activities, and we do not know how sympathetic Shackleton Helliwell would have been to his wife's new responsibilities. There may have been a class issue: the Guild rapidly became centred in

London and the south-east and some of the leading figures were from more markedly middle-class backgrounds. Some evidence of the gap between southern and northern attitudes can be inferred from a spat in the correspondence pages of *Co-operative News* between Martha Helliwell and a Reading woman 'S.A.A.'. The latter had enthusiastically suggested that a halfpenny out of every shilling paid in co-operative dividend should be given to the Guild. Martha Helliwell replied, asking 'S.A.A.' to consider the position of the working classes: 'Many of their earnings average only 18s a week. Out of this they pay at least 2s 6d per week for rent, in addition to taxes; where, then, is the sum she names to come from? These anxiously look forward to their dividend in order to clothe their children, or may be pay a doctor's bill, besides a great many things people of means never think about.' A halfpenny out of a shilling was quite unreasonable, she argued.[221]

Unwisely perhaps, S.A.A. returned to the fray, drawing out the following firm riposte from Helliwell: 'I would advise her to start a branch in Reading (if she has not already done so) and when she has persuaded sixty members to pay one halfpenny out of every shilling for making grants, I will undertake to pay her expense to Hebden Bridge to instil the same into the minds of our members.'[222] S.A.A. withdrew her suggestion.

There may been a much more straightforward reason, however, for Martha Helliwell's decision not to continue on the Central Committee: in 1885 she was pregnant with her fourth child, Albert.

The Hebden Bridge branch of the Guild continued meeting on a monthly basis throughout 1885. In December, for example, the focus was on handicrafts, with members bringing their sewing and knitting work – the antimacassar made by the President drawing particular admiration.[223] Marianne Sutcliffe was a regular correspondent to *Co-operative News* through the early months of 1886 and in August the branch sent in five shillings for central funds, but by this stage there is clear evidence that the impetus has been lost. By 1887, the Guild had grown nationally to 31 branches, but Mary Lawrenson had to report at the Co-operative Congress that two of the branches 'have unfortunately not fulfilled the hopes entertained'. One was certainly Hebden Bridge, which now drops out of the story for a decade.[224]

We do not know how many of the active members of the original Hebden Bridge branch of the Women's Co-operative Guild earned their living at the Nutclough Mill (some certainly did), but the collapse of the venture does suggest a missed opportunity to reinforce the message of co-operation among the women workers there. Joseph Greenwood certainly supported the Guild in his comments at the February 1884 tea party, but Martha Helliwell's remarks about the lack of funding for activities suggests that neither the Hebden Bridge Industrial Society nor the Fustian Manufacturing Society thought fit to support the Guild financially. It is interesting that, by contrast to the Nutclough, the Ruskin-inspired mill-owner George Thomson in Huddersfield who had turned his Woodhouse Mills into a registered co-operative society was later to arrange for a Women's Guild branch to operate within the workplace.[225] One wonders if the fortune of the first branch of the Guild might have been different had Joseph and Sarah Greenwood had six daughters rather than six sons.

There was, however, to be a second chance. In 1892 the Women's Co-operative Guild staged its first independent national gathering, held in Manchester over three days in late July. The event finished on the Thursday, and on the Friday morning a party of Guild women took the train to Hebden Bridge to see for themselves the celebrated Nutclough Mill. Joseph Greenwood did his usual tour of the works and then took the visitors to the top floor of the main mill. Thereupon, as the *Co-operative News* reported,

> Mr Greenwood announced there would be a short cessation of work in order that a little meeting might be held with the workers and on entering the tailoring department – a long airy room where some 150 women and girls sit making up the garments – some of the central committee were quite besieged with eager inquiries about the guild, and were told there had been a branch formed some years ago, which had struggled for some time against adverse circumstances and finally dropped out, leaving in the hearts of its best workers an earnest desire to 'try again' when opportunity should serve. The meeting was held in the tailoring room, the visitors sitting on the little low stools of the workers, the workers grouped around them on the benches and other available seats, the women and girls to the front, and the men forming an interested background.[226]

At the prompting of the visitors, an interim committee to reconstitute the branch was set up there and then, but even this effort failed to take off. It was not until November 1896 that the Hebden Bridge branch of the Guild was successfully re-established.[227]

The top floor of the mill – the floor which had the most daylight, and was therefore most suitable for the sewing work necessary for making up the clothes – was very much women's space, although the room was shared with the small number of male workers who undertook the task of cutting the fabric to size. There were women engaged in other operations at the Nutclough – as winders, and also as 'enders and menders' repairing the holes in the cloth pieces when the fustian cutters made mistakes – but most of the other activities in the mill were considered male work. There were to be no female weavers at Nutclough until the very particular circumstances of the First World War, even though women weavers were a feature of the fustian industry in Lancashire towns.[228]

Women played an important part generally in the Hebden Bridge economy at this stage and dominated the tailoring side of the clothing industry. As the nineteenth century had progressed, the town had become more and more associated with the production of ready-made fustian clothes. There were other centres of fustian weaving across the Pennines but Hebden Bridge led the way in terms of the ready-made side of the business. It has been suggested that the town was turning out 20,000 pairs of trousers a week.[229]

The women sitting at the long rows of sewing machines in the top floor of the Nutclough, and in the other Hebden Bridge mills, were predominantly young people. Indeed, it is easy to overlook the significant fact that probably a majority were still in their teens. Most were single (all the volunteers in 1892 for the committee to reform the Women's Guild branch were unmarried, for example) and although there were married women in the fustian society workforce their numbers were small.[230] Certainly the strong social convention was that women once they had children would be at home. George Thomson's co-operative Woodhouse Mills in Huddersfield did not permit any married women to continue working, although the firm did give a cash award to longer-serving women on their marriage.[231] However, the age at which young women who were working in the mills married was going up; according to one Hebden Bridge writer in 1895, the age at which women chose to marry had by then become on average about 24, significantly up from twenty years earlier when women had married at 18-21.[232]

The Fustian Manufacturing Society, like other local firms, put its women machinists on piece rates. However the co-operative supplied all the equipment and material they needed; elsewhere women were sometimes obliged to buy sewing material from the firm employing them.[233]

There would be girls working in the Nutclough Mill along with the women sewing machinists. The custom in Hebden Bridge was that girls would learn their trade on the job from adult women who would informally supervise their work. One man who started work in the Hebden Bridge clothing trade in 1908 later reminisced that girl machinists in the early twentieth century would work for one month without pay and would then be paid 5s a week by their tutor for three to six months. After twelve months the newly trained girl would be 'on for herself'.[234] We can assume that a similar arrangement operated in the later years of the nineteenth century too.

Although positive accounts from visitors to the Nutclough need to be assessed with care (all companies seek to give visitors the most favourable impression they can), the overall conclusion from contemporary accounts of the sewing room is that the young women there probably did enjoy a pleasant working environment and more companionship than they might have done elsewhere. There were clearly benefits to having your employment in a co-operative workplace.

But there could also be a darker side to being a young woman living in the small community of Hebden Bridge in the Victorian era. In 1896 the local coroner was compelled to comment on the large number of suicides he had noted in the neighbourhood, the 'catalogue comprising a large proportion of young women'. He was back in the town that January for another case: a 22-year-old woman, a machinist at the Fustian Manufacturing Society who had drowned herself in the canal. She was a Sunday School teacher engaged to a local grocery worker, but their marriage had been delayed because they were struggling to find somewhere to live. She had, according to her family, been recently in poor health and suffering depression. A note left behind for her fiancé read 'Dear Lad – I shall never be right again. If I live I shall never do you any good, and I can't live without you.' The note was found in her bedroom by her brother Sam Craven after she had gone missing. Her name was Emily, and she was the daughter of Joseph Craven.[235]

CHAPTER 7

OXFORD UNIVERSITY

From the late 1880s and throughout the 1890s there was to develop, in the words of the Rev Canon Sowden the vicar of Hebden Bridge, 'almost a romantic attachment' between Hebden Bridge and Oxford University. He had many friends at Oxford University, he said, 'and the mention of Hebden Bridge to these called forth an exclamation of pleasure'.

Sowden was speaking at the 1891 Coming-of-age banquet of the Fustian Manufacturing Society, and he was probably looking across as he spoke at the Oxford don who had also been invited by Joseph Greenwood to be present for the occasion. E.L.S. Horsburgh was shortly to make his own speech. In the past, he would say, Oxford and Cambridge had lain dormant, full of 'fat fellowships and comfortable sinecures'. But these were democratic days. Today the universities were waking up. They were 'showing that they existed, not for the mere purpose of privilege but for the purpose of bringing the great boon of cultivation to everybody within reach'.[236]

In the case of Hebden Bridge, 'everybody within reach' meant the working men and women of the town's textile mills. They were not Oxford University's usual students, but they were to turn out in large numbers for the lecture series which Oxford dons such as Horsburgh were to give in the town. And for a small number of men and women from the working classes of Hebden Bridge the opportunity to participate in the intellectual life of Oxford was to be literally life-changing.

The link between Oxford University and Hebden Bridge was made possible by the Hebden Bridge Fustian Manufacturing Society which arranged the lecture series, hosted the lecturers on their visits and met almost all the costs. Generally speaking the lectures, which were staged (of course) in the Co-operative Hall, were free of charge. In a town of a few thousand inhabitants, many hundreds would turn up. Another Oxford don, G.W. Hudson Shaw, describing his course of lectures on English history which he delivered in 1888-9, said that the attendance began with 300 and by the course end had reached 700. He could hardly have been more enthusiastic in the course report he filed later at the university: 'Intelligent questions, animated discussions, absences of trivialities, attention to the really vital problems of English history, intense and eager interest in important matters – those were the features of the work at Hebden Bridge throughout the course'. The results from the lecture series were the most encouraging that he had experienced in any of the lectures he had been giving in the north of England, he added.[237]

Hudson Shaw and Horsburgh were two of the young and idealistic group of Oxford lecturers to visit Hebden Bridge during this period. Others would come too: people such as the writer Hilaire Belloc, the future Archbishop of Canterbury Cosmo Lang, and the geographer H. J. Mackinder, later to be appointed the director of the London School of Economics.

The lectures which were being run at Hebden Bridge were part of the work of Oxford University's Extension scheme. Joseph Craven offered this explanation of the idea behind it when he took the chair for one of Hudson Shaw's early lectures in the town: 'Some people were puzzled to know what it meant. He would tell them. It was an attempt to bring the learning of the Universities within the reach of the working classes, and as it was impossible for working-people to go to Oxford, the Scheme tried so to speak to bring Oxford to the working classes.'[238]

This was a worthy aim, but it was not an easy one to achieve. The desire to successfully attract working-class people from the industrial areas of the north of England turned out, in most places, to be much more difficult to bring about in practice than it did in theory. University Extension in the years of its heyday (especially during the last decade of the nineteenth century) attracted large middle-class audiences in many towns and cities across England and can be seen as having made a significant contribution to middle-class young women's education at that time. But the goal of taking university learning to the working classes, by and large, remained elusive. Oxford lecturers reported that there were only a handful of centres where they got to address large audiences made up primarily of working-class men and women. Oldham, where the co-operative movement locally was also supporting the initiative, was sometimes mentioned in this context, as were, for a short time, Todmorden and Sowerby Bridge. Hebden Bridge was almost invariably mentioned. It was seen as an exemplar.[239]

The link between Hebden Bridge and Oxford stemmed from 1882, when the Co-operative Congress was held in Oxford. Joseph Greenwood, Joseph Craven, John Hartley and J.C. Gray were all delegates. In Greenwood's words, the Oxford Congress 'brought together the active workers in the co-operative movement and some of the trained minds of the kingdom'.[240] The speech from the social reformer Arnold Toynbee, then not quite thirty years of age, was clearly particularly inspiring. Toynbee challenged co-operatives to play an active part in education, particularly in the 'education of each member of the community as regards the relation in which he stands to the other individual citizens, and to the community as a whole'.[241]

Greenwood must have been delighted to hear this. Education was what he had only been able to obtain as a child with great difficulty; it was why he had been so committed to the Hebden Bridge Mechanics' Institute in its early days; and it was what he believed should be central to the co-operative movement's mission. In a paper read at a conference of Yorkshire co-operatives in 1875 he had argued (against some opposition) for every store to have its own reading room and lending library. 'How is all this to be provided for? The answer must be – out of the profits,' he said.[242]

It was no surprise, therefore, that the Oxford Congress was a topic of conversation at the next general meeting of the fustian society, held in Hebden Bridge as usual at the end of July. Joseph Craven as chairman proposed that the Society organise three lectures 'on the economics of labour by some Oxford or Cambridge gentleman who understood the question and could give to co-operators and working men a clear statement of the relation of capital and labour'.[243]

This was why A.H.D. Acland and his wife had visited Hebden Bridge that following winter. Acland (who came wearing a fustian suit made in Hebden Bridge) addressed Toynbee's call, his lectures being on the theme of the education of co-operators as citizens. Some leaders of the movement from outside the town, including Neale, Abraham Greenwood and J.T.W. Mitchell of the CWS came along for the final session. But in general it would seem that Acland did not pull in particularly large crowds.[244]

In March 1883 Acland reciprocated the invitation from Hebden Bridge, inviting Joseph Greenwood to Oxford for a meeting of local co-operative supporters (the 'Co-operative Guild') there. This was held in Corpus Christi college, with the President of Trinity College in the chair. Greenwood was beginning to move in interesting new circles. He gave his account of the formation of the Fustian Manufacturing Society, and (as the report of the meeting said) 'there was not one person in the room who was not carried away by his simple eloquence'.[245]

Despite these links between Acland and Greenwood, it was to take a few more years for something longer-lasting to be achieved. Cambridge University had taken the decision to launch a university extension programme in 1875 and Oxford had taken a similar decision three years later. It was part of a wider debate by the two long-established English universities to redefine what their role was to be in an industrial Britain which was about to have its Parliament elected by universal male suffrage. In fact, despite the 1878 decision very little happened at Oxford until a year after the 1884 Reform Act, when Michael Sadler was appointed as Secretary to the Extension Lectures committee.[246] The first formal set of Oxford Extension lectures in Hebden Bridge took place in the autumn of 1886, when Hudson Shaw gave two lectures on English history; on average, about 230 people turned up. These were intended as a taster before the first six-lecture course proper, which Cosmo Lang gave in January and February 1887 on economic and social history. Lang's audiences were smaller, about sixty on average, but he reported positively on the town's potential. 'Possessing as it does a body of vigorous men deeply interested in the work of education, Hebden Bridge ought to be the most successful centre for the extension of University Teaching,' he wrote in his official report. Two of the attendees took the optional examination at the course conclusion.[247]

Hudson Shaw was back in Hebden Bridge that autumn and winter, for what turned out to be, in his words, 'probably by far the most successful course of lectures we have yet had at this most interesting little place'. The theme was social reformers. Hudson Shaw congratulated the 'remarkable' fustian society for the fact that its educational work was starting to bear fruit. This time five students took the course examination, all receiving distinctions. Among them were the fustian society's secretary Leonard Stocks and Stocks' assistant in the Nutclough Mill's office, Joseph Greenwood's son Crossley.[248]

A series of public lectures, however good the lecturer, could not replicate the opportunities for study open to undergraduates, but the University Extension movement did its best to offer something at least a little closer to the Oxbridge tutorial system. Smaller classes were held, either before or after the main lectures, where those who wanted to discuss the subject with the lecturer in more detail could do so. Class students were encouraged to contribute written essays which were then marked by the lecturer. In Hebden Bridge Hudson Shaw had twenty in his class for the 1887-8 social reformers course, and a reading group complementing the lecture series also began to meet fortnightly, using Thomas Carlyle's *Past and Present* as the set text; about fifteen came to that.[249]

The idea of University Extension really seems to have taken off in Hebden Bridge the following year. Hudson Shaw gave eight lectures from October 1888 to March 1889, and reported that he was averaging six hundred over the period. If there was a disappointment, it was the relatively low number of students who took up the opportunity to submit papers or take the examination. 'But taking into account the character of the centre, and the fact that the great majority of the audience are busy artisans, this is easy to understand and perhaps scarcely to be deplored; only those who are themselves engaged in manual employments can adequately understand the enormous difficulties with which an artisan who desires to think and read has to contend,' Hudson Shaw wrote in his report.[250]

That year eight students took the end-of-course examination, two of them women.[251] Crossley Greenwood participated again, and there were also two thirteen year olds sitting the examination. One of these was a boy called George Herbert Pickles, who was living at the time with his parents and his seven younger brothers and sisters in one of the fustian society's terraced houses at Nutclough. He was – almost certainly – working as an assistant warehouseman at the Mill behind his house; his father, Thomas Henry Pickles, had joined the fustian society's management committee about four years earlier.[252] The other thirteen year old was Joseph Craven's son Sam Craven.

The Fustian Manufacturing Society celebrated the end of the 1888-9 series of lectures, the third year of the link with Oxford University, with a social event in Hebden Bridge. It was an occasion, perhaps, to take stock of their progress. Hudson Shaw and Cosmo Lang were both back, and Neale and J.C. Gray were also in Hebden Bridge for the occasion. The main speech, however, was made by Michael Sadler, the Secretary of the Oxford University Extension scheme. Sadler referred back to Arnold Toynbee's speech at the 1882 Oxford Congress, and went on to encourage the co-operative movement to take education even more seriously. Why should there not at some point be at one of the universities a Co-operative College, he asked?[253]

Hudson Shaw added his own contribution, saying that when Hebden Bridge's history came to be written, 'there would be found in it a record of the attempt to spread university education'.[254] He had already shown his commitment to his working-class audiences. He had told Hebden Bridge a few weeks earlier that he had been offered a Balliol post but had decided to pledge himself to another five years for the Extension movement (in fact, he carried on lecturing, although not in Hebden Bridge, until 1906).[255] But being an extension lecturer could be a demanding job. N. A. Jepson in his history of University Extension *The Beginnings of English University Adult Education* describes how in one term Hudson Shaw was taking fourteen class and receiving probably about ninety essays a week to mark. Horsburgh was conducting sixteen classes, with a similar workload.[256] This was a lifestyle which involved much train travel between centres and which could be gruelling. You could be very dependent on the hospitality you were given.

In Hebden Bridge hospitality was provided by the leading members of the fustian society, a responsibility which undoubtedly fell particularly heavily on the women who managed the homes: Sarah Greenwood, Joseph Craven's wife Hannah and Leonard Stocks' wife Mary. Cosmo Lang later described his visits as a lecturer to northern towns and the welcome he was afforded by the working men he met, recalling 'I often stayed in their own homes, sharing their simple but delightfully courteous hospitality. It was especially at Hebden Bridge that I made some lasting friendships.'[257]

Sometimes visitors could be hard work. Beatrice Potter spent three days in Hebden Bridge at the time of the March 1889 event as part of her research for what was to become the book *The Co-operative Movement in Great Britain*. Potter, very consciously concerned to develop her reputation as a social scientist, does not always come across in the most attractive light in her autobiography. She describes, for example, how she arrived in the Lancashire mill town of Bacup and passed herself off as a Miss Jones, a farmer's daughter from near Monmouth, come to learn all she could about co-operation. 'The dear people have accepted me so heartily and entertained me so hospitably as one of themselves that it would be cruel to undeceive them,' she wrote at the time.[258] Her diary entry from her research trip to Hebden Bridge, where at least she was travelling under her own name, is caustic: 'Young Oxford men are down here; and they and the co-operators form a mutual admiration society between intellectual young Oxford and co-operative working class. Co-operative working man: common condemnation of the capitalist class and money-making brain-workers: a condemnation the form of which bordered perilously on cant, and was clearly the outcome of ignorance.'[259]

Interestingly we have another insight into Beatrice Potter's time in Hebden Bridge, this time from Cosmo Lang: 'She [Potter] had asked to be allowed to come to the Hebden Bridge Society. She came. I was there. We met in Joseph Greenwood's house. The wives considered that it was only proper that they should be with their husbands and they sat silent in their best beaded gowns. All went well till Miss Potter asked if she might smoke – an innocent request nowadays. But the ladies were obviously greatly shocked and became suspicious. I had arranged to take a long walk with the men next day to Haworth Moor, the home of the Brontës. Miss Potter said she would like to come. The ladies were now all the more convinced that they must be at hand to protect their lords. We started, an odd-looking party. But the good women, in their long dresses and elastic-sided boots, wholly unaccustomed to walk further than the distance between their homes and shop or chapel, soon gave up. They intimated to the New Woman that they must return. "I'm so sorry," said she, with engaging frankness, "but I'm going on". Then one guardian of the proprieties turned to another and said grimly: "The impident huzzy!"[260]

The autumn afterwards, in October 1889, Hudson Shaw was invited back to Hebden Bridge to lecture on the Age of Elizabeth. The lectures continued until March and the audiences averaged 500. In autumn 1890 the fustian society decided to experiment with a twelve-week series of lectures, with Cosmo Lang as lecturer and with Victorian literature as the theme. For the first and only time a small charge was made for attendance and numbers were down to between 100-150. Nevertheless Lang reported himself delighted at the 'deep and sustained' interest being shown in the course. It ran from 4 October1890 to 21 March 1891. Thereafter it was decided to revert to six-lecture series, for the first time on a scientific theme: H.J. Mackinder ran a course on physiography (physical geography) from 10 October 1891 to 17 February 1892, with numbers climbing again to average 220.[261]

The examination result for these year's courses are available, and in the Spring 1891 list from Hebden Bridge we read for the first time the name of Robert Halstead. Halstead was briefly mentioned in the opening chapter to this book. It is time to give him a proper introduction.

Halstead's entry in the Dictionary of Labour Biography describes him as a 'co-operator and educator'. But at this stage in his life, when he was in his early thirties, he was a weaver. He was born in the village of Walsden, just outside Todmorden on the road towards Rochdale, and was left an orphan as a child. He started work at eight as a half-timer in one local cotton spinning mill and later learned the weaving trade. He lived for a time in the home of his older brother and wife in Walsden before himself marrying a local girl. He was active in the co-operative movement in his home village where was instrumental in establishing an education committee ('after,' he wrote later, 'the usual struggle with the sluggy Philistines who call themselves hard-headed practical people').[262] Sometime in the early 'nineties, probably in 1893, he got a job in Hebden Bridge as a four-loom weaver at the Nutclough.[263] He and his wife Martha moved in due course to the town, where they lived close to the mill. Martha was to be on the committee of the Calderdale association of Women's Co-operative Guilds for two periods in the later 1890s.[264] Robert himself was to become one of the most committed of the Hebden Bridge Oxford Extension students.

Rather as with Joseph Greenwood himself, there is a sense that Halstead was marking time in his early adult years, waiting for the opportunity he needed to blossom. For him it was the discovery of the life of the intellect.

There is a fascinating glimpse of Halstead's worklife in the Nutclough weaving shed from a friend W. Henry Brown, writing years later in an obituary for Halstead in *Co-operative News*. Brown had visited the Mill sometime in the early 1890s and been given the conducted tour: 'Joseph Greenwood took me through the works and in a corner was a young man reading a book. "That is unusual," I remarked. "Yes," he replied, "He is an unusual man; just have a word with him".'[265]

Looking after four looms was demanding work in a very noisy environment, but when the looms were working smoothly there was occasionally time for weavers to snatch a moment, if they wanted, for study. Some weavers taught themselves languages while minding their looms.[266] When Henry Brown visited, Halstead was reading John Ruskin's *The Crown of Wild Olive*. This popular book of its time included Ruskin's lecture entitled *Work*. Given the content, it seems appropriate as subject-matter for reading in a co-operative mill. Here are two short extracts:

> Money is now exactly what mountain promontories over public roads were in old times. The barons fought for them fairly; the strongest and cunningest got them; then fortified them and made every one who passed below pay toll. Well, capital now is exactly what crags were then.
>
> I have not time however to-night to show you in how many ways the power of capital is unjust; but this one great principle I have to assert – you will find it quite indisputably true – that whenever money is the principal object of life with either man or nation, it is both got ill, and spent ill.[267]

Once again it is Cosmo Lang we can turn to, for a brief insight into that 1890-91 course on Victorian literature. It can only be Halstead he is referring to in the following extract: 'It was at Hebden Bridge that I made the acquaintance of a weaver-scholar, whom I have often taken as my text in speaking about Adult Education all over the country. I had begun some lectures on Browning – a sign that these were Victorian days! I told my working people that they would not make much of him unless they possessed some keys to open his treasures. I gave them one: "Ay, but a man's reach should exceed his grasp, or what's a heaven for?" After the class my friend walked with me very silent to the station. We walked still silent along the platform. Then he said: "Tell me that key again: I haven't got it yet". I repeated the words. After another length of the platform he said: "Tell it again" and I did so. Then the train came in and he said: "I haven't got it yet". Next week he met me with a radiant face: "I've got it now".'[268]

Halstead had probably already encountered the University Extension lectures in Todmorden, where the co-operative there had followed the fustian society's lead and had put on two sets of six-lecture courses, in the autumns of 1889 and 1890. Hudson Shaw was the lecturer in Todmorden, the first course being on Irish History, and the second (as at Hebden Bridge the year before) on the Age of Elizabeth. At Hebden Bridge, after 1890, Halstead became a regular member of the University Extension lectures and classes, year after year. He was usually awarded distinctions in the examinations he took.[269]

He also began making his mark in other ways. There had been no Extension course in Hebden Bridge over the winter of 1892-3 but perhaps to make up for this a conference on the role of University Extension was staged in Hebden Bridge in mid-March 1893. About 150 were present, including Horsburgh. Halstead had the privilege of reading the main paper, which he entitled Working Men and University Extension.

He began forcibly:

University Extension is an attempt to make the old Universities in reality, as well as in a metaphorical sense, national institutions. To the average working man a University training, in the ordinary sense of the phrase, is about as possible as if all the Universities were situated at the north pole. Some of us have had it hammered into us by hard personal experience, or the experience of our fathers, as a curious moral anomaly in the management of national affairs, that the working class who actually form the bulk of a nation should, up to the present date, have been so largely ignored; and having done the lion's share of the world's work, should have been only furnished with so many kicks and so few halfpence in the practical schemes adopted for sharing out the good things of life.

The University Extension movement, he went on, was providing a large and enthusiastic band of University men anxious to help working men appreciate the vast intellectual heritage 'left as the common property of all men'. But Halstead also wondered aloud if the Extension movement was meeting its goals: apart from a few promising centres such as Hebden Bridge, Oldham and Todmorden, and a few other towns elsewhere in Yorkshire and the North, there seemed very little engagement by working-class communities.

Halstead referred back to Arnold Toynbee's inspiring lecture at the 1882 Co-operative Congress, calling for an understanding of the economic and industrial system which went deeper than political slogans. He continued,

Fortunately for the poor, the highest pleasures of life are not inseparably connected with material possessions. Wealth of intellect has other laws of distribution than material riches and those who are poor in material goods need not succumb to the greater curse of poverty of ideas.

He concluded with some specific comments for Hebden Bridge, the town which had already 'gained the proud distinction of leading the way for the Oxford University Extension movement among working men of the north of England'. He called for much more systematic access to higher education in the district. With the involvement of the local School Board authorities, why not create 'within our midst what would practically be a University Extension College'?[270]

His lecture was well received: a paper which had in it 'the quality and character of the highest education in the land', according to the conference Chairman Rev Edward Talbot, previously Warden at Keble College, Oxford, and presently Vicar of Leeds.[271]

By this stage Robert Halstead and several of his fellow students on the Hebden Bridge courses had discovered something else that the Oxford University Extension movement could offer them. They had discovered the Summer Meetings.

As mentioned above, when Joseph Craven had explained the nature of University Extension to his Hebden Bridge audience he had said that it was impossible for working people to go to Oxford so the university was coming to them. He was not absolutely correct. Life as an undergraduate was out of the question, but from 1888 the Extension movement had invited its students to come to Oxford itself, to share a short but intensive time with Oxford dons and fellow students in lectures, discussions and social activities in the heart of the university. It was for many of those who attended an extraordinary experience, bringing personal as well as intellectual changes to their lives.

We get a sense of the power of Summer Meetings in the account given by Vera Brittain in her *Testament of Youth*. As a middle-class young woman she went to Oxford 'in a state of ecstatic excitement'. Oxford did not disappoint: 'There was a light on my path and a dizzy intoxication in the air. The old buildings in the August sunshine seemed crowned with a golden glory and I tripped up and down the High Street between St Hilda's and the Examination Schools on gay feet.'[272]

Halstead was later to say that 'when its [University Extension's] students go to Oxford or Cambridge they feel they are stepping into the midst of something to which University Extension is but the threshold. The University spirit seizes them.'[273] Certainly in the reports of working-class co-operators there is the same sense of heady excitement that Vera Brittain describes. A collective report from the 1889 cohort of students in *Co-operative News* offered a breakneck account of some of the activities: 'Time and space do not permit of a detailed description of the conferences, the garden parties, the geological and other excursions, the visits to colleges, halls, museums, and libraries, with which Oxford abounds.' And then there were the 'social tea parties, and glorious boating excursions'.[274]

Crossley Greenwood was a student at the inaugural Summer Meeting, a relatively short affair, held in 1888. Records of students' names at Summer Meetings are very patchy until 1893, so we know only that four students went from Hebden Bridge in 1889, one of whom was Crossley Greenwood's fellow student on Hudson Shaw's history course, Henry Crabtree. Henry Crabtree was to call his experience in Oxford one 'never to be erased from my memory'.[275]

There is a strong probability that Robert Halstead was at Oxford in 1890, as the winner of a scholarship from the Todmorden class.[276] Samuel Fielding from Hebden Bridge was certainly there. He described the moving experience of visiting Christ Church college and being able to wander 'at our own free will among the costly art treasures' of Michelangelo, Raphael, Turner and others. He implies in a report that Joseph Craven and Vansittart Neale were also in Oxford that year.[277]

Robert Halstead and Samuel Fielding were to co-author a paper which Fielding read at the Calderdale Co-operative Association's meeting in December 1893.[278] Fielding's day job, like Halstead's, was as a weaver in the Nutclough's weaving shed. He was nine years older than Halstead and therefore already in his forties by the time University Extension really got going. He was a self-taught botanist who had begun to lecture locally, particularly on botany and geology (in 1885, for example, he gave a lecture under the auspices of the Hebden Bridge Mechanics' Institute on the perhaps unlikely topic of salmon disease and potato blight).[279] He was a temperance supporter, a Rechabite, and for twenty years chairman of the Mytholmroyd co-operative's education committee. Later he was to have a period of residential study at Ruskin College and in 1915 he was instrumental in founding the Calder Valley Poets' Society. Bernard Jennings has given the following tribute to him: 'Samuel Fielding is one of the finest examples of the Pennine workman-scholar, all of whose activities in learning, teaching, and the promotion of good causes had to be fitted into the spare time of a weaver, until he retired a few years before his death'.[280]

From the middle of the 1890s, although there remain gaps in the records, there is more archival material surviving on Summer Meeting attendances. In 1893 Cambridge University hosted the Summer Meeting for the first time but the only local student appears to have been from Todmorden. In 1894 the Meeting was in Oxford again, with Robert Halstead and George Herbert Pickles from Hebden Bridge sharing lodgings together in Walton Street. There were also four students from Todmorden and one from Walsden. Pickles, by now in his late teens, was, in Halstead's words, 'a very diligent student [who] has declined some very good business offers in order to follow up his studies'.[281] Pickles was set to be one of the new generation of co-operators in Hebden Bridge. It was not to be: six years later, in 1900, he was to volunteer for the St John Ambulance during the Boer War and to die of dysentery in South Africa. Halstead was to write a short poem in memory of his friend.[282]

There seems to have been no Hebden Bridge representation at the Summer Meeting in Oxford in 1895 and records for 1896 in Cambridge are not available, although we know Halstead was present. Halstead was at Oxford the following summer, together with a Mytholmroyd man Samuel (S.C.) Moore. S.C. Moore, like many of the other cohort of students from University Extension, was to go on to play a significant part in Hebden Bridge life in the early years of the twentieth century, becoming a leading figure in the local Labour party. He was also, in 1909, to become the Fustian Manufacturing Society's new Traveller.

After 1898, when a Summer Meeting was held in London (Halstead attended), Oxford hosted the event the following year. A whole group of men from the Hebden Bridge area went down and shared lodgings at the boarding house run by a Mrs Mueller at 18 St John St, Oxford: they were Halstead, S.C. Moore, two men from Mytholmroyd, three from Todmorden and one from Halifax. Another leading Hebden Bridge student, William Nowell, was staying that year in Ruskin Hall (later Ruskin College) which had been founded the previous February. Jemima (Jeannie) Rushworth from Halifax was staying at St Hugh's Hall.

Rushworth was an independent young woman, committed to the co-operative movement and active in the Women's Guild; in 1903 and 1904 she was to spend time in one of Sunderland's poorest areas, working as a residential worker based at the Coronation Street co-operative store.[283] This venture, primarily a Women's Co-operative Guild project and modelled to an extent on the university settlement movement, aimed to reach out to very poor communities not normally catered for by co-operative societies (the fustian society donated colourful fustian curtains for the store).

Jeannie Rushworth was at Summer Meetings again in 1900 (in Cambridge) and 1901 (in Oxford). William Nowell was at the 1901 event. To complete the story, it could perhaps be added that in 1906 these two young people, both with the shared experiences which came from University Extension and Summer Meetings, became husband and wife.[284]

Rushworth reported on her 1899 Summer Meeting, her first, in the pages of *Co-operative News,* so we have from her an account of the debate staged in the Oxford Union chamber where Hebden Bridge students played a leading role. The motion was that war is a necessary ingredient of the national character. S.C. Moore was the main opposition speaker, backed up by a contribution from Halstead. Students from co-operative backgrounds seem to have done much of the debating, and Rushworth reported with pleasure that Moore and Halstead carried the day.[285]

In general, though, the number of working-class co-operators at Summer Meetings was small. This was partly because of the general difficulty that University Extension was facing in reaching working-class communities. Then there was the cost. Oxford charged in 1894 £1 for the two-week 'half' of the Summer Meeting (which was what most co-operative students booked for) and £1 10s for the full period of three and a half weeks.[286] In 1900, Cambridge was charging £2 for the whole Meeting and £1 5s for the two-week half.[287] Add on the cost of travel and lodgings and the total ended up typically £10 for the whole time or £5 for two weeks, although sharing cheap lodgings could reduce the amount a little.[288] This was a period when weavers at the Nutclough were averaging about £1 3s a week pay,[289] so even two weeks at Summer Meeting amounted to three or four weeks' wages. Admittedly both Oxford and Cambridge did institute discounts for parties of co-operative students booking through the Co-operative Union – Oxford brought down its fees for co-operators for 1899 to 15s and 10s for co-operators, for example[290] – and there was also the possibility of a scholarship or grant, usually dependent on how well you performed in the University Extension examination. The Co-operative Union coordinated a small number of grants nationally, and one Hebden Bridge Sunday school, perhaps the Birchcliffe Baptists, was reported in 1893 offering up to six £1 bursaries to students connected to University Extension.[291]

There was also a more insidious cultural problem, in that working-class students may simply not have considered the Summer Meetings designed for them. Halstead tried on several occasions in the co-operative press to drum up more interest and other Summer Meeting students also submitted letters and reports, but numbers stayed low. In May 1897 Halstead was ready to go public with what he thought was the solution. Why not, he said in the pages of *Co-operative News,* organise a Summer Meeting specifically for co-operators? It could be organised by the Co-operative Union, with costs paid for partly by the national movement, partly by local societies and partly by students themselves. It could be run for a week, so the time commitment would not be great. And, initially at least, it could perhaps be run in conjunction with the established University Extension Summer Meetings. 'An eight year experience as a University Extension student, and my attendance at most of the Oxford University Extension Summer Meetings ... have prompted me in making this suggestion,' he wrote.[292]

By 1897, Halstead had become increasingly prominent in national co-operative affairs. Three years earlier, in November 1894, he had been one of the co-operative representatives appointed to give evidence at the Royal Commission on Secondary Education. He was later to recount the background to this:

> Mr Gray came down to Hebden Bridge, and I was asked out of the weaving-shed to meet him in the office of the Fustian Society. To my astonishment, after Mr Gray had explained the object of the interview, he asked me if I would give evidence on working-class education for the Co-operative Union. After some natural hesitation, and with many misgivings and much trepidation as to my qualities and fitness for such a responsible task, I consented.

As Halstead later acknowledged, the experience was a learning one for him; it has to be admitted that his evidence before the Commissioners does not come over particularly coherently.[293]

When the 1896 Co-operative Congress resolved to set up a Special Committee of Inquiry on Education to explore what more co-operative societies could do in the way of educational work Halstead was again selected. He served on the committee alongside, among others, Margaret Llewelyn Davies and J.C. Gray. As the 1896 Congress was Halstead's first as a delegate, backroom planning must have gone on beforehand, presumably between Greenwood and Gray.

The committee reported back to the following Congress, held in Perth, with a series of recommendations. One was that all societies should set aside a fixed part of their profits for educational work, with 2½ per cent the suggested amount. Another was that societies where possible should have permanent paid secretaries for their educational work. Regular meetings of members concerned with education should be held separately from general business meetings. Foreign languages should be taught.[294]

It was an idealistic report and it was effectively parked by Congress, who deferred discussion for a year pending regional debate. Unhelpfully for Halstead, too, the society which had been supposed to propose a motion on the Co-operative Summer Meeting idea had failed to send in the wording in time. But Halstead had at least had the opportunity to lobby for his proposal. There was also a forthcoming meeting he was promoting. This had been arranged to be held in Oxford in early August during the Summer Meeting period, to focus on the relationship between University Extension and the co-operative movement.

Halstead wrote to J.A.R. Marriott, who had replaced Sadler as Secretary of the Oxford University Extension scheme and who was hosting the meeting, to advise him on how Congress had gone:

> I got at the President of a rather large association of co-operative educational committees who promised that I should have the chance of laying my scheme for a Co-operative Summer Meeting before them. I also got at a few influential persons connected with the bigger societies such as Oldham, Woolwich, Kettering and Leicester. I should particularly wish that some of our Midland Productive Societies should be represented at the Conference as they are at the present time somewhat at a loss what to do with their Educational Fund.

Nevertheless, Halstead's experience of his second Congress had been somewhat sobering:

> I am convinced from what I saw and heard at the Congress that if the Summer Meeting is to be organised at all within any reasonable period it will have to be largely through personal influence and agencies working to some extent independent of the official machinery of the Co-operative Union.[295]

The Oxford meeting duly went ahead in the Examination Schools on 4 August 1897. The Marquess of Ripon took the chair and Joseph Greenwood attended. Halstead had also been found a place. He had had to write to Marriott earlier in the year, dropping a rather heavy hint: 'I should enjoy being at the conference myself and at the [summer] meeting myself but as my chance of attending the latter depends on winning a scholarship for which I have not the time to compete I have little hope of being with you unless I am appointed in some official capacity to be at the conference.' Halstead was given the role, it seems, of proposing the resolution. This called for 'some organised attempt being made to secure a larger attendance at the University Extension Summer Meeting of students drawn from the wage-earning classes'.[296] The desire was there, but execution was still proving difficult.

As we saw, the Special Commission of the Co-operative Union had called in 1897 for co-operative societies to consider putting 2½ per cent of profits towards educational work. Hebden Bridge Fustian Manufacturing Society was at this stage dedicating £60 a year for educational purposes, or about 1.3 per cent of its profits. The first contribution specifically for education had been made in the second half of 1885 and during the University Extension course years the education grant had tended to be £60 a year (Table 4). This was, it must be said, much better than many co-operative societies managed, but it was still less impressive than the Hebden Bridge Industrial Co-operative Society which dedicated almost exactly 2½ per cent of profits to education between 1889 and 1895 and kept the contribution at over 2 per cent for the rest of the decade. Todmorden co-operative society was also contributing well over 2 per cent of profits for much of the 1880s and early 1890s.[297]

Table 4
Hebden Bridge Fustian Manufacturing Society, spending on education 1886-1905[298]

Year	Education grant (£)	percentage of profits
1886	40	1.45
1887	40	1.42
1888	40	1.35
1889	40	1.25
1890	60	1.71
1891	60	1.61
1892	60	1.16
1893	60	1.35
1894	60	1.44
1895	60	1.16
1896	60	1.26
1897	60	1.31
1898	70	1.56
1899	80	1.76
1900	20	0.53
1901	25	1.18

1902	30	1.03
1903	55	1.68
1904	0	0
1905	0	0

University Extension lectures continued in Hebden Bridge each year until December 1897. Horsburgh was the lecturer in 1893-4, when the theme was the French Revolution, and again in the autumn of 1894 (Europe after the French Revolution). Hilaire Belloc stepped in at short notice for Hudson Shaw from Nov 1895-Jan 1896 (the Making of England) and Horsburgh was back for October 1896-Jan 1897 (Social and industrial questions since 1789) and in the autumn of 1897 (the Expansion of England). Numbers at the lectures varied, but were typically around 200-250. Class sizes varied from 10 to 20.[299]

In 1898-9 the fustian society decided to go it alone and invited the trade unionist Fred Maddison, elected the year before as a Sheffield MP, to give a set of six lectures on the theme of 'the Organisation of Labour'.[300] Thereafter, three further Oxford University Extension courses were put on, each taught by Horsburgh. In the autumn of 1899 his theme was 'Six nineteenth century statesmen'; in the autumn of 1901, he returned for a course entitled 'Culloden to Waterloo'; finally, in the autumn of 1901 his subject was Shakespeare. Attendance averaged respectively 175, 200 and 350.[301]

By the end of the nineteenth century something of the initial drive was beginning to go out of the University Extension vision. Halstead's idea for Co-operative Summer Schools had also achieved only limited take-up. Halstead himself was to give his verdict at the 1900 Congress: 'The experiment of bringing University men into contact with co-operators had not been a success. We should have to do a great deal more general educational work before that desirable result would be accomplished.'[302]

But nevertheless seeds which had been sown were germinating. The previous year, in August 1899, another meeting had been arranged at Oxford to take stock of progress in the two years since the 1897 meeting. Halstead was there and so too was a young man in his early twenties who worked as a clerk for the CWS in east London. Albert Mansbridge, like Halstead, had close links with both the University Extension movement and the co-operative movement. He had on two occasions written to the *Co-operative News* supporting Halstead's proposal for a Co-operative Summer Meeting.[303]

Mansbridge presented a paper on the theme of the co-operative movement in citizen education which was highly critical of what had so far been achieved: 'aggressive' was how one report described his paper, and Halstead himself dissociated himself from some of Mansbridge's arguments.[304] But Halstead and Mansbridge were thinking on similar lines. Four years later, in August 1903, they were to meet again at another meeting in Oxford, this time with a firm proposal on the table: to launch a new Association to Promote the Higher Education of Working Men.

Mansbridge had been preparing for this with a series of articles in the *University Extension Journal* which discussed ways that the links between university education and co-operation could be extended also to the trade union movement. Halstead responded with an article in April 1903 supporting Mansbridge, although pointing out some practical difficulties.[305] Mansbridge had in July gone on to form a provisional committee for the new association at a meeting which was held in London, at Toynbee Hall.[306]

Halstead had been primed to prepare a paper for the Oxford launch. No one really interested in higher education among working men could be satisfied with the progress made, he said. 'It seems to some of us that the prospects are not so promising now as they were some years ago,' he went on. University Extension had become very successful in reaching other classes of society but its aspirations for the working classes were receding. 'The promoters of this Conference, in the light of these considerations, believe that if the higher education of working men has to make desired progress, it will have to consolidate itself into a special movement,' he added.[307]

Hudson Shaw warmly supported the proposal. Mansbridge moved that the draft constitution already prepared for the Association be adopted and a coordinating committee which included Halstead, Mansbridge and Hudson Shaw was elected.[308] The organisation which two years later was to rename itself the Workers' Educational Association was launched.

But by August 1903, much had changed in Robert Halstead's life. He was no longer a four-loom weaver in the Nutclough's weaving shed, but instead the Secretary of a national co-operative body, the Co-operative Productive Federation. And he and his wife Martha had left their home in Hebden Bridge to make a new life in Leicester, which was rapidly becoming the heartland of productive co-operation.

The Nutclough Mill as it was when first acquired by the co-operative in 1873
Pennine Heritage – Alice Longstaff Collection [PH – ALC]

The mill in 1887, shortly after completion of the weaving shed (seen here to the left of the main building) *PH – ALC*

A plan of the mill at the end of the nineteenth century, showing the location of the weaving shed, dyeworks and main mill
Co-operative Heritage Trust [CHT]

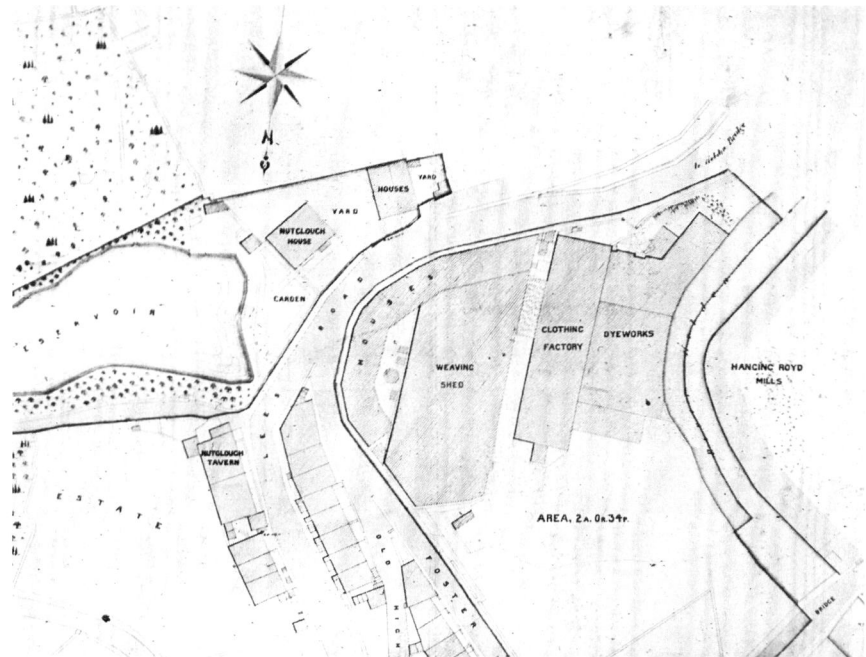

The mill with the wooded clough behind, around the start of the twentieth century. The darker outline of the original mill can be seen against the lighter stone of the later extensions *PH – ALC*

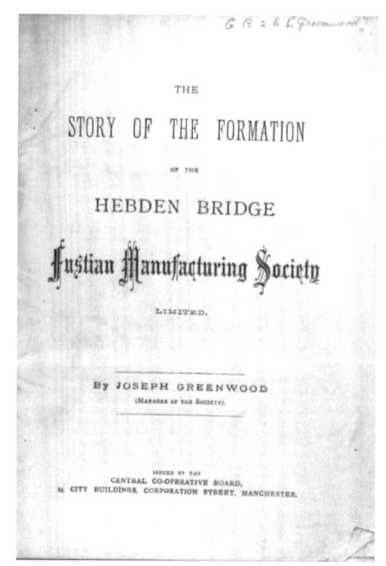

The front cover of Joseph Greenwood's booklet on the early days of the co-operative *CHT*

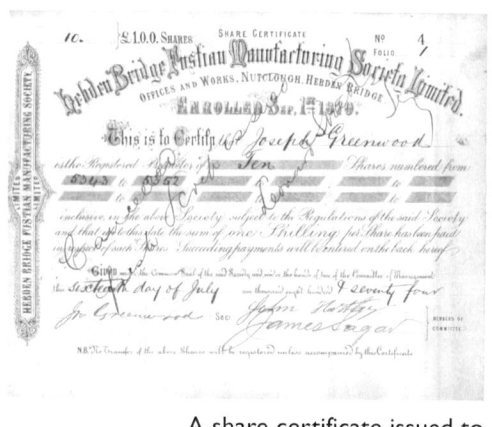

A share certificate issued to Joseph Greenwood in 1874, later cancelled by Leonard Stocks *CHT*

Joseph Greenwood *CHT*   Jesse Clement Gray *CHT*

Reportedly taken at the annual stocktaking, probably in the early 1890s.
In the central row: (from the left) Crossley Greenwood, Leonard Stocks, James Johnson (committee member), Joseph Greenwood, John Hartley and Sam Greenwood. Two of Joseph Greenwood's sons are in the back row: Fred (far left) and Lloyd (above his father) *CHT*

Martha Helliwell, responsible for launching the first branch of the Women's Co-operative Guild in Hebden Bridge *CHT*

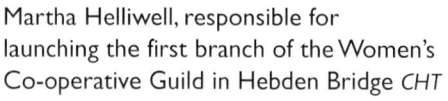

Robert Halstead *PH –ALC*

Twisting the yarn, one of the early processes carried out in the mill. This and other photographs of the co-operative at work date from the early twentieth century *CHT*

A general view of the looms in the weaving shed CHT

The art of fustian cutting by hand, probably photographed at a demonstration CHT

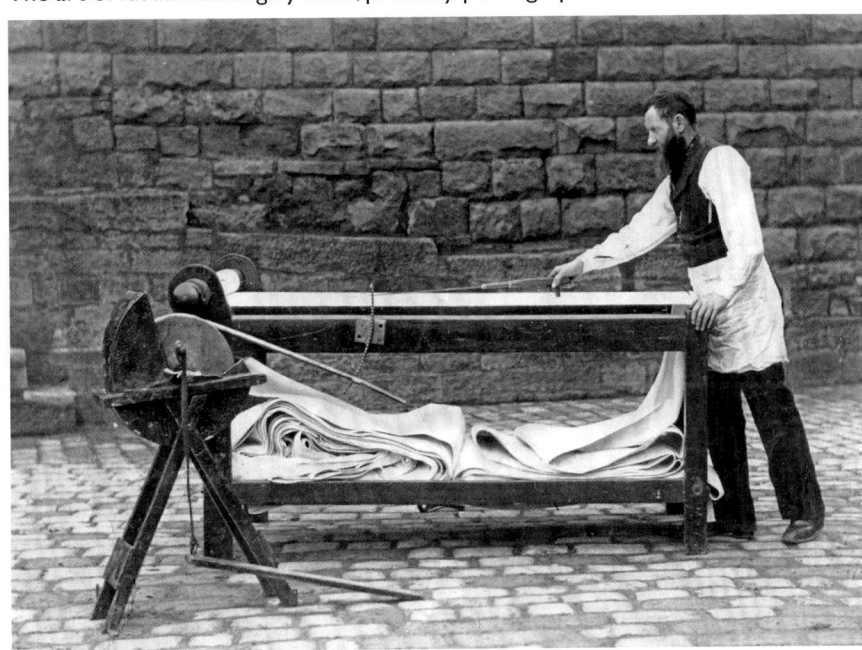

In the dyeworks, c. 1914 *CHT*

Scouring and dyeing, c. 1914 *CHT*

Wholesale clothing shop, pre-First World War *Hebden Bridge Local History Society*

Cutting cloth prior to the making-up process *CHT*

Clothing cutting room, c. 1914 *CHT*

A general view of the top floor, showing the women sewing machinists *CHT*

Another view of the machinists, pre-First World War *Hebden Bridge Local History Society*

Women hand finishing garments, pre-First World War *Hebden Bridge Local History Society*

Sam Moore with the co-operative's travelling exhibition case, believed to have been taken at a co-operative congress, c. 1910 CHT

CHAPTER 8

CO-PARTNERSHIP

In the pile of general correspondence received by J.A.R. Marriott at the Oxford University Extension scheme office came a letter which started like this:

> For three or four years some of us have been anxious to secure for Mr Halstead of Hebden Bridge better opportunities to help forward the cause of education. Mr Halstead, as I think you know, is by no means strong and we feel that the continued strain of mill life and educational work combined is likely to seriously affect his health. If an arrangement can be made to free him from the work in the Mill, there is much good educational work that he would be able to undertake among the working people of Lancashire and Yorkshire.

The letter went on to suggest that Halstead would be able to form small classes of working men for study in connection with co-operative societies and to attend conferences more regularly. 'You know Mr Halstead well enough to judge of the kind of work he would do.'

There was, however, a question of money. The letter listed a number of people who had been approached and agreed potentially to help contribute to a fund to support Halstead, at least for a year, but there was still a shortfall. 'I am now writing a few letters to those that I feel are likely to be interested, with a view to securing their support ... I shall be glad to know whether I may add your name to the list of supporters.'[309]

The letter is undated, but almost certainly written in the summer of 1898. The writer was a man called Henry Vivian, who had turned thirty in April that year and who had been secretary for several years of an organisation called the Labour Association. The Labour Association was intended as a propagandist body, one which promoted not only productive co-operation in general but worker participation in particular, or what was coming to be called co-partnership.

It had been set up at the 1884 Co-operative Congress at a fringe meeting which Joseph Greenwood had chaired and had been given a formal launch the following January at a high-profile conference in Hebden Bridge, organised by the fustian society.[310] E.O. Greening, Neale and Lloyd Jones had been among the originators.

A second letter from Vivian to Marriott dated 27 July 1898 filled in some of the details of his proposal:

> Our present ideal with regard to Mr Halstead is to raise a £100 a year ... Of this 30s a week will go in salary and 10s a week in expenses. He will be pretty much of a free lance but we shall arrange for him to form small classes of working men for the study of the questions he is able to deal with ... What some of us feel is that freedom from the Mill would enable him to pick up his strength a bit.[311]

Vivian said he already had pledges for more than two-thirds of the £100, including £5 from Marriott's predecessor in his office, Michael Sadler. We do not know if Marriott also contributed but in September Vivian was able to report to the Labour Association committee that three-quarters of the target had been met, and it was agreed to offer Halstead the position, initially just for the twelve month period.[312] Halstead was to switch from weaving to working as an itinerant lecturer and propagandist from his home base in Russell Place, Hebden Bridge.

The funds seem to have been found to keep him engaged into a second year, for in the spring of 1900 we find him lecturing in Scarborough (14 Feb), Bury (21 Feb), Peterborough (22 Feb), Kings Lynn (23 Feb), Mytholmroyd (1 March), Padiham near Burnley (13 March), Peterborough (15 March), Kings Lynn (16 March) and Norwich (17 March).[313]

1900 was Halstead's last year working in this way for the Labour Association, however. In September that year the Co-operative Productive Federation (CPF) advertised for a new Secretary for their organisation; twenty-three applied, and Halstead was chosen.[314] From then on until his retirement in 1921 he was to live in Leicester and work for the CPF.[315]

The CPF had been founded in 1882 as a body bringing together the leading productive co-operatives in the country. Many of the people who were behind the Labour Association, including Neale, Greening and Joseph Greenwood, also gave the CPF their support.[316] Both organisations were part of the same tendency within the co-operative movement, the one which was strongly committed to the participation of workers in their places of work and strongly opposed to the way that the CWS was choosing to develop its own productive works.

In other words, to understand the background to the Labour Association and the CPF and to Robert Halstead's later career, we need to revisit the issue which had nearly torn apart the Hebden Bridge Fustian Manufacturing Society in 1876 (chapter 3) and to trace the way that the arguments around bonus to labour and profit-sharing continued to develop in the co-operative movement in the 25 years after that. This is an important part of the history of British co-operation, probably the single most important ideological issue that was confronted, even if watching the story unfold is not always an edifying spectacle. To quote an editorial from *Co-operative News* from this period, 'we find ourselves plunged into a fierce controversy in which we shall endeavour to bear ourselves as philosophically as possible'.[317]

It will be remembered that the CWS, the 'Wholesale', took the decision to begin manufacturing in 1872 and for a short time thereafter introduced for its employees a complex profit-related pay scheme. This was voted out in 1876 on the primary grounds that it had not noticeably improved worker productivity. A more limited bonus scheme was brought in again by the CWS in 1882 for certain departments, extended to other employees in 1885 but abandoned in 1886.

The independent Scottish Wholesale Co-operative Society, by contrast, adopted profit-sharing for all its employees in 1870 and extended this in 1883 when it began production. The exact arrangements were changed periodically, but from 1892 until 1915 it paid a bonus on wages at the same rate as the dividend on purchases to its member societies. One half of the bonus was retained in a profit-generating loan fund, withdrawable on termination of employment.[318]

Most distributive co-operative societies did not pay any kind of profit-share to their store employees, but some did. In 1899 Halstead researched this for an article for the magazine published by his new employing organisation the Labour Association; he found that 229 (15 per cent) of societies featured in the Co-operative Union's annual returns paid a bonus to labour, worth on average 6¼ per cent of wages. Some powerful and influential societies were in this category: they included (according to a slightly later list) Belfast, Leicester, Derby, Birmingham, Nottingham, Huddersfield, York, Woolwich, Portsea Island, Plymouth and Bristol.[319]

In other words, practice varied within the movement. The case for giving the co-operative movement's employees a share in the benefits of their labour was particularly associated with the Christian Socialists, and therefore with London and the southern section. Neale, Lloyd Jones, Hughes and Greening were all at one time or another to take to the platform at Co-operative Congress to argue the case. Lloyd Jones' critique of the CWS approach at the 1874 Congress can be taken as an example: 'If the stores joined together in the Wholesale are to establish workshops all over England, under absolute managers appointed solely by themselves, employing thousands and perhaps tens of thousands of workpeople, who will be merely wage-paid labourers without shares, without votes, without meetings, we shall soon have two hostile classes with divided interests – one concerned in getting all it can for money and the other concerned in giving only what it must. The workers in our so-called co-operative factories will be merely so many underlings of the staff of the Wholesale,' he said. The Wholesale would get round this, Lloyd Jones argued, if it conceded to its workers three things: firstly a direct share in the profits, secondly a voice and a vote in the management of their factories, and thirdly the right to invest their savings in the places where they worked.

Lloyd Jones's three points demonstrate the way that, already by the mid 1870s, the issue of bonus to labour was extending into demands for other forms of worker engagement.

It is easy to caricature the disputes in the co-operative movement over these issues as a simply a south/north affair, or as one between middle-class supporters of co-operation and working-class practitioners. However as G.D.H. Cole pointed out in his landmark history of the co-operative movement in 1944, the battle lines were much more complicated than this.[320] Neale may have come from a privileged background but Lloyd Jones had been a fustian cutter. Lloyd Jones's position was one shared too by Joseph Greenwood, of course, even if Greenwood's was a minority position in the north-west section of the Co-operative Union.

The arguments – we can begin calling it a conflict – remained live throughout the 1870s and early 1880s at Co-operative Congresses, and indeed the voices were raised louder the more the CWS demonstrated its intention of expanding its manufacturing operations. A boot and shoe operation was opened in Heckmondwike, West Yorkshire, in August 1880 and a woollen mill in Batley was taken over in 1887 after its failure as an independent manufacturing company. A cocoa works was started in London the same year. Currying of leather was added to the Heckmondwike operation in 1888 and a corn mill on the Tyne completed in 1891.[321]

There was an easy opportunity for point-scoring at the 1879 Congress, held in Gloucester, where delegates such as Holyoake and Lloyd Jones were able to draw attention to a strike of workers which had taken place at the CWS's Leicester boot and shoe factory. Holyoake said that the CWS's move to Leicester had been a 'calamity' for the town's workers, and Lloyd Jones backed him up. 'You will have strikes and you will be ruined, if you do not turn round and deal justly with working men,' he told Congress. It was left to other delegates, including Abraham Greenwood, to argue back. 'With regard to the strike at Leicester, if the workmen there considered they had a grievance, they ought to have represented it to their employers; but they had not done that. They had struck without submitting their case to the manager,' he said.[322]

Whether the strike was well-founded or not (and there was to be another strike at the Leicester works seven years later), the CWS did not seem on the path to ruin. Just the opposite. It was at this time growing into a great commercial undertaking. Its turnover increased from £1.15m in 1873 to £3.34m in 1880 and £4.79m in 1885[323]

On the other hand, independent co-operative production was turning out to be quite a challenging concept. One of the highest profile failures was that of the Ouseburn Engine Works in Newcastle-upon-Tyne, established in 1871, which went under a few years later taking with it considerable capital from co-operative societies including the CWS and the Halifax society.[324] Nearer Hebden Bridge, there was also the disappointing failure of the Lancashire and Yorkshire Flannel society at Littleborough, which had been an early united attempt by neighbouring co-operative societies to collaborate in a manufacturing venture. Set up in 1872 with much enthusiasm (and with several thousand pounds of co-operative capital), it was in serious difficulties by 1878. Greenwood's view at that time was that it was greatly undercapitalised; John Hartley's blunt verdict was that local societies would be unable to find the extra funds needed.[325] The Littleborough works were dissolved as an independent society in 1878 but continued to operate under the control of the liquidator J.T.W. Mitchell of the CWS, who in the end successfully turned the business around.[326]

These were two examples from a long list. The deep economic downturn of the late 1870s which had caused difficulties at the Nutclough Mill added to the problems. It should of course be added that it was not just co-operatively structured businesses which were failing at this period in the country's economic development, but the evidence certainly could be made to look damning. William Nuttall, a central figure in the CWS at this time and no friend of the profit-sharing viewpoint, analysed co-operative returns to the Registrar for an article in the CWS Annual of 1883 which claimed to demonstrate that 224 productive co-operative societies had failed. Greening fought back through the pages of *Co-operative News*, arguing that the article had been written simply to try to prove a foregone conclusion. 'No one reading the article and accepting its facts and figures as reliable could come to any conclusion other than adverse to the plan of making the workers partners in their workshops,' he said. His own claim was that only 24 of the 224 failures had been definitely profit-sharing concerns; Nuttall's list included corn mills and co-operatives which had incorporated but never traded, he argued.

Greening also argued that the role of productive co-operatives in the movement should not be judged just by their numbers:

> I ... claim for this small knot of really co-operative producing societies a success which cannot be measured by money results. If anyone will look at the composition of our annual Congresses, our frequent local conferences, our central board of management, the committees of our newspaper and other propagandist bodies, they will find everywhere a number of active, earnest and thoughtful men who have been contributed to the movement by these productive societies.[327]

There was, of course, no template for the British co-operative movement to follow in relation to manufacturing and production: they were having to work out for the first time the best way to progress and feel their way forward to a sustainable solution. Particularly in the 1880s there was pressure on the CWS to restructure their manufacturing plants as separate, but federated, co-operatives. Neale proposed something on these lines at a meeting in Hebden Bridge in January 1885, when he called for a gradual transfer of CWS businesses into employee ownership. 'Then the managers of the Wholesale would have the pleasing duty of handing over a well appointed and thriving business to a body of workers trained under its fostering supervision to the efficient management of the work by which they were to live,' he said.[328]

The most thoughtful exploration of this sort of solution came from J.C. Gray, by that stage Neale's deputy at the Co-operative Union, in two papers prepared in 1886, one for the Plymouth Congress and the other, a follow-up, read at a conference in Derby the following autumn. Gray's view was that the co-operative movement, having successfully tackled distribution, should approach production by focusing on the role played by labour. 'Labour, in my opinion, holds the position of first importance ... It is impossible to deny that there is much more value in a man's labour than, under the present system, he can ever obtain for it.' Workers just got their wages, he went on, capital enjoying the vast bulk of the added value. This had to change: 'The usual condition of things should be reversed and ... the worker should hire the capital, and not capital hire the worker,' he wrote. Give capital its 'wage', of say 5 per cent, and nothing more. Make inanimate capital the servant of the human labourer.[329]

This was the theory, but how could it be realised? Gray's proposal was that co-operative production in Britain should be completely restructured so that each manufacturing works was independently constituted but federated together through the CWS which would hold shares in each. The CWS would not run the businesses from the centre, Gray stressed. 'On the plan I propose, each productive workshop would have a separate existence in name, and would be independent in action so far as it did not clash or compete with others, and manufactured articles for which a ready sale could be found. These independent societies would each have a link with the centre by means of the representatives appointed from that centre to sit on its committee of management,' he wrote.

The current independent societies (Gray went on to enumerate some of the best known) would be gradually integrated with this new approach: 'Hebden Bridge, Paisley, Airedale, Coventry, Printing Society, Leek, the Flour Mills &c would all have to take in the Wholesale Society as part proprietor to the extent of at least one-fourth of their share capital ... On the other hand, the Wholesale would have to separate all its present productive works and have them registered as independent societies.'[330]

When first reading Gray, it is perhaps easy to write off his plans – as with his 1906 'single national society' speech – as being idealistic and impractical. But his paper does offer a coherent way in which co-operative production could have developed in Britain. If such a framework seems unwieldy, we need only look at the Mondragon co-operatives in the Basque Country today, the world's largest industrial co-operative group, which are federated in a way very similar to that Gray proposed in 1886.

It was not Neale, or Gray, or indeed Co-operative Congress, which decided how the CWS would run its affairs, however. The CWS was itself an independent co-operative society controlled by its members, the distributive societies who held its shares; its strategy was decided by the Board appointed by the members and ratified at the general meetings held quarterly at several centres around the country. The CWS's way of running its manufacturing operation was not necessarily better than that followed by the independent societies such as Joseph Greenwood's in Hebden Bridge. To take one period more or less at random, the CWS made a loss of £365 at its Durham soap works, a loss of £265 at its Batley ready-made clothing factory, and a loss of £186 at its Batley Woollen Mills during one of its trading quarters in 1889, although it offset these comfortably with profits at Heckmondwike and Leicester.[331] But the CWS's approach was not one it was prepared to change.

Gray returned to his proposal once more, in 1890, but accepted that he had to admit defeat. 'We had been divided in our opinions into the two extremes... and he had tried to make them meet and kiss each other. It was not his fault they would not agree', he said.[332]

At the 1887 Congress Thomas Hughes let rip. When we speak of what the Wholesale is doing in its workshops, he said to Congress, we have to bow our head in shame and humiliation. Neale backed him up: 'Nobody was more determinedly opposed to the principle upon which the Wholesale carried out its productive business than he was,' he said, attacking J.T.W. Mitchell by name. But Hughes' diatribe may have been counter-productive, and there was a sense that this was not the year for the show-down. The issue, Neale proposed, should be discussed further and the final decision taken the following year, at the 1888 Congress which was to take place at Dewsbury.[333]

This meant twelve months to mobilise, and things were put in motion straight away by Greening and the Labour Association. In late July 1887 following a committee meeting E.O. Greening wrote to Hughes calling for a united strategy: 'The Executive of the Labour Association... think yourself, Mr Neale, Mr Sedley Taylor, Mr Holyoake, Mr Joseph Greenwood and other recognised leaders on this question should meet and agree as to how our work is to be done.'[334] Greening went on, 'What is to be done if Dewsbury refuses our motion?'

The Labour Association by this time was three years old. Its creation could be seen as a convenient device to give an organisational base for that grouping of Christian Socialists and others who were campaigning in the Co-operative Union's Central Board and at Congress (there were now other opposing viewpoints being heard on the Co-operative Union's southern section of the Central Board, for long the de-facto power base). Neale, despite his position as the General Secretary of the Co-operative Union, regularly attended committee meetings in London for the first year or so, and Lloyd Jones was linked to the Association until his death in 1886. The driving force in the early years, however, was Greening.

Joseph Greenwood remained a close collaborator. He had bluntly expressed his own views in a personal letter to Greening a few years earlier, when he had written:

> There is no doubt but that those of us who are in favour of participation of capital and profit by the workman in productive operating will have a task to get anything done ... In any case we must reassert and maintain the true principles of co-operation and never give way to the teachings of Messrs [Dr John] Watts and [J.T.W.] Mitchell or the whole of the Wholesale Board and its perverseness in regard to these things.[335]

Greenwood had been part of a Labour Association delegation to the CWS in 1886, calling unsuccessfully for it to reinstate the profit-sharing scheme for its workers.[336]

There was an ideal opportunity coming up in the autumn of 1887 for those wanting to get together to caucus before Dewsbury, and it was to be in Hebden Bridge. The Labour Association's minute book for 4 October reads, 'Resolved that we ask Mr Greenwood to call meeting of gentlemen to whom overtures had previously been made for a private consultation on the present condition of the Productive movement'.[337] The private meeting happened on Sunday 16 October,[338] most of the main protagonists being in Hebden Bridge that weekend for the series of events on Saturday linked to the 'christening' of the fustian society's recently installed new steam engine (it was named 'Thomas Hughes'). Hughes himself was out of the country at this point, but Neale, Greening, Holyoake and the Marquess of Ripon were all in Hebden Bridge.[339]

The result of their meeting can be found in the Labour Association's minute book, which reads for 25 October: 'Mr Greening reported private consultation on Sunday morning. Mr Neale agreed to the issue of a manifesto calling attention to the present crisis and urging care in selection of delegates to Dewsbury Congress and Central Board. Decided to ask Mr Hughes to draw up manifesto ....'[340]

After all the build-up, it has to be added that the Dewsbury Congress resolved very little. Congress debated the subject on the first day and then continued again on the afternoon of the second. Holyoake, Hughes, Neale and others had put forward one resolution, proposing federation on grounds very similar to J.C. Gray's 1886 proposal. An alternative resolution from the CWS side stated 'We cannot conceive of any organisation more fitted to carry out the work of co-operative production than the Federation known as the Co-operative Wholesale Society'. In the end a compromise amendment was voted through. This began 'Congress recommends that by whomsoever productive enterprises are established – by either the Wholesale or distributive societies, or by organisations of the workmen themselves – an alliance be formed on equitable conditions for the sharing of profits and risks between the worker, the capitalist and the consumer'. A second part of the resolution referred to the Wholesale societies:

> Congress invites the Co-operative Wholesale Societies of England and Scotland, and all distributive societies which carry on production on their own account to adopt in the conduct of their works the principle formulated above, and to assist the United Board by suggestions and plans for perfecting it.[341]

The giveaway words here were 'recommends' and 'invites'. Congress had implicitly recognised that it was a forum for debate and discussion, not a body which could establish policies over individual parts of the movement. 'We were under the impression that something more than the assertion of a principle was expected from the Dewsbury Congress,' said a *Co-operative News* editorial later. Instead, it said, a resolution had been passed that was 'practically meaningless and worthless'.[342]

There was an attempt made in 1891 within the CWS's own structures to reverse its policy on profit-sharing, the impetus coming from the Norwich society. The Norwich motion was debated at the CWS's various regional meetings and overwhelmingly defeated.[343] By 1892, when Congress reconvened in its spiritual birthplace of Rochdale, it was J.T.W. Mitchell's turn to go on the offensive. 'It is time that namby-pambyism was crushed in these Congresses,' he said, speaking from the chair. 'According to my conviction consumption ought to be the basis of the growth of wealth in this country.'[344]

Mitchell had a formidable new weapon he could flourish, in the shape of *The Co-operative Movement in Great Britain*, the book which Beatrice Potter had been researching on her visit to Hebden Bridge and which had now just been published. Potter came down firmly, indeed aggressively, against the model of independent productive co-operatives of the kind promoted by the Labour Association. She highlighted, as William Nuttall had done in the 1883 CWS Annual, the numbers of co-operatives which had failed. She critiqued the role of the Christian Socialists, dismissing them as those 'excellent and talented gentlemen who spent time and money on the formation of working-class associations'. She failed to find more than a handful of successful productive co-operatives which she felt lived up to the rhetoric. 'Granted that the ideal form of democratic industry is the self-governing Co-operative workshop, in which the workers elect from among themselves the director of their labour, again I ask, Has the ideal been actually realized?' Answering her own question she claimed that 'forty years of persistent self-devoted effort' had left only eight societies which more or less fitted this description. The 'fair vision of a brotherhood of workers' vanished into 'an industrial phantom'.[345]

The Hebden Bridge fustian society plays a walk-on part in the book. It gets credit from Webb as the 'exceptional success' but does not divert the thrust of her argument. Anyway at Hebden Bridge as elsewhere, Webb said, 'the balance of power is in the hands of non-workers'.[346]

From his perspective, Holyoake summed up Potter in five words as 'very clever and very wrong'.[347] Potter certainly spares the distributive side of the movement the same sharp scrutiny she gives the productive side where no quarter is allowed for the compromises and messinesses of the real world. Potter's book does demonstrate, however, that there were arguments which could be raised on the other side, against the Labour Association's position.

So what, in broad terms, were the arguments for and against being raised during all these endless years of debate? There were both practical and ideological issues.

A writer in 1892 summarised the dispute as being between 'warm-hearted enthusiasts for social improvement and hard-headed administrators of co-operative business'[348] which certainly might be one way of describing, say, Holyoake or Neale on one side and J.T.W. Mitchell on the other. But this is not quite an accurate summation, because the Labour Association and those who supported it argued that their way of structuring business was better in practice as well as in principle. Workers who were joint owners, who had a place in the management of the business, and who shared the profits were likely to be more committed workers, they claimed. If Britain was to continue its economic development at a time of growing pressure from overseas competitors, this approach to running business was the way forward. Productivity, in short, would be higher in labour co-partnership firms.

This was contested, as we have seen, by the CWS which claimed to have seen no particular improvements in productivity when it had experimented with profit-sharing. The CWS and those who shared its approach also raised a whole series of practical issues over the exact way a profit bonus could be worked out. Should there be one bonus paid across the whole workforce, even if some parts of the business had been making a loss? But if bonus was paid on a departmental basis this would mean differential pay levels, and was this fair? What about hard-working and efficient workers in a productive department where, through a management fault, a loss had been made – why should they be penalised? Where did, say, a CWS bank clerk fit in? Should bonus be paid only to workers in productive works or those on the distributive side as well – and anyway, how could you fairly draw the dividing line between what was productive and what distributive?[349]

Behind these sorts of detailed questions lay perhaps the underlying problem that, as we have seen, profit itself was a flexible concept in a co-operative business, something which could be increased or decreased depending on how prices were set for the ultimate co-operative customer.

The philosophical arguments are more profound. Beatrice Potter used the term 'federalist' and 'individualist' to describe the two viewpoints, a usage which had begun a short time earlier and was popular with the CWS and its allies and particularly unpopular on the other side. Under this terminology, the 'federalists' were those who organised production through the CWS, which was after all a federation of independent local co-operative societies; the 'individualists' were those who argued for individual productive co-operatives benefiting their individual workers.

For Mitchell and his CWS colleagues, the fact that the CWS's profits were distributed out to member societies meant that all could share the fruits of the business. The community as a whole would be elevated by the sharing of profits in this way. 'We want to put the profits of trade into the pockets of people, not a section of them,' Mitchell said during Congress in 1893.[350] There was a simple solution for the employees of the CWS: all they needed to do was to be a member of a local society in membership of the CWS and they too like everyone else would benefit from the dividend.

This was an influential argument for a working class which was trying, collectively, to improve its position. It reflected the importance of the co-operative dividend in many working-class household budgets. There could be a sense, too, that a 'federalist' approach was fairer to the vast majority of those active in the co-operative movement who had to earn their living in conventional businesses and who drew simply wages. Was it just and reasonable that a small number of their peers, those fortunate enough to be working for co-operative employers, had their wages augmented above market levels through an extra bonus?

Against all this we can perhaps turn to Robert Halstead for the alternative view. In an 1898 essay *Co-operative production viewed in the light of some first principles* he sought to rebut the federalist argument: 'The federalistic system of co-operative production does not introduce anything new which will serve to distinguish co-operative from any other forms of production which owe their origin to competitive influences. It does not solve the labour problem, but simply adopts the joint-stockism of middle-class competition.' Co-operative production of this kind has adopted the 'highly-centralised system of industrial despotism', giving the worker no special economic advantage and left at the mercy of competition, just as in other forms of business structure. The workers' sole form of self-protection was to try to defend their wage levels through trade unionism.

There was an alternative:

Under the system which gives bonus to labour, the worker's share in the success of the firm is economically and practically recognised. Labour has hitherto passed through three stages of progress, viz., slavery, serfdom and wagedom. The next stage is the complete industrial emancipation of labour, and profit-sharing, joined with a systematic capitalising of the workers' share for securing co-partnership, is a well-organised attempt to assist labour out of mere wagedom into the freedom of self-employment and self-management. The self-emancipation of labour is thus ensured ...[351]

This is Halstead offering the theory. What perhaps does not come through in his words is the sense of passion that those supporting this viewpoint felt, the idea that they were upholding the original principles of the co-operative pioneers who had been struggling to change a world which was based on a fundamental injustice. For the passion we can look to Holyoake, speaking to a Hebden Bridge audience at the October 1887 event to name the fustian society's new engine:

> Labour is taken without security, is given no interest, has neither first or second award of profit, and can be cast off at a week's notice ... Capital has no care nor toil to perform. It lives in opulence or saunters into sunny climes ... All the while labour is chained to the workshop. From morning to night it toils out its dreary or cheerless years. All the strength and light of its life, which it will never see more in this world, is unrequited. All that capital does for labour is to feed it, so that it can work, and only as long as it can work, and then leaves it to die. All the profit which labour has created by its ceaseless and cheerless industry is swept away by capital, even to the last penny, and paid over the counter to its banker. Is this fair play to labour? Is this equity to industry? Is it common honesty or common humanity? Yet there are some who tell us that this should be the co-operative policy in our workshop.[352]

As might be expected, the Dewsbury Congress did not see an end to the wrangling. Holyoake and Mitchell clashed at the 1890 Congress, for example, and Holyoake was back criticising the CWS in 1894 in *Co-operative News*, arguing that 'retrogression treads on the heels of business success'.[353]

It was a fractured movement, in other words, which J.C. Gray inherited from Neale when he took over the General Secretaryship of the Co-operative Union in the autumn of 1891. Gray's introduction to co-operation of course had been in Hebden Bridge at the Fustian Manufacturing Society but he was to demonstrate considerable political adroitness in holding the ring between the warring parties and putting in place the framework of an effective modern organisation.

Although they were events which were greatly mourned in the movement, the deaths of Vansittart Neale in 1892 and of J.T.W. Mitchell in March 1895 aided this process by removing from the scene two of the individuals most closely associated with the conflict. The 1895 Congress, held in Huddersfield, was branded as the conciliation Congress, one which would bring the movement back together. Reaching across the divide, Thomas Hughes gave a tribute to Mitchell, who despite his role in building up the mighty CWS had continued to live a frugal working-class lifestyle and had died leaving only a few hundred pounds. Holyoake talked of looking forward, rather than going back to old debates.[354] A committee for co-operative conciliation was set up, with five members of the Central Board and three each from the CWS, the Scottish CWS and the Co-operative Productive Federation. Joseph Craven, chairman of the CPF as well as the fustian society, was one of their delegates.[355]

Gray's role in defending the central role of the Co-operative Union through this period brought strains with Robert Halstead who before he had started working on a paid basis for the Labour Association was already an enthusiastic promulgator of the Association's message. Hebden Bridge, the location for the Association's launch event a decade earlier, had remained its northern base. Greenwood himself was strongly committed to the Association's work, as a minute from its 1895 AGM demonstrates: 'Joseph Greenwood urged the necessity of an active propaganda. Difficulties there no doubt were in abundance but we must not be deterred by them, and in the end we should make our own impression on public opinion.'[356] In 1897, it was agreed to set up a Lancashire and Yorkshire section of the Labour Association – an echo perhaps of the original Co-operative Union's two divisions of London and the North-West – and in May that year the new Lancashire and Yorkshire Council was launched at a meeting in the Hebden Bridge Co-operative Hall. Greenwood chaired and Halstead was appointed one of the secretaries.[357] Halstead offered himself as a lecturer for the Association on a series of themes, including voluntary and state socialism, trade unionism and co-operation, the Italian social reformer Giuseppe Mazzini, and – naturally – working-class education and co-operation. Greenwood himself offered two lectures, one entitled the organisation of productive workshops and the other 'How we made co-operative production a success at Hebden Bridge'.[358]

The Labour Association's work was on occasions beginning to make Gray's life difficult, however. In the aftermath of the 1895 'conciliation', Gray and Halstead were both at the North-West sectional conference held in Bolton the following March, designed to discuss the way forward. Halstead, speaking for the Labour Association, tried to get through a motion in support of co-partnership principles. Gray responded very firmly:

Is it wise for the Union to depart from its position as the general adviser and propagandist agency of the movement, and become a partisan or financial agent of one part of the movement? We cannot overlook the fact that co-operators are divided in respect to co-operative production. The Union up to now has been the head of the movement; are we to make it a one-sided partisan affair, with one side marshalled against the other?

Gray was also irritated with the Labour Association because it had been working with a new start-up co-partnership business in competition with an existing co-operative society; Gray maintained the new venture was effectively the private business of a number of wealthy businessmen. He carried on with surprising vehemence, 'I begin to wonder whether people who talk about co-partnership really know what is meant by it. Mr Halstead represents the Labour Association; I wish he represented a more sensible association, after the pattern of the Hebden Bridge Fustian Society.'

For good measure Gray also addressed a few negative comments against the Co-operative Productive Federation, which was represented at the Bolton conference by none other than the Nutclough chairman Joseph Craven. The CPF was 'good as far as it goes' but its powers were limited, Gray said, adding 'I cannot understand how a productive federation consisting of other productive societies can assist co-operative production at large'.[359]

It was true that the CPF did not have a great deal to show for its first years of life. It had been started as a way of bringing together the most successful of the independent productive co-operatives and by 1897 had 51 member firms, with the Hebden Bridge Fustian Manufacturing Society providing not only the CPF's chairman Craven but also a significant annual membership subscription. But a proposal in 1893 to bring the productive societies into a much more formalised federated structure was abortive: only a small number of societies came to what was supposed to be a key preparatory conference.[360]

Instead the CPF turned its attention to the task of helping productive co-operatives find capital, by borrowing at 4 per cent and lending on to co-operatives at 5 per cent. By 1897 it had £4,000 out on loan. 'This method of dealing with funds for Co-operative Production meets a long-felt want. It offers a reliable and convenient means for societies and individuals to invest Loan Capital,' the Federation explained.[361] Much of the capital came from well-heeled supporters looking to put their money into what today would be described as an ethical investment. In 1897, for example, the CPF committee was reporting £200 from an Alice Vaughan, £150 from Miss

Madden and £100 from the Hon T.A. Bassey.[362]

These loan funds were not necessarily administered particularly efficiently. Later on, in 1904 when Robert Halstead was in charge at the CPF, it was found that several loan agreements were not legally stamped (in other words, the loans had been left unsecured) and for others the loan books could not be found. There were also, predictably, bad debts. Making business loans is, then as today, a skilled business and the CPF seems to have got better in taking loan decisions as the years went by.[363] Its role in this regard can be seen as an interesting forerunner of the various co-operative and community enterprise loan and finance schemes operating in Britain today.

The CPF was later to work closely with the Labour Association around propaganda work and the Labour Association's Henry Vivian was represented on the CPF committee. The CPF's main role, however, was as a supplier of business services to its member firms. One of its most long-lasting initiatives was the introduction, in 1906, of a joint invoicing scheme enabling local co-operative societies to settle up for purchases made from several productive co-operatives in one payment.[364]

Robert Halstead's appointment in 1900 followed the death of the CPF's then Secretary Thomas Blandford and a short period when Henry Vivian stood in. Vivian would seem to have pushed Halstead's candidacy strongly against some opposition from those who felt that Halstead was more a scholar than an administrator, and presumably CPF's chairman Joseph Craven would have been pleased to have seen an ex-Nutclough man appointed. It is possible that the sceptics were right, however. Halstead's time at the CPF was not necessarily particularly rewarding. 'Halstead entered an office and gave to routine the visionary nature that was meant for propaganda among small groups and guilds,' said a friend much later. He was 'wearing himself out in clerical labours that wearied him to weakness'.[365] From about 1910 ill-health confined him to routine clerical labours.

The CPF also took him away from his direct involvement in the educational movement: it was Albert Mansbridge who built up the Workers' Educational Association in the years after the 1903 launch and who is remembered as the organisation's primary founder. Halstead's contribution has slipped out of the story.

Nevertheless, Halstead did his best at the CPF to defend the interests of his member firms, in the process coming into conflict once again with J.C. Gray at the Co-operative Union. It needs to be said that the 1895 attempt at conciliation did not put an end to disagreements; the conciliation committee produced a majority report in 1896 (supported by the CPF), and a minority report from the three CWS representatives. The Scottish CWS equivocated between the two positions. And though Gray had successfully managed to take some of the heat out of the arguments, another dispute between the CWS and advocates of co-partnership flared up in 1900.

The CWS, arguing that it was participating in exhibitions of co-operatively produced goods along with independent societies only to find itself coming under attack for its position on profit-sharing, announced it would cease to participate in most of these exhibitions. To resolve this another committee was established, with Gray as its chairman. Halstead sought to ensure that three nominations from productive societies for this committee were CPF nominees but Gray argued back that the CPF was not fully representative of all the independent productive co-operatives. An unseemly spat between the two former Nutclough employees developed in *Co-operative News*. Halstead accused Gray of showing 'the temper of a narrow officialdom'. Gray replied, 'I refrain from making any remarks on the last paragraph of Mr Halstead's letter ... because I might, perhaps, be tempted down to the same level of argument'. Gray drew attention to his credentials: 26 years active service in the co-operative movement, 'ten of these years being spent in connection with a productive society of whose success I am as proud as anyone can be'.[366]

Gray was only four years Halstead's senior and the roles they now found themselves in did not perhaps help their relationship. Halstead was, however, to pay handsome tribute later to Gray's contribution, in a speech made after Gray's early death in 1912. If there were two men who had done more for him in the co-operative movement than any others, Halstead said, it was Joseph Greenwood and Mr Gray. 'About Mr Gray one discovered more of the comrade than the official.'[367]

CHAPTER 9

CAPITAL AND LABOUR

J.C. Gray had been encouraged to come across to Hebden Bridge from Manchester to take the chair at the public meeting arranged by the fustian society in early November 1893. The larger of the two Co-operative Halls was almost full for the occasion. The speaker was Tom Mann, the trade union and labour leader.

Gray earned some early laughter from his audience: 'He could imagine some of his friends saying, 'Why should I come to hear Mr Mann lecture? Mr Mann is a Socialist – he's a horrid man',' Gray started. 'This word Socialism frightened a good many people, but they had never attempted to understand it,' he went on. 'Could they honestly say that all was right in this country of ours? The relations between capital and labour, and between capital and the consumer, were they as they ought to be?'

Mann took to the platform to address the theme 'The faults of our present industrial system and how to remedy them'. He talked of the social and industrial discord in Britain, of adulteration in manufacturing, of some workers working 14 hours a day while others were unemployed, of the position of women who were considered cheaper than men, of the 'shockingly low' standard of living of working people. He called for co-operators to work for the general reconstruction of the industrial system on democratic and ethical lines. To achieve this reconstruction, the principles of co-operation could be applied at national and municipal levels, too, he said. Bring the railways under national control, for example.

'Some people said that he was a disturber of the peace. He wanted to disturb their peace of mind who seemed content to let wages remain at the shockingly low standard they were at to-day,' he added.[368]

Tom Mann was at this time close to the co-operative movement, and his Hebden Bridge visit was part of a lecture tour he was making under co-operative auspices. Others from an earlier generation had also seen co-operative endeavour as prefigurative of a socialist society. Karl Marx, although he may later have moved to a more state-centric approach, had in 1864 spoken highly favourably of 'co-operative factories raised by the unassisted efforts of a few bold 'hands'". By deed, rather than by argument, they were demonstrating that production on a large scale could be carried on without a class of masters, Marx said: 'The value of these great social experiments cannot be over-rated'.[369]

By the time of Tom Mann's visit to Hebden Bridge, the industrial north of England was (this time using Engels' words) experiencing something of a 'rush to socialism'.[370] The Independent Labour Party had been launched a few months earlier, in January 1893, at a well-attended conference in Bradford. The *Clarion* newspaper, the widely read and non-sectarian socialist paper, had started in 1891 and its editor Robert Blatchford's influential socialist pamphlet *Merrie England* was published in the summer of 1893. In 1896, when the Yorkshire ILP organised a Whit Monday rally just outside Hebden Bridge in Hardcastle Crags, hoards of people headed up the hill past the Nutclough Mill to hear Keir Hardie and his fellow ILPer Caroline Martyn call for socialism. The local paper claimed that as many as 12,000 people had been in Hardcastle Crags that day for the speeches and the mass performances undertaken by the various local Clarion choirs.[371]

It was against this background that some of the arguments within the co-operative movement were being played out. J.C. Gray had himself urged his movement not to forget the higher purpose of co-operation. In powerful language he had typified the approach of unbridled capitalistic competition in the following way:

> You are an independent unit, existing without responsibility of any kind beyond your own personal desires or wishes – before you lies the world and society, make them your prey – so conduct and order your business life that it shall bring you wealth. The world is an orange, to be sucked – a sponge, to be squeezed – squeeze it to the utmost of your power and if, in one direction, you do not succeed in your purpose, try another way; but in all your exertions have in view your own material benefit, no matter who sinks or swims in the struggle.

In competition, Gray went on, there would always be antagonism and always losers as well as winners. Those who were the greatest losers were the poorest of the working classes, upon whom 'the greatest evils of competition' fell.[372]

Offering a critique of the way industry was organised in the late nineteenth century Britain was the easy part, however. Putting forward practical solutions was more problematic, and that word 'socialism' could cover all sorts of proposals for change. As increasingly the idea of socialism came to be associated more particularly with state socialism, and with a form of industrial organisation focused on state ownership, Joseph Greenwood in particular had misgivings.

In 1886 at a Yorkshire co-operative conference in Hebden Bridge Greenwood had called on his fellow labourers in the movement to have confidence in one another and use their abilities for the benefit of all: 'If that was Socialism, then he was a Socialist,' he said. Later, in 1895, he was to describe himself as a Christian Socialist, in the tradition of Neale, Hughes and those others who had promulgated the Christian Socialist message almost half a century earlier.[373] Greenwood was less sure about the ILP approach to socialism: 'There were the Independent Labour men who meant very well, but could the representatives they sent to Parliament do for the working classes what the working classes could do for themselves?' he said at the Huddersfield Congress of 1895.[374]

Greenwood's approach was a resolutely bottom-up one, based on worker self-organisation. And the reason co-operative production was so important was because it meant, as he put it at Huddersfield, that workpeople 'controlled their own workshop and shaped its destinies and received the fruits of their own labour'.[375] Elsewhere he expressed considerable scepticism that any centralised approach could achieve the desired results.[376]

Greenwood's view was similar to that of Robert Halstead: 'While admitting the moral enthusiasm and ability of working men who were joining the ranks of the Socialists he had little hopes of any highly centralised system making much improvement of the present system,' Halstead was reported as saying in 1899. 'Socialism, as compared with Co-partnership, involved the clumsy expedient of using a political agent to realise what was an industrial end. In his opinion, Socialism would fail because it mistook the capture of an autocratic system by the democracy for the evolution of a democratic system answering to the ideals and aspirations of the industrial population.'[377]

Halstead was to expand these views more fully in a feisty exchange in a magazine called *The Commonwealth* with a Fabian Society member and advocate of a state-focused route to socialism, Henry Macrosty. Macrosty had attacked profit-sharing and co-partnership as still leaving labour in the thrall of capital. The truth is, he went on, 'that bonus on wages is nothing but wages after all, a form of wages which is perhaps occasionally useful as a stimulus to apathetic workpeople'. There was nothing revolutionary, nothing socialistic about it.

Halstead let rip in response: 'I have to confess that the idea of a well-drilled, well-conditioned, wage-earning, labour population such as Mr

Macrosty wants in order to stifle the craving for the bracing incentives of Labour Co-partnership is to me morally repulsive. Unless we workers can realise that the best part of the Industrial Democracy is, like the kingdom of Heaven, within us, to be worked into outward realisation, there seems very little heaven for us but one of 'fatty cakes and something worse than herb beer', or very little democracy except an exchange from capitalistic to official domination from the top, with the same disinherited wage-earners at the bottom eating such messes of pottage as the Jacobs of a centralised collectivism can find it in their hearts or in their power to give to us.'[378]

In the light of the difficulties which emerged in Britain during twentieth century ventures into nationalisation, and the failure too of the state socialist model developed in the Soviet Union, there is space once more on the British left to look at Halstead's vision of a very different, bottom-up route towards the transformation of society. Halstead can be an attractive figure in other respects too. In 1896, for example, we find him arguing against gender inequality and for women to be paid on the same basis as male workers in productive co-operatives.[379]

But we also have to recognise that there was a core ambiguity in the message of co-partnership. We can call on the independent productive co-operatives' old antagonist Beatrice Potter, now in her married guise as Beatrice Webb and writing jointly with her husband Sidney, to put the charge. The Webbs, in a report for the Fabian Research Department published in the *New Statesman* in 1914, offered a critique of productive co-operatives which remained little changed from Beatrice's original *The Co-operative Movement in Great Britain*. They argued that, notwithstanding the occasional success, the achievements of self-managed co-operative workshops were so paltry and limited that they offered no model for any radical transformation of industrial life. The Webbs, like their fellow Fabian Macrosty, saw state intervention as the necessary agency.

But the Webbs also sharpened their knives at the concept of co-partnership. This was 'not the finding of a new organisation of industry, so that it may be governed in the interests of the community rather than those of individuals, but the discovery of a way to avoid conflicts between the capitalist employer and the wage-earners in his service'.[380]

There had been an element of the idea of bringing together capital and labour in a harmonious partnership at the very start of the Co-operative Union; the 1869 London conference agreed that the new union's objects included 'conciliating the conflicting interests of the capitalist, the worker, and the purchaser through an equitable division among them of the fund commonly known as profit'.[381] This was a stance which particularly reflected the approach of Neale and of other Christian Socialists.

As labour unrest gathered pace in the 1880s, and particularly with the emergence of an active Marxian current in British socialism with the foundation of the Social Democratic Federation in 1881, the call for co-partnership to be promoted as a way to create harmony between labour and capital grew louder. Indeed, we can detect a definite transition taking place from this period onwards, associated with the growing popularisation of the term co-partnership itself. Whereas one can interpret Greenwood's defence of bonus to labour in 1876 as a radical, 'left', position against an increasingly commercialised and pragmatic distributive co-operative movement, the issues become much more complex and ambiguous in the later years of the century.

We can get a sense of this from a speech made by Thomas Hughes in Hebden Bridge in March 1886. Referring to the mass socialist demonstrations in London which had taken place a few weeks earlier (and had ended in the bloody repression known subsequently as 'Black Monday'), he told his audience: 'A great deal of cant was talked by these Socialists about capital and labour. The foundation of such talk as went on in Trafalgar Square was the notion that there was an antagonism between capital and labour.'[382]

This was similar to the perspective held by Earl Grey, who began to take over from the Marquess of Ripon, more than twenty years his senior, the role of upper class supporter of co-operation and co-partnership. Albert Grey, born in St James's Palace, London in 1851, has been described by his biographer as an idealistic imperialist. He served the empire in Rhodesia and South Africa and later was to be appointed Governor-General of Canada. He held family estates in Northumberland. A vice-president of the Labour Association, he was invited by Greenwood to visit the Nutclough Mill in 1898. He told his Hebden Bridge audience at a public meeting during his visit that profit-sharing would create a contented working population. 'The great advantage of the industrial partnership system was that it minimised the likelihood of labour disputes by the establishment of complete solidarity of interest between capital and labour, and made every worker feel that he was not merely a hired labourer but a partner in the undertaking'.[383]

There was another element to the co-partnership message, and that was the strong moralising dimension which came across from some of its adherents. This element, too, can be traced back to the Christian Socialists where it was certainly an important part of Neale's support for co-operation. Earl Grey expressed this in his address at Hebden Bridge in 1898: 'Co-operative production furnished each man with an ideal, which became to him a religion. It helped to form character.'[384]

Character-building, which in this context has to be read as meaning improvements to the moral character of the working classes, was a theme Grey returned to a few months later in a Presidential address at the National Co-operative Festival at Crystal Palace in August. He was forthright in his criticism of the CWS and the retail co-operative movement which he said had 'degenerated' and no longer 'had the qualities which are necessary to stir the soul'. But there was hope yet in co-operative production. Follow the lead of Hebden Bridge, and of the productive co-operatives in places such as Leicester and Kettering, he went on, and these principles 'cannot fail to improve the character, the status and the efficiency of the worker, and to consolidate the interests of capital and labour, thereby strengthening the nation both in character and wealth'.[385]

It should be added that the annual co-operative festivals every summer at the Crystal Palace in south London which had begun in 1888 were a rallying-point for the Labour Association and for proponents of co-partnership. The idea for them had been E.O. Greening's. What had started in 1886 as a small-scale Flower Show run under the auspices of his Agricultural and Horticultural Association had developed into a major summer event, combining Flower Festival competitions with mass performances by co-operative and temperance choirs and with other entertainments. The festivals also included each year a national exhibition of co-operative production, at which the Hebden Bridge Fustian Manufacturing Society was a regular participant. Over the years the Crystal Palace events were to attract very large numbers: over 60,000 were claimed for the 1903 event, for example.[386] Greening was directly involved for the first fifteen years as the festival's chairman, and for most of its life (it continued until 1910) it was run entirely autonomously from the Co-operative Union.[387]

The list of vice-presidents of the Labour Association at this time is an interesting one. Earl Grey was joined in this list of patrons by, among others, the Duke of Westminster, the Earl of Stamford, Lord Wantage, the Bishop of Durham and the Bishop of Ripon. Joseph Greenwood was on the list too, along with stalwarts such as Holyoake and Greening, but nevertheless the Labour Association is sending out a clear signal that it wishes to be a long way from the socialist activism manifesting itself in, say, Trafalgar Square – or, for that matter, in Hardcastle Crags with Keir Hardie and Caroline Martyn on a Whit Monday holiday.

This tendency – what we can call the class harmony approach – was eventually to overshadow the earlier worker 'self-employment' impulse which had seen Greenwood be such a passionate defender of bonus to labour. Ultimately the Labour Association was to veer away from the mainstream co-operative movement to support what today would be considered an employee share-ownership approach to business. It changed its name in 1901 to the Labour Co-partnership Association, changed it again in 1928 to the Industrial Co-partnership Association, again in 1972 to the Industrial Participation Association and eventually in 1989 renamed itself the Involvement and Participation Association. It continues to operate today, using the strap-line 'raising performance through workplace engagement', perhaps not exactly the slogan Joseph Greenwood would have chosen.[388]

What was Greenwood's attitude to all this? Did he see capital and labour as having identical or antagonistic interests? The answer is that he held a rather more finessed position, one which distinguished between capital itself in its simple economic sense and capitalism, as a system of industrial organisation.

Capital and labour, if they properly understood each other, might work for their mutual benefit, he said at the 1882 Co-operative Congress.[389] He elaborated on this ten years later in his hearing before the Royal Commission on Labour. The Chairman, Sir Michael Hicks-Beach MP, began the questioning. Do you consider, he asked Greenwood, that there are conflicting interests between capitalists and labour? Yes, Greenwood replied. And the remedy then?

> We believe that there can be no quarrel between capital and labour as such, because each is necessary to make the other remunerative, but we also believe that there must always be an amount of friction between the capitalist who is also an employer and the labourer who has nothing but his labour to sell.

Greenwood went on:

> We propose to substitute for this system of opposing interests either one of identity of interest by uniting the worker and the capitalist in one person, as may be done by the workers in the different industries providing the capital necessary to employ themselves, or otherwise eliminating altogether the employing capitalist and for the worker to hire from the capitalists the capital necessary to employ himself and pay interest on wages for the use of the same.[390]

The problem for Greenwood was that capital generally had all the cards to play:

> Capital is necessary, and should be valued by workmen in co-operative production. It should be secured from loss as much as possible, and if labourers are about to ally themselves with it they should take care that it has its due and no more ... If it be left open to capitalists to claim more they will probably strive to get the utmost return upon their capital.[391]

Holyoake put the same point more picturesquely: 'The co-operator is not against capital. Capital is exactly like fire – an excellent servant when it warms the inmates but a bad one when it burns down the house'.[392] Holyoake's remark is one that the twenty-first century British co-operative movement might want to take to heart.

There is one central issue which has been implicit so far in the story of Joseph Greenwood, the Nutclough co-operative and the wider co-partnership movement, and which we should address explicitly: the always vexed question for the British of social class. The success of the Hebden Bridge Fustian Manufacturing Society had taken Greenwood far beyond his roots as the son of an impoverished hand loom weaver, born at a time when the family was barely managing to get by on a diet of oatmeal porridge and skim-milk. He was in friendly contact now with some from the highest social circles in the country, including those aristocratic patrons of the Labour Association like Earl Grey. He had been feted at Corpus Christi college in Oxford, where he had met senior Oxford dons; Anglican bishops knew of him and his co-operative mill, and some had come visiting.

Nevertheless, despite all this, in late Victorian Britain the differences of social class could not be willed away: it was reflected in almost every aspect of life, in wealth, in the clothes worn and not least in accent (Greenwood, we have to assume, would have had a broad West Riding accent).[393]

Even with goodwill on both sides, the risk of patronising or being patronised was ever present. Here, for example, is an account from a friend of Robert Halstead's about Halstead's experience in the early days of university extension: 'Halstead was brought from the works at Hebden Bridge and taken to West End drawing rooms as a typical workman with ideas that sought the better relationship of labour and capital. Duchesses and dames held their lorgnettes steady to see him plainly.'[394]

Class attitudes emerged almost regardless of intention. For instance, the passage quoted in chapter 7 (pages 88-89) from Cosmo Lang where he describes Beatrice Potter's visit to Joseph Greenwood's house gives away almost as much about Lang's own class and his relationship with his working-class hosts in Hebden Bridge as it says about Potter herself.

Potter was indeed right to draw attention to the class contradictions which working-class co-operators faced when in *The Co-operative Movement in Great Britain* she bemoaned the fact that they had to suffer 'sharp rebukes and fervent exhortations from bishops, nobles, politicians and economists and other would-be foster-parents of working-class associations'.[395] One of the strong defences which can be made of the other wing of British co-operation at this time, that represented by the CWS and the distributive societies, is that they were almost exclusively working-class organisations under working-class leadership.[396] But then the same, too, could be said of the Hebden Bridge Fustian Manufacturing Society, not to mention the other productive co-operatives who lined up within the broad co-partnership camp.

Is there an argument that Greenwood and others at the Nutclough allowed themselves to be seduced too much by the attentions of those higher up the social hierarchy and in doing so somehow betrayed their class? A hostile reading of the evidence could perhaps find material which could be mustered to make a case (it is possible to raise an eyebrow at the motivation which sent Halstead in 1894 to London to attend a meeting of an embryonic 'Industrial Union of Employers and Employees', for example).[397] But it has to be said that, despite the vehemence of the internecine disputes within the co-operative movement, this was never a charge which the opponents of co-partnership levied at Greenwood, at Halstead or indeed at the fustian society in general.

There was another way of addressing this issue, an appeal which one feels Greenwood would want to advance: that better relations between people from different social backgrounds, including more social interaction and friendship, was a sign of a more equal and less class-ridden society, the sort of society which co-operators such as Greenwood were attempting to build.

There is a touching comment from Greenwood, written in 1909 just after the death of Joseph Craven, remembering the times when he and Craven had visited Thomas Hughes, Rugby schoolboy, Oxford student, barrister and by this point a county court judge:

> We used to visit the late Judge Hughes together once a year and on the last occasion we went together to Chester, Mr Hughes's home on the Dee, we all went for a walk round the walls of the city and into the cathedral, talking together as equals and then back to his house; and when we parted at the door, Mr Hughes was too full to speak.[398]

Talking together as equals – this was, in late nineteenth century Britain, indeed a prize to be sought and celebrated. It was a sign of a better society in the making, one which, just possibly, co-operation could help bring about.

CHAPTER 10

INTERNATIONAL CO-OPERATION

Joseph Greenwood left Hebden Bridge late in October 1896 to catch the train to London. From there he continued on to the south coast and across the Channel to Paris. It was, almost certainly, his first time abroad.

His destination was number 5, rue Las Cases, a small street on the Left Bank not far from the Assemblée Nationale. This was the home for le Musée Social, not a museum in the conventional sense but more a research centre dedicated to France's co-operative and working-class movements. Founded two years earlier, le Musée Social housed a specialist library of books and newspapers and also offered a ground floor conference hall. It was in this hall (still there today, at what has become CEDIAS, the *Centre d'études, de documentation, d'information et d'action socials*) that the second Congress of the International Co-operative Alliance was to take place, between 28 and 31 October. Greenwood was one of the relatively small number of British co-operators to make the journey.

It was to be quite a memorable few days. Le Comte de Chambrun, who played a similar role in the French co-operative movement to that played by the Marquess of Ripon in Britain, opened up his opulent Parisian home known as l'Hotel de Bourbon-Conde for an evening reception and dinner on the first night. There, overlooked by the statues of Faith, Hope and Charity from the nineteenth century sculptor Eugène Guillaume, the delegates got a taste of Paris life as lived by the fortunate few. There were the usual speeches. Holyoake, a few months from turning eighty and speaking on behalf of the British contingent, seized the opportunity to plug the benefits of profit-sharing. The evening ended late, some of the delegates getting back to their hotels after midnight.

The next evening the reception was in the even more splendid surroundings of the Elysée Palace, as delegates participated in the reception offered by the President of the French Republic Félix Faure. Faure had spent two years in England in business and took time that evening to talk to the British party. He also offered them the chance to use his Presidential box at the Grand Opera later in the week. Holyoake was to recount how the British party, Joseph Greenwood among them, had difficulties in gaining admission to the Opera House because of the crush and had finally (after overcoming language difficulties of the kind the English often have in France) managed to be escorted into the building through the back of the stage.[399]

But Joseph Greenwood had not come to Paris for a holiday. The 1896 Congress of the International Co-operative Alliance marked an important second step in the attempt to establish a representative worldwide organisation for the co-operative movement, the first being the inaugural Congress held a year earlier in London. Greenwood was to return from Paris as the ICA's elected Treasurer and member of the six-strong Executive Bureau, charged with ensuring that the fledgling Alliance's financial and administrative affairs were managed in good order.

Today the International Co-operative Alliance is recognised as the global voice of the co-operative movement. It has over the years had both highs and lows but encouragingly is currently on something of an upward trajectory. One of the ICA's most important achievements in recent times has been to bring the movement together around a shared definition of what constitutes a co-operative, an agreed statement on co-operative values and a set of seven co-operative principles. These values and principles, which have at their root some of the original beliefs of the Rochdale Pioneers, were adopted at the centenary conference of the ICA in 1995 and are widely used globally to distinguish co-operative ventures from other forms of joint enterprise. The ICA today operates from a small office in Brussels.

It was no coincidence that the first two ICA conferences, in 1895 and 1896, took place in London and Paris for it was the co-operative movements in Britain and France which had most to do with the ICA's establishment. The co-operative movement in Britain had been internationally minded from the earliest days; as we have seen, it was the example of the worker-run productive co-operative businesses in France in the period immediately after the 1848 Revolution which had been an inspiration for the Christian Socialists. Reports on the progress of co-operation in several countries, including Denmark, France, Germany, Italy, Sweden and Switzerland, were presented at the London Co-operative Congress of 1869 and international reports were a regular aspect of Congresses thereafter.[400]

An attempt to bring together an international co-operative alliance had been tried in Paris in 1867 but cancelled at the last minute. By the 1880s visits from fraternal delegates from abroad were a feature both of French co-operative conferences and of the British Co-operative Congresses. The French co-operative leader Edouard de Boyve from Nîmes raised at both the 1886 and 1887 British Congresses a French proposal for the establishment of an international alliance. However, nothing at this stage was realised.[401]

When Neale and Greening tried again, with the issue in 1892 of a short pamphlet entitled *Proposal for an International Alliance of the Friends of Co-operative Production*, they had something slightly different in mind: a body which could carry forward into the international arena the battle in support of co-partnership that they had been waging in Britain. This proposed alliance was to be a kind of Labour Association writ large. As originally planned by Neale and Greening, it was not a body which would welcome in those from the CWS end of the movement. Indeed Neale (now no longer General Secretary) was effectively working outside the Co-operative Union's own internal committee structures in order to progress these aims.

The new alliance took form for the first time in Rochdale during the time of the 1892 Congress, at a fringe meeting held at the Greyhound Hotel. There was a large British attendance although only two foreign delegates were present (de Boyve and Charles Robert, another French supporter of profit-sharing). The meeting approved the principle of the Alliance 'on the basis of the participation of the worker in profits' and agreed to hold a follow-up meeting. The obvious place to hold this was at the Crystal Palace festival the following August.[402]

Neale did not manage to get to Crystal Palace, however. He wrote to Greening from his home in Bisham Abbey that he was confined to bed and added 'I do not see when the imprisonment is likely to end'.[403] Sadly, he was now at the end of his life and was to die the following month.

Joseph Greenwood was also absent, although the fustian society sent both Joseph Craven and Leonard Stocks as delegates. Greenwood's absence is out of character and unexplained, but he may have been needed by his wife at home. Sarah Greenwood, the woman who had married a young fustian-cutter in 1855, had lived with him through the difficult years of the Cotton Famine in the early 1860s and had borne him six sons, was to die at the end of 1892, still only in her mid-fifties.

Craven and Stocks would have been able to report to Greenwood on their return to Hebden Bridge that the Crystal Palace meeting had reaffirmed the decision of Rochdale. A resolution had been agreed to set up 'an International Alliance of the Friends of Co-operative Production based on the co-partnership of labour' in order to 'establish relations of mutual helpfulness between those who are working in all countries to end the chronic warfare between Capital and Labour and to establish industrial peace'.[404]

Neale's death halted the momentum, however. Plans to hold the inaugural Congress, originally intended for 1893, were re-arranged for 1894 and were then postponed again until 1895. The event, when it finally happened, was held in the Society of Arts (now the Royal Society of Arts) in its headquarters near the Strand from 19-23 August, arranged so as to allow participants also to visit the Crystal Palace festival taking place at the same time.

Until a few short weeks before the ICA Congress opened, the planning had been overseen by an executive committee made up of committed co-partnership adherents, including Greening, the CPF's Thomas Blandford and Henry Vivian, with the elderly Holyoake offering moral support. Henry Wolff, an Englishman with first-hand experience of the German co-operative banking movement, had been recruited after Neale's death by Greening and was another key participant. The main body of the British co-operative movement, as represented by the Co-operative Union, was absent.

Greening and J.C. Gray had been in touch with each other during the spring of 1895, however, and immediately after the Huddersfield 'conciliation' Congress the opportunity was there for Gray to bring his organisation into the preparations. At a meeting held on 6 July it was agreed that Gray would join Greening as a joint convenor of the Congress and that the Co-operative Union would be represented on the executive committee. Gray also ensured that the Co-operative Union would be recognised as the British section of the soon-to-be established Alliance.[405]

It would be too easy to imagine, however, that more than two decades of bitter disputation in the British movement could be reconciled quite so readily. The Congress of what was now to be the International Co-operative Alliance (the new name had been agreed in 1893) had to be presented with a draft set of words to express the Alliance's objectives. There was a predictable disagreement over how prominently profit-sharing should feature in this and a special meeting of the ICA's embryonic executive was held on the Tuesday afternoon of the Congress to try to reach an acceptable compromise. The minute book reads that 'Mr Joseph Greenwood of Hebden Bridge was also present by invitation to consult with the committee'. It seems likely that Greenwood was seen as the senior figure whose views were respected both within the co-partnership fraternity and by J.C. Gray and his Co-operative Union colleagues, and who therefore could help broker an agreement.[406]

Despite the Tuesday meeting, a row broke out on the Thursday morning of the Congress with Holyoake leading the charge: 'This Congress was called together as a Congress to promote profit-sharing,' he pronounced, arguing once again against the CWS being recognised as eligible for ICA membership. Gray responded, contradicting Holyoake, and Joseph Greenwood felt impelled to try to obtain a consensus. 'I think it is desirable that we should carry as far as possible the true principles of co-operation in the formation of this Alliance,' he said. 'Of course we have agreed that profit-sharing, with participation in the control of the business and workshops, ought to be in the hands of the employees. At the same time, I think it hard to exclude a body of co-operators who are at variance with the majority on one point. I would suggest … that all may take part in this Alliance'.[407]

There was, it has to be said, almost a re-run of the same debate the following year at Paris, where once again there was an attempt to restrict ICA membership to firms practising profit-sharing, this time promoted both by Holyoake and by a group of productive co-operatives, mainly from France. Both Gray and Greenwood spoke again for a compromise. Greenwood argued (his words are in French in the official Congress report although he would have spoken in English) 'Je supplie le Congres de ne pas occasionner, par le vote de l'obligation de pratiquer la Participation aux bénéfices, une scission, irréparable peut-être entre les coopérateurs'.[408]

One of Greenwood's objectives for the new ICA was a practical one: to encourage trading internationally between co-operatives. The Hebden Bridge Fustian Manufacturing Society was at this time doing some international sales through the offices of an intermediary, and had exported according to Greenwood 'many thousands of pounds' worth of goods. (Greenwood must mean in total, rather than annually: in 1895 his society's sales outside the co-operative sector were only about £8,500 in all). Greenwood also pointed out that his co-operative was an importer: much of the market in dyewoods for the British textile trade at this stage was in the hands of German businesses and imported from Germany.[409]

Greenwood would have been pleased, therefore, that the 1895 Congress agreed to establish an International Committee of Co-operative Commercial Relations and particularly pleased to be chosen as its chairman, even if the practical development of international trading between co-operatives was inevitably more challenging than the theory. Since it was deemed too expensive to bring foreign delegates to Britain Greenwood's committee sought information through circulars, only some of which were returned. After a year little concrete had been achieved. The Paris Congress was told that chairs from a co-operative of cabinetmakers in Milan had been imported into Britain, as had been some Italian gloves; conversely, British manufacturing co-operatives in Macclesfield (silk), Alcester (needles) and Walsall (padlocks), as well as the boot and shoe co-operatives of the Midlands, were all hopeful that overseas markets could soon be found for their goods. A year later, there was only a little more to report. Greening had put the Agricultural and Horticultural Association's contract for seed envelope printing to a co-operative printing business in Paris, for example, and British co-operators were trying to find a market for co-operatively produced Dutch butter. There were cultural misunderstandings to overcome along the way, however. J.C. Gray had to explain patiently to French wine co-operatives that the vast majority of British co-operative societies were not licensed to sell alcohol. There is no evidence that the Nutclough Mill itself had managed to find any overseas co-operative outlets for its goods.[410]

The structure developed for the ICA, the creation of national sections which operated more or less autonomously between Congresses, mirrored in many ways the framework of regional sections put in place for the Co-operative Union more than a quarter of a century earlier. The administrative work of running the Alliance was undertaken from London by a small executive committee helped by some paid secretarial back-up. J.C. Gray and E.O. Greening continued to be joint secretaries, Gray travelling down regularly from Manchester. Henry Wolff was another regular at these meetings, as was Aneurin Williams, a Labour Association activist and associate of Greening's who was later to become an MP.

Greenwood's appointment at Paris as the ICA's Treasurer and as a member of the Executive Bureau needs to be understood in this context. There was indeed a need for a competent person to oversee the organisation's finances. The London Congress in 1895 had been bankrolled by Greening, who when the accounts were prepared afterwards was a creditor to the extent of £384.[411] Gradually the debt to Greening was to be paid off; in 1900 the outstanding amount was down to £100 and by 1902 the ICA seemed to have more or less balanced its books.[412]

Joseph Greenwood's role as Treasurer was not a hands-on one: he had a business based in a Pennine valley to run and regular train journeys to London committee meetings for the ICA were not feasible. Nonetheless, he seems to have made an effort in the aftermath of the Paris Congress. He attended a meeting at the ICA's office in Southampton Row on 28 December 1896 and again a fortnight later on 11 January 1897.[413] He was also down in March and July for national section meetings when the opportunity was taken to hold meetings at the same time of the international trading committee. Much of the latter committee's work at this stage was focused on trying to produce a comprehensive catalogue of goods produced by productive co-operatives in ICA member countries.[414]

The third ICA Congress was fixed for September 1897 for Agnetapark in Delft, in the Netherlands, the invitation coming from the progressive Dutch businessman Jacob Cornelis van Marken. Van Marken ran his distilling and yeast production enterprises on co-partnership lines and had built a model co-operative village close to his factories. The Delft Congress attracted around thirty British delegates, including Greening, Vivian, Blandford and Henry Wolff. Joseph Craven from the Nutclough was another delegate, attending his first ICA Congress. George Thomson from Woodhouse Mills in Huddersfield was present, accompanied by his wife. J.C. Gray was present, with his wife. And indeed Joseph Greenwood was in Agnetapark, too – along with *his* wife.

Greenwood, widowed in 1892, had remarried in September 1896. The wedding had been a quiet ceremony in Heptonstall, at which Joseph Craven had acted as the best man; the flag had flown at the Nutclough Mill in celebration. The new wife, Ellen, was ten years younger than him, in her early fifties, but had herself been widowed. Originally from Hebden Bridge, Ellen Walmsley, née Clegg, had more recently been living in Bacup. The new Mr and Mrs Greenwood honeymooned after their wedding on the Isle of Wight, but perhaps the Delft Congress proved an opportunity for a second holiday together. Unlike Sarah, Ellen was also to accompany Joseph regularly to Co-operative Congresses.[415]

The Delft Congress reprised some of the debates from London and Paris, including another lengthy debate on co-partnership, much of it centred on how precisely co-partnership should be defined. Henry Vivian offered one set of words: 'Co-partnership is a system under which the actual employees of any business have, in right of their labour, a substantial share fixed in advance in the profits thereof, and in which they also have an effective share in the capital, control and responsibilities'. Vivian's wording appeared to have been formally agreed, only for Congress the next day to change its mind and decide to proceed without a firm definition. Building a co-operative movement in Britain had been challenging; building an international co-operative movement appeared to require just as much patience.[416]

The International Co-operative Alliance has its own written histories, so we can abbreviate the story here. Greenwood remained ICA Treasurer and continued to travel to London for executive bureau and national section meetings at roughly quarterly intervals during the autumn of 1897 and the first half of 1898. Thereafter he was less often a participant and he is not shown in the official record as a delegate for the fourth ICA Congress, which was held again in Paris in July 1900. Leonard Stocks, the fustian society's secretary, represented Hebden Bridge on that occasion.[417]

In 1902 the ICA Congress took place for a second time in Britain, at an event held from 21-25 July in Manchester. There were delegates from Belgium, France, the Netherlands, the United States, Denmark, Russia, Germany, Switzerland, Italy, Spain and Sweden, as well as sizeable numbers of British delegates. There was certainly a whole party present from the Hebden Bridge Fustian Manufacturing Society: as well Greenwood, Joseph Craven and Leonard Stocks the group comprised almost all the members of the management committee.

The 1902 Congress marked a moment of transition for the ICA. It had begun, rather like the Co-operative Union, as a gathering point for individual supporters of the principles of co-operation, mainly from the middle classes, and representatives of co-operative societies. Already at the 1900 Congress there had been a proposal to restrict membership of the Alliance to co-operative organisations, and in 1902 J.C. Gray on behalf of the Co-operative Union returned to the issue and successfully put through a rules amendment to this effect. In practice, individual supporters of co-operation could easily have been able to get delegate credentials if they so wished, but for Holyoake this was a backdoor way of moving the Alliance away from co-partnership principles. He railed against the move and criticised the Co-operative Union for having among its own members 'the most ignorant of societies'.[418] Elsewhere Holyoake was to scornfully rename the ICA as the International Commercial Alliance.[419]

But the mood was changing away from Holyoake. Indeed, the 1902 Congress heard a strong critique of co-partnership from a French socialist delegate who called instead for the socialisation of the means of production. His report was adopted without opposition, although the French writer Charles Gide was later to wryly observe that 'as there were only seven or eight persons in the Congress who understood French and as his report was read in French, one need not consider that unanimous approbation as very significant'.[420]

What the 1902 Congress delegates did participate in was a lively debate on working-class housing, which included discussion of Ebenezer Howard's proposals for garden cities. There was another debate focused on co-operative agriculture and smallholdings. And on the final day of Congress there was a debate for peace and against militarism. One of the Belgian co-operative and socialist leaders Edward Anseele spoke passionately against the risks of war. Already, more than a decade before the First World War, there were ominous signs of trouble ahead.

The 1902 Congress included the formal business of electing the ICA's executive committee, now called the central committee. Joseph Greenwood was again nominated and again elected as Treasurer, a post he occupied until the 1904 Congress in Budapest, which he did not attend. By this stage in the ICA's development his appointment has to be seen primarily as honorific.[421]

However, Greenwood was to have a central part in the final activity of the 1902 Congress week. A number of trips had been laid on for the delegates during the afternoons of Congress, including excursions to the CWS biscuit works at Crumpsall and to the Rochdale Equitable Pioneers. On Friday afternoon it was the turn of the Hebden Bridge Fustian Manufacturing Society to play host. A chartered train was laid on to bring a large party from Manchester to Hebden Bridge, where they walked the short distance up the hill from the station to the Nutclough Mill. 'The inhabitants stood in groups at the corners, or stretched far out of windows to get a good view of the foreign visitors,' reported *Co-operative News*' correspondent Catherine Mayo. 'Possibly they hoped that the representatives from different countries would appear in their respective national dresses.' Hebden Bridge was perhaps hoping for a small-scale re-run of Queen Victoria's elaborate diamond jubilee procession of 1897. 'They seemed disappointed to find how much alike we all looked,' Mayo added.

There was tea laid on in the Co-operative Hall, and speeches. J.C. Gray spoke, praising the International Co-operative Alliance for its role in helping create what he felt could be a new era of justice and equality throughout the world. Joseph Craven, as the fustian society's chairman, responded on behalf of the hosts. But the main speech was from Edward Anseele the Belgian socialist, who spoke on behalf of the visitors. They had visited the cradle of distributive co-operation at Rochdale the day before, he said, and now they were saluting the birthplace of productive co-operation. 'To compete against capital, to try and produce a cheap and yet a sound article, and to do that with little or no capital to start with was a tremendous work, nay, a work of genius,' he said. 'They were creating a condition of society when the workman would be his own employer, his own task-master, criticise the value of his own work, and decide what use and destiny that work should be put to. It was a grand ideal. A humane and moral evolution to attain.'[422]

Anseele proposed a toast. 'In honour of their enterprise and in the hope of this salvation as well as emancipation of the working-classes throughout the world, he drank to the success of universal co-operation.'

CHAPTER 11

WORKING LIVES

When the ICA delegates visited Hebden Bridge in 1902, before the tea and speeches, there was – needless to say – the guided tour of the works. The party was split into smaller groups of about twenty and taken round to be shown all the different stages of manufacturing carried out by the fustian society. The comprehensive report of the tour which was subsequently published provides us with an opportunity to, as it were, look over the shoulders of the international visitors and to see for ourselves how the fustian society was operating at the start of the twentieth century when the bulk of the business expansion had already been completed. Our guide on the tour of the mill will be the *Hebden Bridge Times's* reporter.[423]

As with the Women's Guild visitors of 1892 (chapter 6), the ICA delegates were taken initially to the fifth floor at the top of the mill, to the long room where the women sewing machinists worked. 'Here were about 170 females making up fustian into garments, the materials being cut out by the men, part of the work done by hand and part by machinery,' we are told. The scores of sewing machines, driven by gas engine, were 'going for all they were worth'.

From the top of the mill the visitors were taken a floor down to be introduced to a much earlier stage in the manufacturing process. This was the part of the mill where the weft of the woven fustian cloth was cut by fustian cutters, a process still being undertaken in 1902 by hand: 'The fustian cutting on the fourth floor, done by a long sword-like knife, aroused the curiosity of the foreign visitors'. (It might be added that machinery to undertake fustian cutting was to arrive very shortly afterwards, being introduced at the Nutclough in 1905.[424] From then on the craft which Joseph Greenwood had learned as a young man would rapidly become obsolete.)

Also on the fourth floor was a warehousing area where the stock of woven pieces and finished garments was held prior to being sent to customers. The third floor of the mill was used as an additional area for holding stock, and the visitors were shown both finished cloth pieces and the fustian 'in the grey', straight from the looms. Machinery used for finishing fustian after it had been dyed, including machines for brushing up the pile, was also housed on the third floor.

'Arriving on the second floor' – the *Hebden Bridge Times* again –

> where the winding and doubling rooms abound, it was explained that here the first process is really commenced by the Society. They buy the cotton yarns from the spinners of Lancashire, and in this room is the first process towards the finished garment. The yarn is bought in the single thread and the doubling and twisting machines make it two or three-fold as required. Adjoining this room were noticed machines for raising and shearing the pieces, and in the bottom room were machines for brushing the cords and preparing them for the dyehouse.

The ICA visitors moved on down to the dyehouse at this point, where the local newspaper reporter, who perhaps momentarily lost attention, is unhelpfully unforthcoming. In fact the dyeing process was a skilled job, with something of the distiller's craft about it. Some of the dyewoods used were subjected to a process called stilling in order to get the necessary intensity of colour: dyewoods were put in iron boxes placed over a cistern full of boiling water, with the water passed repeatedly through the dyewood boxes until the full dye colour had been extracted. At this point in the process the liquor remaining was drawn off into overhead vats to be held until the particular dye was required.[425]

The water from the moorlands surrounding Hebden Bridge was soft and considered particularly suitable for dyeing purposes. There was, however, a general problem in the town of disposing of the waste water at the other end of the dyeing process. The fustian society had some difficulty in 1898 in meeting the provisions of the River Pollution Prevention Act (introduced first in 1876) which was an attempt to improve at least to some extent the water quality of rivers in industrial areas. The difficulty may have been the close proximity of the dyehouse to the river Hebden.[426]

The ICA delegates moved on to examine the engine house, where the steam engine 'Thomas Hughes' was still doing its best, providing power for the mill machinery. The Nutclough Mill got through considerable quantities of coal every week to power the engine, the arrangement being that the coal was delivered from the main road above down a shoot. Close by the engine house was the boiler house, holding two boilers each thirty feet long. The visitors had it explained to them that the water was drawn from the two reservoirs owned by the fustian society and located higher up the clough above the mill.

The next stop on the guided tour appears to have been the drying room, to the west of the main mill and close to the river Hebden. Here 'the pieces are dried and size put in, which gives to fustian its objectionable smell,' the *Hebden Bridge Times* reports. Sizing – adulterating the cloth by adding a stiffening agent – was a controversial process and one which the fustian society undertook only with reluctance. Originally a mixture of flour and tallow was used for size in the weaving trade locally, with china clay being included later on. The use of size meant that the finished cloth seemed thicker and therefore more likely to be longer-lasting (even though, of course, the size would eventually wash out). Joseph Greenwood had complained as long ago as 1874 that he was struggling to persuade co-operative societies to buy goods without size, with the Halifax society one of the few prepared to buy pure goods. Neale at the same time had called for co-operative societies to do what they could to educate their members towards buying quality goods.[427]

Sizing had for many years been a major concern for weavers in the cotton industry because of the working conditions under which they were obliged to work. For example in 1871 more than a thousand Todmorden weavers had petitioned Parliament about the conditions in their weaving sheds and the risks these posed to their health. To ensure that yarn which had been sized could be successfully woven without breaking mill-owners had got into the custom of keeping the atmosphere in their weaving sheds very damp, creating almost tropical conditions. Lung disease for weavers was one of the consequences. Parliamentary legislation in 1889 tightened up on conditions but did not outlaw the practice altogether.[428]

At the Nutclough Mill sizing took place after the weaving process rather than before. Nevertheless there was one potential health hazard to be avoided as much as possible, for sized cloth was artificially softened later in the manufacturing process by a machine which was notorious for creating dust. The fustian society took various measures to try to reduce the quantity of dust in the air.

The ICA delegates finished their visit in the weaving shed, on the other side of the mill from the drying room. Here was where the fustian society had its 232 looms, each weaver having responsibility for four. We are not told whether the looms were stopped during the visit – if not, the visitors would have certainly carried with them the memory of the noise of the weaving shed – but we are informed that the whole tour of inspection of the mill lasted a good hour and a half.

'It was a treat to the visitors and they manifested their pleasure,' concluded the *Hebden Bridge Times*. 'One of them remarked to our reporter present that he could not have believed such a large body of men, women and young people could be so happy at their work in the mill.'

This throwaway remark demands some attention. Visitors often made some such comment after their guided tours of the Nutclough Mill, but then the point of such tours for Greenwood and his colleagues was precisely to persuade visitors that co-operation was a better way of organising work. We have to ask the question: just how happy were the Nutclough's workers? Was this a working environment, in other words, which was significantly different from that which workers would have encountered in non-co-operative mills?

The development of the co-operative, as we have seen, had required various kinds of compromise. Beatrice Potter was quite correct – at least in relation to the formal structures of the co-operative – when she wrote in *The Co-operative Movement in Great Britain* that the balance of power at the Nutclough was in the hands of non-workers. It may have been the influence of individual external investors which had troubled Greenwood in the early days, but later on there was a definite shift of power towards the co-operative societies.

As Figure 3 (page 64) shows, there was by chance a broad parity between worker and co-operative society member numbers through the first 25 years of the Fustian Manufacturing Society, with new local societies joining as members at broadly the same rate as the expansion of the workforce. From the early years of the twentieth century the situation changed somewhat. By 1910, for example, at a time when there were 295 worker members the number of co-operative society members had grown to 373; in 1914 the figures were respectively 292 and 400.[429] In strictly numerical terms, the balance was swinging increasingly towards co-operative societies.

But even in relation to the fustian society's formal governance structures, the influence and power of co-operative societies can be overstated. Generally speaking the member societies that exercised their rights and attended the half-yearly general meetings were those in the immediate geographical area. Societies much further afield – and by the end of the nineteenth century these included places such as Arundel, Plymouth and Blaenavon[430] – were usually unrepresented. The management committee was, by custom, made up of representatives of societies within the Calderdale area where there were close personal links between committee members and employees. Indeed, we know that several of Joseph Craven's children worked in the mill, as did the university extension student George Herbert Pickles, the son of management committee member Thomas Henry Pickles. Other management committee members may well have had children or relatives working there.

Although employees were ineligible to join the management committee, by the early twentieth century if not before there appear to have been structures in place which enabled the workers' voices to be heard. A writer in 1908 commenting on the status of women in productive co-operatives described how women workers at the Nutclough 'are eligible for and have for many years sat on the departmental committee on which the employees and General Committee are represented'.

The same writer is complimentary about the general working conditions to be found: 'Hebden Bridge Fustian Society Limited have light and airy rooms and full air-space. No standing is done in the [weaving] shed or where women work. There are fans working to keep away the dust and cotton fluff caused by the raising machines.'[431] Another account drew attention in particular to the good employee dining room facilities offered by the co-operative.[432]

There is a similar message about the conditions at the Nutclough Mill to be found in the writings of Robert Halstead. It might be argued that Halstead, as an advocate of co-operation and co-partnership, is hardly an impartial observer but his comments, written only a short time after moving to the fustian society, ring true. Having described some of the health hazards linked to heavy sizing of cloth he adds, 'Perhaps it is only right and pertinent to say that the writer is now a fustian weaver at the Hebden Bridge Co-operative Fustian Society where the conditions for the workman are a decided improvement on what he has found elsewhere'.[433]

Later, when he was working at the Co-operative Productive Federation, Halstead elaborated on his personal experiences: 'For about twenty-seven years I have worked under ordinary competitive conditions of industry and for about seven years under Co-partnership conditions, so I have been in the position to judge the effects on one's self of these different conditions. For myself, I was greatly impressed with the change. First as to what one might call the general atmosphere in the two sets of conditions, and secondly as to the effects in particular directions. There was a much greater sense of security of employment and more considerations for incidents of life outside those of business in a Co-partnership workshop than in an ordinary factory.'

Halstead went on to offer some observations on management methods, which again we can assume came in part from personal experience:

In considering the matter of internal discipline and difficulties of management under Co-partnership conditions, we have to ask: are these difficulties different or greater than under competitive or other forms of co-operative conditions? The same causes of friction between management, and very much the same forms of it, appear under autocratic management as under the joint management of Labour Co-partnership of the working-class type. The main difference is in the manner of coping with the difficulties. In the case of autocratic management the results of friction accumulate week by week, or it may be month by month, or perhaps even year by year... Co-partnership management reckons, on the other hand, with these same difficulties from day to day or week to week, and tends to get a more exhaustive adjustment between autocratic control and joint control – between the machine side of management and the human side.[434]

Decent working conditions were important not least because workers in the late nineteenth and early twentieth centuries spent much longer in their workplaces than we do today. At the time of its twenty-first birthday celebrations in 1891, as far as we can tell, the fustian society was operating Nutclough Mill from 6am to 6pm from Monday to Friday, with a half-hour break for breakfast at 8am and a further hour's break for dinner in the middle of the day. Saturday was a half-day, with the mill operating until 12.30pm.

In the mid-1890s, working hours were brought down to 56 a week, with working finishing at 5.30pm each day. Another half-hour was shaved off the working week in 1902.[435] (As we shall see, there was to be a further reduction in working hours much later in the co-operative's life.)

Starting work at 6am, particularly on dark cold mornings in winter of the kind which Pennine communities such as Hebden Bridge often experience, may seem unreasonably early today but was taken as normal at the time. The fustian society appears to have more or less accepted the standard mill hours operating in its town, which were longer than those in some of the Lancashire cotton spinning and weaving towns – productive co-operative societies elsewhere engaged in other trades also worked shorter hours.[436] George Thomson at the co-operative Woodhouse Mills in Huddersfield had been much more radical, for example, introducing a 48-hour working week to replace the 56½ hours as early as 1893.[437]

What about the wage levels paid to the fustian society's workers? Greenwood was questioned about wages during his Royal Commission on Labour hearing in 1892, responding that 'we pay rather better than the standard wages in the district'. He gave some examples: women finishers in the tailoring department were paid in some instances one (old) penny more per garment than elsewhere and 'in the dyeing, we pay day wages at a trifle more, 6d, it may be 1s a week more than they do in the private firms'. This is a somewhat different answer to that which Greenwood had given at a Calderdale co-operative district meeting six years earlier, when he said that he 'was not aware' that Nutclough workers got higher rates of wages than were paid by private employers; he may, of course, have been tailoring his remarks then for his audience, who would have been partly responsible for electing his management committee and might have looked askance at the thought that the fustian society was being over-generous.[438]

What Greenwood stressed to the Royal Commission in any case was that the chief benefit was the regularity of employment and the absence of short-time working that the co-operative aimed to achieve.

Among the documentation Greenwood gave to the Royal Commission were statistics for average annual wages for employees at his society (these were reported to be averages taken over employees' whole period of employment, which may somewhat distort the figures). The table below uses Greenwood's data for annual pay levels, from which weekly rates have been calculated. The winders and finishers are women workers; fustian cutters and fustian finishers, dyers and weavers are male, as are the tailor, the warper and the tackler (the tackler being the weaving shed overlooker).[439]

Finishers: 10s 9d – 19s 2d
Winders: 12s 9d – 13s 10d
Dyers: 20s 10d – 25s 4d
Weavers: 21s 10d – 23s
Fustian cutters: 25s 10d – 29s 8d
Fustian finishers: 26s 2d – 27s 3d
Tailor: 32s 3d
Warper: 32s 8d
Tackler: 34s 2d

These can be compared with data about the Nutclough from 1897 from the trade newspaper the *Yorkshire Factory Times*, which we can expect to be reliable:[440]

Machinists: 15s 6d
Finishers: 18s
Winders: 20s
Weavers, average: 23s

Dyers, day workers: 24s
Cutters, day workers: 30s
Warpers and beamers: 34s

('Finishers' here are women finishers in the tailoring department, not the fustian cloth finishers).

Data such as these help identify broad levels of pay during this period of the fustian society's life. For comparisons with rates of pay in non co-operative businesses, we have to turn again to Robert Halstead, and in particular to his closely researched paper *Variation of Wages in some Labour Co-partnership Workshops*, written in 1900. The data for Hebden Bridge were collected by Halstead directly; 'I have taken all the precautions I could to get reliable evidence,' he reports.

In headline terms, Halstead concludes that the fustian society's pay in 1899 was on average 10 per cent better in comparison to non co-operatives. He also reports a 13 per cent increase in wages during the 1890-1899 decade.

Halstead breaks down his data by category of work, giving wages for 1891 and 1899. These show some discrepancies with Greenwood's Royal Commission data and those published by the *Yorkshire Factory Times*, although in broad terms the data are comparable.

Table 5

Pay rates at Hebden Bridge Fustian Manufacturing Society 1891, 1899; In italic: (where available) comparable wages, 1899, in non co-operative businesses[441]

Trade	Wages 1891	Wages 1899
Foreman dyers	40s	55s
Dyers' labourers	24s	24s
(non co-op)		*24s*
Machinist sewers	2½d per garment	2½d
(non co-op)		*(10-20 per cent lower)*
Finishers	20s	24s
Taper	34s	34s
Weavers	Ave 2¼d per lb weft	Ave 2 ⅜d per lb weft
(non co-op)		*Ave 2 ⅛d per lb weft*
Overlookers	28s, 33s-35s	28s, 33s 8d – 36s
(non co-op)		*32s – 33s*
Warehousemen	18s	28s
(non co-op)		*25s – 30s*

Warehouse foreman	42s	45s
(non co-op)		*37s – 45s*
Fustian cutter out	37s	45s
(non co-op)		*37s – 45s*
Fustian cutter	26s	26s
(non co-op)		*20s*

Halstead undertakes a similar exercise for other productive co-operatives, with similar results. He concludes that one reason for the higher wages being paid in co-partnerships is because these businesses show relatively high levels of productivity by their workforce.

Another possible explanation emerged in an exchange between Greenwood and Gerald Balfour at the Royal Commission on Labour hearing. Greenwood had claimed that his firm has 'no difficulty in obtaining the very best class of workers. Indeed when it becomes known that there is a situation open there are a great number of applications for it.' In other words, Balfour replied, you are really giving better wages to better workmen. Greenwood had to concur that this might indeed be the case.[442]

The Lancashire cotton industry in the later decades of the nineteenth century was a highly unionised sector, with powerful union amalgamations in both cotton spinning and cotton weaving. Weavers' associations had been established in Blackburn in 1854, in Bolton in 1865, in Burnley in 1870 and in Rochdale in 1878-80. The Todmorden Weavers' Association was set up in 1880 in response to an attempt by the mill owners to reduce wages by 10 per cent. It had membership of over 400 by the end of its first year and went on to become a significant force in the town.[443]

At a very early stage the Lancashire cotton industry also saw the structures for industry-wide collective bargaining put in place, the form of industrial relations based on negotiated settlements between employers' associations and trade unions of the kind which remain the norm in most European Union countries even if this is a much less familiar model these days in British employment practice. This development of collective bargaining was not achieved without some long and bitter disputes in several major Lancashire towns, but the system of agreeing fixed 'lists' (set wages for particular work tasks) could be seen as bringing benefits for both sides in industry: as well as strengthening the workers' position it helped employers (or at least more enlightened employers) by removing the cost of labour from inter-firm competition. It also helped reduce the likelihood of spontaneous labour unrest. The separate wages lists negotiated for individual Lancashire towns were brought together into a unified list in 1892.[444]

Despite these highly significant developments across the county border in Lancashire and just up the river Calder in Todmorden, Hebden Bridge was notorious during the later nineteenth century for not being a strongly unionised town – and for being a place where wages were low. Its size and relative isolation geographically and its focus on fustian rather than mainstream cotton weaving were contributing factors.

There was in theory a strong sense of shared endeavour between the trade union movement and the co-operative movement. Lloyd Jones had asserted in 1874 that co-operators should not see trade unionism as something standing apart from their own interests: 'Every point gained on the one side is an advantage to the other,' he said then.[445] There were growing links between the TUC and the Co-operative Union from the 1880s, with fraternal delegations sent to each other's congresses. There was also a TUC/Co-operative Union Joint Committee established as an arbitration body to consider and try to resolve any industrial disputes which might develop between management and workers in co-operative businesses.

Joseph Greenwood undoubtedly shared Lloyd Jones's views. Nevertheless, despite Greenwood's engagement with early attempts at trade unionism by fustian cutters, the Nutclough Mill reflected Hebden Bridge's lack of a strong union tradition and was initially not strongly unionised. Greenwood told the Royal Commission on Labour that his co-operative employed both trade union members and non-unionists, and that one of the fustian cutters was the secretary of the local branch. In reality in 1892 the numbers of union members at the Nutclough Mill were probably very low and limited to the fustian cutters and, perhaps, to some of the weavers.[446] It is probable that the majority of workers saw no particular benefit in paying union dues; conditions at the Nutclough were acceptable and there were no wider union activities in the town in which to engage. The women workers were definitely not unionised at this stage.

A strike twenty miles away among the fustian weavers of Bury in 1898 was to change this, at least as far as the Nutclough's weavers were concerned. Trouble had been brewing in Bury over the summer and things boiled over at the start of August when five mills posted notices of a reduction in weavers' rates of pay. The workers at the mills called for the notices to be post-dated to allow for negotiations and when this was refused they went on strike. The strike initially affected a thousand workers.

Hebden Bridge was held to be the guilty party. The low wages being paid there were, it was alleged by the Bury mill-owners, the reason why they had to bring down their own costs to compete. According to the *Cotton Factory Times*, the Bury weavers were paying the price of the 'short-sighted policy of the weavers at Hebden Bridge'.

This was, of course, a reference to the Hebden Bridge fustian sector in general. However, and coincidentally, the Bury co-operative society had just received a report from its delegate to the half-yearly meeting of the Hebden Bridge Fustian Manufacturing Society, and this meeting was also reported prominently in the *Cotton Factory Times*. When the striking workers foregathered on 8 August, a few days into the strike, the finger was being pointed by the men's union leader James Mills not just at Hebden Bridge in general but also at the Hebden Bridge co-operative. Paying a profit-bonus might be all very well, he said, but not if it meant that the co-operative and its employees were undercutting the Bury wage list. 'The co-operators of Hebden Bridge, along with the other employés there, were responsible partially for that [strike] meeting that day,' Mills said.

The *Cotton Factory Times* was widely read in the cotton industry, and the report of Mills' remarks drew an immediate response from Robert Halstead, writing on behalf of the Labour Association. 'It is extremely difficult to see what good purpose can be served by a prominent labour leader going out of his way to lay any of the blame of the Bury labour struggle on his fellow workers who are in a direct way working for the benefit and emancipation of labour.'

In the thick of a strike, there is little room for nuances. Halstead's letter simply led to further criticism of the co-operative from James Mills at another mass meeting of the strikers. 'The happy time had not arrived when everybody were co-operators,' he said. What they needed, he argued, was a strong trade union for all the fustian weavers at Hebden Bridge which would help prevent the Bury list being undercut. What were the Nutclough weavers doing to help? Halstead had said in his letter that 90 per cent of the weavers there were willing to join a union, Mills told his audience, yet previous attempts to set up a union – with Halstead himself as the provisional secretary – had fallen apart after a few weeks. 'It was no use men writing letters to the press if they themselves did not use their intelligence and abilities in a practical way,' Mills added.

Facing a growing threat to their reputation, the fustian society sent Joseph Greenwood, Leonard Stocks and Robert Halstead to speak directly to the Bury weavers at a well-attended meeting held on 5 September, a month into the strike. The meeting was held behind closed doors, but the Nutclough intervention clearly had the desired effect. The *Cotton Factory Times* reported that the delegation 'appear to have conclusively proved that, although their prices are arranged somewhat differently to those lately in force in Bury, they are on the whole fairly on a level'. Leonard Stocks had in fact claimed a week before in *Co-operative News* that, if they switched at the Nutclough from their own price list to the Bury list, the weavers would probably be left less well-off, if only marginally. Greenwood did promise his audience, however, that the Bury list would be instituted if that was what his own employees requested, and it appears that this is indeed what happened.[447]

Back in Hebden Bridge, steps were taken to pick up James Mills' challenge, with Greenwood and Halstead very much to the fore. A meeting was arranged for the end of September in the town at which William Inskip of the national boot and shoe union, representing the trade union movement, and J.C. Gray from the co-operative side jointly explained the benefits of joining a union. Inskip was at that time the co-chair of the TUC/ Co-operative Union Joint Committee.

The meeting, and Greenwood's personal endorsement seems to have helped. The *Cotton Factory Times* reported that 'a feeling now prevails in many quarters at Hebden Bridge that if the existing trade unions were but to repeat at once their previous attempts to form a union at Hebden Bridge they would meet with a success quite as great as have been the failures of the past'. The Nutclough weavers held a shop meeting a few days later in early October and resolved by a large majority to become members of the Todmorden Weavers' Association.[448] By the end of the year Halstead was claiming that all the Nutclough weavers had joined.[449] Todmorden Weavers' Association itself claimed to have recruited 240 new members that quarter, mostly from Hebden Bridge.[450]

From this base, the Todmorden Weavers' Association went on to focus on organising the other Hebden Bridge mills, with various recruitment meetings arranged in the town over the following few years, including one in October 1900 when James Mills from Bury was invited across to be the primary speaker (the Bury strike incidentally had spluttered to a conclusion at the end of 1898). The Fustian Manufacturing Society, both management and workers, appeared to adapt to the new unionised way of working. In 1901, for example, the union was brought in for a demarcation dispute after weavers complained they were being called away to the warehouse.[451]

The Todmorden Weavers' Association did not recruit workers engaged in other activities at the Nutclough. In due course (as we shall see in a later chapter), the fustian society's management would find itself dealing with the National Society of Dyers and Finishers, the United Association of Power-Loom Overlookers and, particularly, with the union which organised the cloth cutters and machinists in the tailoring department, the Amalgamated Union of Clothiers' Operatives (AUCO).[452] The AUCO had begun to become established earlier in the 1890s with a particular focus in Leeds, and had by 1897 gained a presence in Hebden Bridge. There were 25 members locally in July that year, including Joseph Craven's son Sam Craven and at least a handful of other workers we can recognise as working for the fustian society. Only men were eligible for membership at this stage.

Women were members of the unions operating in the cotton industry in Lancashire, and indeed in some towns played a significant role.[453] There were increasing attempts by the late 1890s to organise women workers more generally, and in April 1899 a Hebden Bridge public meeting was addressed by the 26-year-old Mona Wilson of the Women's Trade Union League, whose message was that trade unionism was for women as much as for men.[454]

When in 1900 the AUCO changed its rules to admit women there was an immediate influx locally of 18 women (paying 3d a week, half the men's subscription). They may have found it difficult to have their voice heard, however, for most of these women quickly lapsed their membership. Nevertheless, by 1906, when the Hebden Bridge AUCO branch had grown to 74 members, the women were back in the union in considerable numbers. With Sam Craven an active member, we can assume that some, if not the majority, of the women members were his fellow workers at the Nutclough.[455]

Once a byword for unorganised labour, Hebden Bridge was increasingly to become one of the strongest centres of unionism. It was also, in only a few years' time, to be the locus for the longest and bitterest weavers' strike that the Lancashire weaving unions had experienced.

CHAPTER 12

INTO THE TWENTIETH CENTURY

A new century brings new hope. As the nineteenth century drew to a close there must have been a sense that the twentieth would be the one which would bring fruition to all the high hopes and expectations for which working-class organisations had been campaigning and working towards for so long.

But the twentieth century started badly for the Hebden Bridge Fustian Manufacturing Society. Within the first two years, Greenwood and his committee were to find themselves facing the most difficult trading environment they had encountered for twenty years.

The years until 1895-1896, with some minor hiccoughs along the way, had in broad terms seen an ever-increasing growth both in the fustian society's sales and in the profits it made. There was a strong sense of forward progress. Profits crossed the £5,000 threshold for the first time in 1895 and sales reached a peak of over £46,600 the following year. But thereafter, things faltered, with both sales and profits falling back slightly in the remaining years of the nineteenth century (Figures 4 and 5).[456]

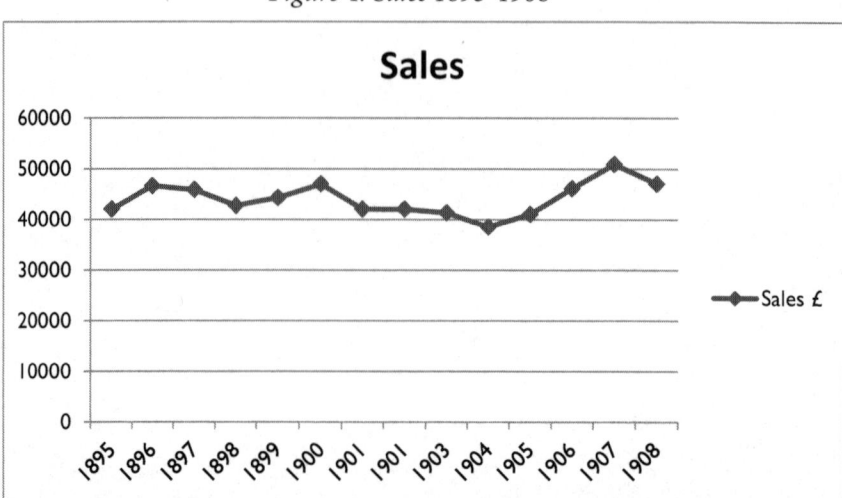

Figure 4: Sales 1895-1908[457]

Sales in 1900 moved forward again, growing by about 10 per cent, but worryingly profits fell significantly, to below £4,000 for the first time for almost a decade. The problem, as reported to members at the July 1900 co-operative meeting, was the significant increase in the prices of cotton yarn and coal, two key business inputs.

The downward trend continued in 1901, which unhelpfully was also a year of slump in the macroeconomic business cycle in the UK. Sales fell markedly and profit collapsed to around £2,120, more than 50 per cent below the profits being generated just two years earlier. The profit to sales ratio in particular fell drastically, to 5 per cent, after years when the ratio had been around 10 per cent. Something had to give, and it was to be the profit dividends given to labour and to co-operative societies on their purchases.

The co-operative had taken the decision in 1891, following the 1890 vote when the fustian society had finally managed to secure the reduction to 5 per cent for interest on all share capital, that the share of profits paid on labour and on purchases would be increased upwards from what had been the previous norm of 3¾ per cent to 5 per cent. From then on until the end of the nineteenth century, this remained the situation: profits were used to pay 5 per cent interest on share capital, to award a 5 per cent (1 shilling in the pound) bonus to wages and to give a 5 per cent dividend on sales to member co-operative societies. This must have seemed a satisfyingly tidy arrangement, even if, as we saw in chapter 3, any idea that the three denominators being used were comparable was in reality spurious.

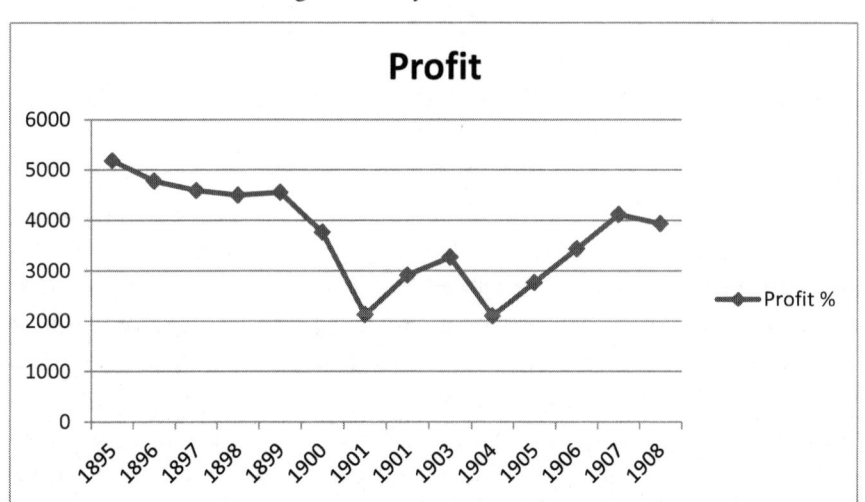

Figure 5: Profits 1895-1908[458]

In 1900 this arrangement came to an end. Investors continued to receive 5 per cent, but the dividend to labour and on sales was reduced, initially to 3¾ per cent. No dividend was paid at all in the first half of 1901, and when it was reinstated it was at the lower rate of 2½ per cent (or 6d in the pound on wages). This was held for eighteen months, before briefly being increased to 3¾ per cent for the first half of 1903 (Figure 6).

If this move suggested optimism, it was ill-founded. In 1904, at a time when the British economy was again suffering from slump, sales fell below £40,000 for the first time for fourteen years and profits were at their lowest level for twenty years. The dividend to labour and on sales was again cut, only returning to 3¾ per cent in 1907. It was to remain at this level until 1913.

Figure 6: Profit dividend to employees and to member co-operative societies, as a percentage of wages/purchases 1895-1908[459]

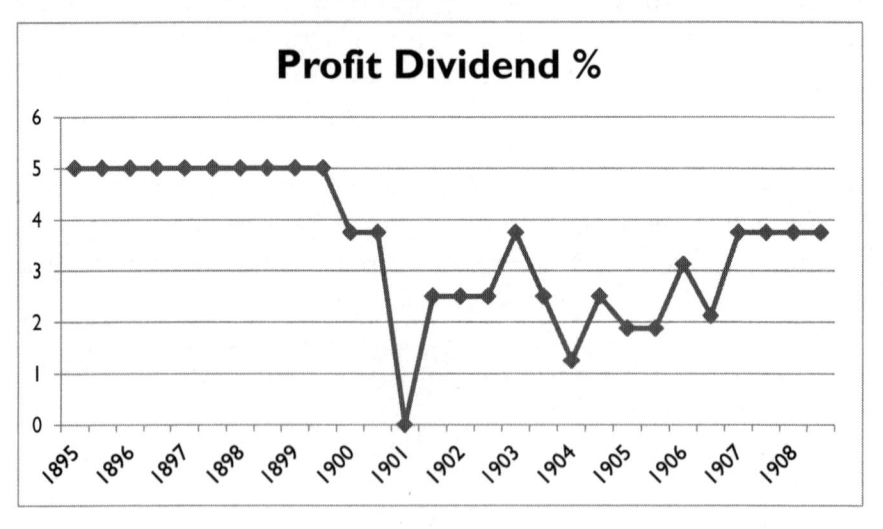

Profit Dividend %

At the same time, there was a clear determination to maintain the interest payable to investors on share capital. Perhaps the battles with investors over the 5 per cent rate in the late 1880s had taken their toll: the prospect of yet further battles over the interest being offered may have seemed too difficult to contemplate. Nevertheless it should also be noted that share-ownership by this stage in the co-operative's development had been changing. By 1908 (when detailed figures are available) the point had been reached where individual workers held £8,195 of the total capital of £28,485. Some of the interest payments being made were going to the Nutclough's workers, in other words – although not, of course, to all employees on a equal basis. Co-operative societies, who held a further £11,930 in shares, were also receiving interest as well as dividends on purchases. There was still however a sizeable legacy of external investors who continued to hold over £8,300 in share capital in 1908. This group remained significant beneficiaries of the profits being generated throughout the life of the co-operative.[460]

Given the financially straitened times, it is not surprising that the fustian society's contribution towards education petered out during the early twentieth century. The University Extension movement had run its course in Hebden Bridge and the Education Act of 1902 had in any case seen major reforms of state educational provision, particularly at secondary level. After 1903 – with just one exception, in 1911 – grants for education by the co-operative were never to be above £10 a year; for several years they were zero. The call by the Co-operative Union commission on which Halstead had served for a 2½ per cent profit levy from co-operatives for educational purposes was long forgotten.

Even in difficult times, however, the fustian society showed itself prepared to look beyond its own members' direct interests, in terms of the donations it made to charitable and other good causes. In 1900, to take one year as an example, its members voted to give ten guineas (£10 10s) to an Indian Famine relief fund and a further ten guineas to the Hebden Bridge district nursing service. £25 was given to a relief fund linked to the Boer War and two guineas were subscribed to a fund for a memorial for the co-operative pioneer Robert Owen.[461]

The contributions made in 1900 reflected the fustian society's general priorities towards charitable initiatives. Local health provision was regularly supported. The Hebden Bridge nursing institution was a frequent recipient of donations, often although not invariably being given ten guineas a year – in 1897, as a special present to celebrate Queen Victoria's jubilee, £100 was given. The Halifax Royal Infirmary on at least two occasions was granted £25. The co-operative also contributed a small amount for a time towards a Lancashire asylum for those with mental illnesses.[462]

There was regular support offered to particular relief funds, including those established after a run of terrible mining disasters in the 1890s. The Thornhill colliery fund received £25 in 1893, the South Wales colliery disaster fund £20 in 1894 and the Diglake colliery fund £10 in 1895, to give three examples. Indian famine relief was supported in 1897 as well as 1900, and the co-operative also gave help in 1898 to relieve distress in the West of Ireland, although on this occasion help was given in kind: three hundred pairs of children's and adult fustian trousers were donated to the relief effort.[463] Contributions to strike funds were sometimes made as well.

Co-operative causes were regularly supported. Individual co-operative societies in difficulties and trying to recapitalise through national appeals received help. The Newbottle society in Co Durham was helped to the tune of £10 in 1894 and the Cowdenbeath society by a similar amount in 1897. Newark got two guineas the same year.[464] The fustian society on several occasions contributed to the costs of staging the Co-operative Congresses when they were held nearby and it also supported the Defence Fund which the Co-operative Union set up in 1902. This fund was to provide resources to respond to attacks by private traders' associations, who had begun to actively mobilise to weaken co-operative societies and victimise their members in a number of northern towns, including St Helens, Wigan and Burnley.[465]

As well as its charitable donations, the fustian society also supported sister productive co-operatives on several occasions by acquiring their shares or loan stock. Its approach here tended to be a cautious one, which was perhaps advisable for by no means all these investments came good. £500 was placed with the Brownfield Guild Pottery co-partnership venture in 1895, for example, three years before the business went into liquidation – a further £200 was put in at that stage as part of a recapitalisation attempt.[466] There were smaller investments in, among others, a Macclesfield silk manufacturing co-operative, the Burnley Self-Help (cotton) Manufacturing Society, the Bradford Cabinet-makers co-operative and the quarrymen's co-operative in North Wales established following a bitter strike and lock-out there.[467] As with some ethical investments today, there might in some of these cases have been a sense that the contributions were quasi-donations as much as straightforward commercial investments.

Finally, the fustian society was scrupulous in paying its membership dues to co-operative bodies. It paid subscriptions to the Co-operative Union, to the Co-operative Productive Federation and to the Labour Association, as well as to the International Co-operative Alliance.

The fustian society continued to host the northern centre of the Labour Association following Robert Halstead's move from Hebden Bridge to Leicester, the task of acting as secretary in the north passing to Joseph Greenwood's son Crossley. It will be recalled that Crossley was working as Leonard Stocks' deputy in the Nutclough office. One of the cohort of University Extension students in Hebden Bridge, he turned thirty in January 1901 and was increasingly making his mark in local co-operative circles. In 1903, for example, he led the discussion at a meeting of the Calderdale Co-operative Association by reading a paper he had written on the issue of co-operatives selling on credit. Later that same year he was to take over from his father the position of Secretary of the Calderdale Association, a post Joseph Greenwood had held for three decades.[468]

Crossley's work for the Labour Co-partnership Association, as it became after 1901, was probably initially undertaken on a voluntary basis. However, in almost an exact repeat of the way Henry Vivian tried to help Robert Halstead a few years earlier, moves were made in 1903 to turn this into a paid position. In late June Vivian floated the idea at the Labour Co-partnership Association's committee that Crossley Greenwood be paid fifty shillings a week, to use his bookkeeping and accounting expertise to help new societies with their accounts, to write articles 'and generally do propaganda and other work for the Association'.[469]

It is not clear whether this was exactly the deal eventually agreed. Vivian reported to the August meeting that a discussion had been held with Crossley Greenwood, and the committee agreed that they would 'try and work him in gradually in the matter of lecturing, calling on societies and for the Journal and that the Secretary discusses payment with him when we find out what the work involves'. An honorarium was paid for the first time in April 1904, and reports began to be published of lectures undertaken by him. In March, for example, he addressed an audience of over three hundred at Great Harwood in Lancashire on the theme 'co-operation at home and abroad', on behalf of the Association. He also lectured on several occasions on Le Familistère, the model co-operative village and factory at Guise in northern France established by Jean-Baptiste André Godin.[470]

The Labour Co-partnership Association had cause to feel in good heart during this time. The number of co-partnership productive co-operatives had grown steadily during the later years of the nineteenth century, and this new wave of co-operatives appeared to have considerably more staying power than some of the earlier unsuccessful ventures. Leicester, Kettering and other Northamptonshire shoemaking towns were established by this stage as the heartland of productive co-operation.

But nevertheless late in 1902 something had happened at one of the most successful Leicester co-operatives, Leicester Hosiery, which had left a very dark cloud over those who, like Joseph Greenwood and his allies in the Labour Co-partnership Association, were making a stand for autonomous worker-run co-partnerships. Once again it was the CWS which was cast in the role of villain.

Leicester Hosiery, under the leadership of its manager George Newell, had been an active member of the Co-operative Productive Federation and a strong supporter of the idea of greater federation between independent productive co-operatives. But Newell had died in May 1901, in his early fifties.[471] A year later, the CWS approached the members of the society, proposing a deal to take the business over and run it as a CWS factory.

The story, as told by E.O. Greening who raged against the proposal, was that the Hosiery society had originally gone to the CWS as its banker to ask for a loan to help expand the business but instead had found themselves receiving a takeover offer. 'This astonishing transaction had been sought to be carried out by the sudden calling of a meeting of shareholders to receive an offer to buy, no details being given,' he thundered in the pages of his magazine *Agricultural Economist*.[472]

Greening and his co-partnership allies mobilised immediately they were aware of the threat. Halstead wrote to Greening in October, 'The feeling here in Leicester so far as I can ascertain it runs very sharply against the Society going over. A few of us are meeting here tonight to discuss informally what we can do.' The decision was taken to hold a meeting on November 7 aimed at the Hosiery Society's workers, to rally them to vote against the CWS deal. Halstead agreed to speak, as did Henry Vivian and the MP Fred Maddison. Joseph Greenwood made the journey down from Hebden Bridge to speak as well.[473]

The meeting had the desired effect. At the first meeting of the Hosiery Society members, there was a strong majority against the CWS takeover. The meeting was adjourned until late in November, when the definitive vote was taken. Joseph Greenwood immediately sent the elderly Holyoake in Brighton a telegram with the news. The telegram read: 'For committee recommendation 204, against 286.' It meant victory.[474]

Or, at least, it seemed initially like victory. The CWS, however, was not prepared to leave matters like this. It pointed out to those co-operative societies which were members of Leicester Hosiery Society that it felt itself now free to set up its own hosiery business in competition – a development, it pointed out, that could mean the societies' investments in the Hosiery Society might rapidly lose their value. Was this really what they wanted? 'The war drums beat in earnest. The 'Great Wholesale' had been insulted!,' Greening wrote in *Agricultural Economist*. 'The societies became alarmed for their property and relentless pressure was brought by them to bear upon the workers.'[475]

Halstead piled in, trying to defend the society's workers as the pressure grew: 'Here is an organised body of co-operators who have been deeply concerned in ensuring the success of a society which embodies the principle they stand for, and because they simply organise to protect their threatened cause they are denounced for their interference,' he told *Co-operative News*.[476]

Nevertheless the CWS worked behind the scenes and it rapidly became clear that the November decision would be reversed. Leicester Hosiery disappeared as an independent co-operative society in May 1903; a year later CWS closed the Leicester plant, in order to open a new factory on a greenfield site outside the city. By 1907 the story was very old news: the CWS Chairman dismissively referred to Leicester Hosiery as 'one of those small concerns started in connection with another phase of the co-operative movement'.[477]

In the aftermath of this event the Labour Co-partnership Association's Aneurin Williams wrote a thoughtful paper drawing out some lessons he felt should be learned. He warned other co-partnership co-operatives of the 'fatal mistake' of depending on co-operative societies for capital and the equally fatal mistake of depending on co-operative stores entirely for custom. Instead, he wrote, co-partnerships should look to their workers to provide the capital and for should pay profit bonuses in the form of accumulated shares rather than distributed. 'The second part of the cure is of course for the societies to push out into the open market for trade,' he went on. 'My third point is to put the representation of your worker shareholders on your committees ... I would have the workers elect their representatives on the committee by themselves.'[478]

Williams' paper was presented at the March 1903 AGM of the Co-operative Productive Federation which was attended by Joseph Craven as the CPF chairman. What he thought of Williams' analysis we do not know, and we do not know if Greenwood also read the paper, although it is very likely. Were there lessons here for Hebden Bridge? It was true that the Fustian Manufacturing Society was not *entirely* dependent on co-operative societies for either share capital or custom, although increasingly societies were coming to occupy a dominant position in the Nutclough's membership, and some of Williams' concerns should perhaps have hit home. On the final point he raised – that of worker representation – no effort appears to have been made after the early 1890s to consider this step for the fustian society. Even if the proposal had been put forward, it is not clear whether by this stage Craven would have been able to carry his committee with him.

Times were changing. In May 1903, his friends at the Nutclough Mill bid a sad farewell to John Hartley, who had died aged eighty-one whilst still in post as the fustian society's Traveller. Flags were flown at half-mast at both the Nutclough and the main store of Hebden Bridge Industrial Co-operative Society, the co-operative he had helped found in 1848. The old Chartist had never reached the American co-operative community he had once dreamed of, but he had done much for his home town.[479]

Other senior management figures at the fustian society were growing older. Both Joseph Greenwood and Joseph Craven turned seventy in 1903, not that Greenwood was showing much sign of wanting to retire. He was, however, planning ahead. In 1902 he purchased for £309 a plot of land and old cottages in Sandy Gate, Hebden Bridge, very close to the Birchcliffe chapel he attended. He pulled down the buildings and had a terrace of six substantial modern villas built in their place. Later he was to occupy 1 Sandy Gate himself. The houses were, effectively, his pension pot.[480]

Every year from 1879 Joseph Craven had been re-elected to the presidency of the Society: it had become a formality. When he clocked up 21 years of service on the committee in 1896 his contribution to the Nutclough was marked with an honorarium. The original proposal had been for £25, but at the July meeting the Accrington society delegate successfully proposed to double this to £50, equivalent to many months' income. Craven, out of the room for this discussion, came back in to be given the news. 'He was somewhat overcome', reported the local paper.[481]

In January 1906, however, Craven faced a challenger for his position as President. The move, it would seem, was not one he had expected. Even more unexpectedly, the challenger won, by 111 votes to 92. Although Craven was elected back as an ordinary committee member at the July 1906 meeting, for the first six months of the year he was out in the cold, with no formal link to the co-operative.[482]

The new president had for some years been serving as the secretary of the small Cragg Vale co-operative society, in the valley south of Mytholmroyd. His name was Arthur Ainley, and he was at that time in his mid-forties. Originally from the Calder valley village of Sowerby, he had initially worked in one of the valley's textile mills before becoming an insurance agent. He became the poor-rate overseer for the Mytholmroyd urban district council early in the twentieth century, and later became the general district rate collector. He had been elected to the Fustian Manufacturing Society's management committee in 1893 and had been a committee member each year since then. He was to remain the society's president for the remaining years of the co-operative's life.[483]

The palace coup against Craven suggested that the committee were concerned to bring younger blood into the business's strategic management. The move was probably a direct result of the disappointing trading conditions over the previous few years. It was certainly a clear signal that change was in the air.

There were other changes in 1906 as well. Crossley Greenwood, in addition to his work for the Labour Co-partnership Association, was heavily involved in the creation at the very end of 1905 of the Hebden Bridge Literary and Scientific Society, an initiative which brought together many of the cadre who had emerged in Hebden Bridge through the University Extension Summer Meetings. The idea of the Lit & Sci (still going today) had been proposed by William Nowell, and Samuel Fielding and S.C. Moore were among those at the launch meeting. Crossley volunteered in February 1906 to be its first secretary, but within weeks had had to give up the post.[484] Aged 35 and still single, he had made a dramatic decision to move from Hebden Bridge to Letchworth Garden City.

The move had almost certainly been facilitated yet again by Henry Vivian at the Labour Co-partnership Association. Greenwood's role there was to use his accountancy experience to work for a co-partnership housing co-operative, the Garden City Tenants, which had been established in Letchworth, as well as to continue his collaboration with the Association; following the move he was co-opted to the Labour Co-partnership Association's committee. He left Hebden Bridge for the south in February or very early March 1906.[485]

If the story of Britain's nineteenth century productive co-operatives has up to now generally been ignored, the same could also be said of the history of housing co-operatives in this country. Such an account, if one were to be written, would certainly cover the extensive involvement of distributive co-operative societies in housing their members. In 1907, at the request of the Co-operative Union, around 400 societies reported on what they had done in terms of housing. Between them they had lent £6.5m as mortgage loans to members with which 32,600 houses had been bought; they had themselves directly spent £1.2m on building over 5,500 houses which were then sold; and they had also spent approaching two million pounds on building 8,530 houses which were being rented out.[486] In the Calder valley, most of the societies had engaged in some house-building, even small societies such as Heptonstall and Cragg Vale; as we have seen the fustian society itself had erected eighteen houses for rent.[487] Co-operatives had been motivated partly because of the evident need for decent working-class housing but also because many societies found themselves with excess capital, for which housing proved a useful outlet.

A history of co-operative housing would have to go beyond this, however, to cover those early ventures which much more closely resemble today's housing co-operatives. The Tenant Co-operators Ltd would certainly require a mention. This was established in 1888 (with Edward Vansittart Neale as one of the founders), the idea being to obtain capital at 4 per cent and to use it to build groups of houses near London which would be let to members at ordinary rents. Tenant-members (and all tenants were required to be members) would, it was hoped, receive a dividend on profits made. By 1906 the Tenant Co-operators had grown to have 320 members and properties valued at £28,680 in various locations in the London area. However, the aim of engaging tenants in the co-operative's management had proved rather more challenging.

The Tenant Co-operators model was adapted slightly for the Ealing Tenants co-operative which was established in 1901 with Henry Vivian playing a key role. By 1906 it had 104 houses worth over £50,000. Another similar co-operative – Sevenoaks Tenants, set up in 1903 – had 47 houses and 46 members, and there were also embryonic housing co-operative societies of this kind becoming established in Leicester, Bournville, Manchester, Hampstead, Oldham and elsewhere.[488]

The Garden City Tenants which Crossley Greenwood moved south to support was set up in a similar way, with the strong involvement of the Labour Co-partnership Association leadership, particularly Aneurin Williams and Henry Vivian who acted as its chairman. It was established in 1905 to bring a housing co-operative society to the new community which was taking shape at Letchworth Garden City, inspired by the vision of a new form of urban living as proposed by Ebenezer Howard. Howard's book *To-morrow* published in 1898 and reissued four years later as *Garden Cities of To-morrow* had received considerable attention – and indeed is still influential today. In addition to the Letchworth venture, which aimed to create a self-contained residential and industrial town with a permanent agricultural belt, the Hampstead Garden Suburb Trust was at this time also working to develop 240 acres which it had purchased from Eton College.

Aneurin Williams, as well as his engagement in the co-partnership movement, was a director of the First Garden City company which had acquired the freehold of the land at Letchworth and which was overseeing developments there. He claimed to the 1907 Co-operative Congress that the garden city movement was 'essentially a part of the co-operative movement', and certainly there was some cross-fertilisation of ideas. With Williams and Henry Vivian involved, the Garden City Tenants became one of the earliest developers to get established in the new town. In its first year it erected thirteen cottages of various sizes round a communal garden, each cottage having its own private allotment.[489] By the end of 1906 it counted 111 members and 130 houses, valued at £37,670.[490]

Letchworth Garden City was growing fast when Crossley Greenwood arrived, from a population of 400 in 1904 to 2,500 in 1906.[491] As well as his responsibilities as Secretary for the Garden City Tenants society he was also asked to work for the Co-partnership Tenants' Housing Council. This body, equivalent in some ways to the role played by the CPF for productive co-operatives, was intended to bring the Garden City Tenants together with other co-partnership housing co-operatives, both those established and those being planned.[492] The Housing Council was also a convenient conduit to raise capital for future house-building: George Bernard Shaw was among the investors, putting in £5,400.[493]

By the middle of 1907 the Garden City Tenants Society had progressed to the stage where it had obtained funds in excess of £29,000 and had built 285 houses. In July that year it staged an event attended by, among others, Joseph Greenwood, who had come south to see what his son was up to. (Robert Halstead was there, too, from Leicester). Joseph Greenwood, it seems, may have been expecting Letchworth to be a little on the alternative side, a little cranky; he was surprised, it was reported, at the 'absence of curiosities'.[494]

Given the family connection now with Letchworth, it was predictable that the idea of a garden city – or in this case, a garden village – would take root in Hebden Bridge. Plans for what were intended to be both a co-operative cotton weaving works and a settlement of co-operative houses in the Eaves valley, just to the west of Hebden Bridge, were in fact already being progressed at the time of Joseph Greenwood's trip to Letchworth.

The story of the Eaves Bottom Self-Help Manufacturers Society venture is the story of Joseph Greenwood trying a second time, almost forty years on, to pull off what he had managed to achieve at the Hebden Bridge Fustian Manufacturing Society. The background was a bitter Hebden Bridge weavers' strike which had broken out at Foster Mill in July 1906, had rapidly pulled in workers at Richard Thomas's Hangingroyd Mill adjacent to the Nutclough Mill, and had then a month later spread more widely in the town. It was to be a very long battle, the longest strike in the history of the weavers' unions and one of the most costly for the union. Before it finally came to an end, after two and a half years at the end of 1908, many thousands of pounds had been paid out in strike pay: over £13,600 was paid out in 1907 alone, for example. The Todmorden Weavers' Association had to seek financial support from the Amalgamated Weavers' Association, at that stage the second largest union in Britain, to which it was affiliated. 'This dispute ... is one of the most stubborn fights our district has ever been engaged in,' the Todmorden Weavers' Association said in October that year.[495]

Although the Nutclough Mill was not directly affected by the strike, the whole town was effectively caught up in what was happening. The use by mill-owners of 'knobsticks' (scab labour) gave a particular bitterness to the dispute. There were street disturbances in November 1906 and a number of strikers found themselves facing legal proceedings. On 28 January 1907 the suffragette leader Emmeline Pankhurst came to the town for a series of meetings nominally called by the Trades Council in support of the strike when, according to the local paper, the majority of Hebden Bridge inhabitants were on the streets. As well as the planned meeting at the Co-operative Hall, several overflow meetings were held including an open-air one in St George's Square in the centre of town. A brass band of striking weavers accompanied a 400-strong march. The evening finished with some minor disturbances, when windows were broken at one of the mill-owners' houses.[496]

The fustian society's management was approached early in 1907 and asked to consider extending its weaving operation to provide employment for some of those on strike, but declined the proposal.[497] In strict business terms, the decision was probably the right one: it is not clear that a larger weaving shed could have been commercially viable. Nevertheless, Joseph Greenwood undoubtedly felt a strong obligation to do something to help and he set up a meeting to look into the possibility of establishing a new venture. By June plans were taking shape. A meeting at the Weavers' Institute in June resolved to try to raise £15,000 capital for a new co-partnership, which would purchase two disused mills together with 48 acres of land in Eaves Bottom.

The mills would weave cotton whilst the land was intended to be turned into the garden village, 'planned on model modern lines, restoring the old English village green'. It was a captivating vision of a better future. According to the *Co-partnership* magazine, 'the site is fitted to become an arcadia and to ring with song and happiness'. The garden village would be one 'where its people will live lives free from carking care, free from lock-out or strike, happy in their beautiful surroundings on their own hillside'.[498]

It is perhaps surprising that the success of the Hebden Bridge Fustian Manufacturing Society had not previously attracted many other attempts at productive co-operation in the upper Calder valley. An abortive effort had been made in 1895-6 to establish a Mytholmroyd Manufacturing co-operative which had successfully raised capital, had briefly employed around eighteen workers but had failed to get beyond the start-up phase and had quickly disappeared.[499] Much more successful was the Calderdale Co-operative Clog Sundries Manufacturing Society, based beyond Todmorden at Walsden. This co-operative was begun in 1892 with nine workers to manufacture sole irons for clogs. Never a large venture, it was nevertheless profitable and long-lasting, servicing the very substantial market for clogs in Lancashire and Yorkshire at that time. In 1909 it was doing trade of a little over £3,000, turning a profit of around £200 – and paying a bonus to labour from that profit of 6d in the pound.[500]

If we leave to one side the Sowerby Bridge Flour Society, Calderdale Clog Sundries was the only co-operative society of its kind in the neighbourhood apart from the fustian society at the time the Eaves Bottom venture got under way. The Eaves project had an eminent group of people to help it get established. The committee was chaired by Greenwood himself – not only manager at the Nutclough but by this stage a highly respected elder statesman on the Urban District Council – and included among others the president of the Hebden Bridge Industrial Co-operative Society, the manager of the local electricity works, and another local councillor. The co-operative movement rallied round. The Hebden Bridge society put up £1,000, the Heptonstall society contributed £250, and other societies put in smaller amounts of between £20-£100. The strikers themselves reportedly invested approaching £2,000. The capital raised meant that the Eaves mills and estate could be purchased, and the sale went through in September 1907 for £3,750 (£3,500 as cash, £250 as shares in the new co-operative). Henry Vivian was invited to Hebden Bridge for an inaugural ceremony in August and Greenwood enthusiastically briefed E.O. Greening as the work got under way: 'we are making bargains for good old looms, taking care they are in good condition,' he wrote, sending photographs to his friend of the voluntary work being undertaken by the strikers to get the old mill reservoirs cleared of sludge.[501]

And yet by 1908 it was clear that not everything was going to plan. The shareholders' meeting in May, chaired by Joseph Greenwood, heard an urgent call for more capital. The original capital had been spent on acquiring the estate and purchasing sixty-four looms, not enough to run a commercially successful business. The largest investor, the Hebden Bridge co-operative, seemed to be having cold feet, its President resigning from the committee and being replaced by the ever-faithful Joseph Craven. The idea now was to build a new weaving shed and acquire altogether 300-400 looms.[502]

More difficulties were ahead. Greenwood and Craven must have hoped that the fustian society would help bridge the capital gap and a motion was submitted to the July meeting proposing an investment of £500, half in share capital and half as a loan. The meeting voted the motion down. Greenwood no longer had the power he once had to influence his members.[503] By September the Eaves Bottom committee had stopped the weaving, partly on account of bad trade. The auditors' report two months later showed a trading loss of £249.

1909 was to be even worse, with a loss of over £560 made for the half-year until May. 'The state of trade during the half year has been most difficult,' the members' meeting heard. By November there was a cumulative loss of £1,250. In April 1910 the directors bowed to the inevitable and decided to suspend operations and liquidation followed.[504] 'The starting of a co-operative workshop is beset with the utmost difficulty and to start through a strike the difficulty is much greater,' Greenwood was to write a short time later in his memoirs.[505] The weavers' strike itself was by this stage history, having petered out without the weavers achieving the success they had originally hoped for.

1909 brought sad news of a different kind for Joseph Greenwood. As he put it in a letter to Greening sent on 5 September, 'I am sorry to write that our old friend Joseph Craven died last night. I called to see him on my return from Manchester. He was then alive and fully conscious. He put out his hand, and it seemed to me as a last farewell. I took both his hands in both of mine, and we exchanged our last hope for God's help.'[506] Craven had, Greenwood said elsewhere, dedicated the last few months of his life to his work as a committee member of the Eaves Bottom co-operative: 'His last wish was for its welfare'.[507]

Another co-operative pioneer had gone. 'The aspirations of his life and all his efforts were for a betterment of the condition of his class,' said Greenwood in tribute.[508]

Greenwood had himself had a close shave nine months earlier, when he had suffered a serious accident in the Nutclough Woods. On his way to the mill on 22 December 1908 he lost his footing when crossing the goit (water channel) which linked the upper and lower reservoirs and fell about six feet, banging his head on a slab of concrete and becoming unconscious. He lay in this position for at least an hour before finally coming round sufficiently to crawl away and seek help. He suffered facial injuries and bruising and was off work for some days. He was a few days short of his seventy-fifth birthday. It was, said the local paper, a miracle that he was not killed outright.[509]

All things considered, it was becoming time for Joseph Greenwood to take the big decision to step aside. On 6 April 1909 he formally took his retirement from the co-operative he had done so much to establish and develop. Ten days later a celebration was held in his honour at the Co-operative Hall.

There were to be other honours for Greenwood at this time. The Labour Co-partnership Association, for example, commissioned the Manchester artist Reginald Barber (later to tutor the young L.S. Lowry) to paint an oil portrait of Greenwood. The portrait was hung for many years in the Association's London office but has now disappeared.[510]

The *Co-operative News* offered its own tribute. 'Gentleness, kindly humour and faithful devotion to the cause of the people are among the admirable characteristics of Mr Joseph Greenwood. Mr Greenwood is one who belongs to the 'old guard' of co-operators who had to do the spadework at a more troublesome period of the social history of the people ... In his retirement he will carry with him the love of his fellow-men. And that is something worth cherishing.'[511]

CHAPTER 13

A TIME OF CHANGE

Given that the fustian society's management committee had had many years to anticipate this moment, it managed to handle the business of the succession with curious maladroitness. Perhaps committee members had found it simply impossible to anticipate that Greenwood would ever *not* be at the helm. To be fair, Greenwood himself does not seem to have given any active thought towards preparing for his succession.

The management committee went to the co-operative's secretary, Leonard Stocks, at that point two years short of his fiftieth birthday, whom they assumed would take over. But Stocks, to their evident surprise, turned the job down. Instead they hurriedly devised a plan B, promoting the co-operative's Traveller to the post of manager.

This being Hebden Bridge, the heartland of the Greenwood clans, it should come as no surprise to learn that the new manager of the fustian society shared the same surname as the old. The new manager's name was Sam Greenwood and although he was not related to Joseph Greenwood (or, at least, not closely related) he had the curious coincidence of having as his father a man called Joseph Greenwood. A further coincidence was that Sam Greenwood had – just like the Nutclough's Joseph Greenwood – taken a wife whose maiden name was itself Greenwood. There were other surnames in Hebden Bridge, but sometimes it just didn't feel that way.[512]

Sam Greenwood enters the history of the Fustian Manufacturing Society at this point with almost no back-story. He was born around 1866, the son of a weaver and one of the youngest of a large family, and married his wife Emma Greenwood in Heptonstall in 1892. He had begun work at the Nutclough in 1882 in his mid-teens and had worked at different times as a warehouseman, a weaver and in the dyehouse.[513] He was promoted to the position of Traveller on John Hartley's death in 1903 and had worked for 27 years for the co-operative when he was given the manager's position.

What is missing is much evidence that Sam Greenwood participated before his appointment in the wider co-operative movement. There is no record of him having attended any Co-operative Congresses, for example, and he does not show up in records of the meetings of the Calderdale Co-operative Alliance. We do know that he attended several Crystal Palace exhibitions, although this may have been only after his appointment as Traveller. He did not produce papers or write to the co-operative press and he does not seem to have been active in the University Extension scene either, although there is a solitary record of an S. Greenwood qualifying for the end-of-course examination in 1889, which may be him. A much later account describes him having an interest in educational matters, and as being a keen photographer.[514]

There is also remarkably little documentary material left in the co-operative's archives from his time in charge: little more than a clutch of picture postcards sent by him to Leonard Stocks when he was on holiday.

Sam Greenwood was not an old-style co-operator. We can deduce that he did, however, know the fustian society business well, not least from the various different jobs he had undertaken at the Nutclough, and he seems to have had an adequately effective working relationship with Stocks, who stayed on as secretary. Given the formidable task of following on from Joseph Greenwood he may not have been particularly pleased at the way that Arthur Ainley, with perhaps unnecessary candour, spilled the beans about his appointment at Joseph Greenwood's retirement party: 'Mr Stocks, to my surprise and I think to the surprise of the Board, declined the offer of the Board [to be manager]... Failing Mr Stocks the Board offered the position to Mr Sam Greenwood,' Ainley said. He went on to add, again perhaps not giving his new manager the most ringing of endorsements, 'I want to appeal to you to give him all the help you can'.[515]

Why did Leonard Stocks turn down the post? His background was as an administrator and the position of manager was a very different one, comprising among other things the role of production manager and the responsibility for oversight of the workforce. Stocks may have been correct in knowing that he would not have been well-suited to these responsibilities. He may also have known that the times ahead could be challenging. In turning down the position he may however have suggested to the committee that a more collegiate management approach to the business could be tried. Certainly in 1918 both he and Sam Greenwood were on the same salaries.[516]

During Sam Greenwood's first few years as manager the co-operative saw a welcome gradual return to growth in sales and profitability, with profits crossing the £5,000 threshold in 1913 for the first time since 1895. Sales grew past £50,000 in 1911 and were over £61,000 in 1913 (Figures 7, 8). One sign that the co-operative was planning for the future were the capital investments undertaken in the business. In the spring of 1909 the firm's usual architects were commissioned to design an addition to the weaving shed and in April 1913 they were asked again, this time to design a new roof for the dye-house and a warehouse to be built alongside.[517] The most substantial investment came a little later, during the war period in 1915-16, when a new engine was commissioned to replace the venerable 'Thomas Hughes' and a new engine house was built to accommodate it. The new engine was named 'Unity'. The total outlay was substantial, over £10,000 according to one report, but Arthur Ainley pointed to the considerable savings to the coal bill which the more efficient new engine and boilers would bring about. In any case, as he pointed out, the society's balance sheet was in very strong shape with much of the past capital investment undertaken by the business already written down to zero. Ainley paid tribute at the celebratory launch event in April 1916 to the technical advice which the fustian society had been able to enjoy from the CWS's engineering department.[518]

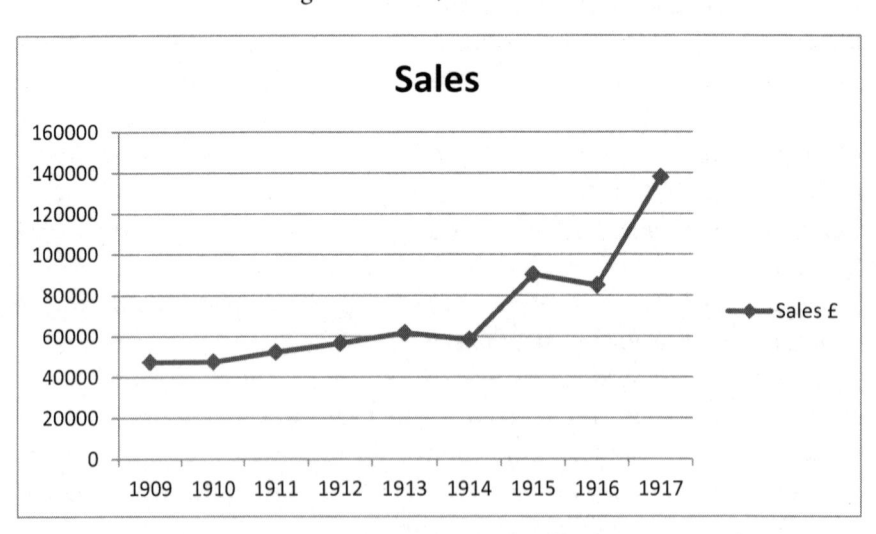

Figure 7: Sales, 1909-1917[519]

The broader context in which these developments were taking place was a very different one from that of an earlier period in the fustian society's history. Sam Greenwood's period as manager would see conditions in the fustian industry, and more widely in the cotton trade, change in almost every respect. The war, as we shall see, brought unprecedented government levels of intervention in industry, with direct government engagement in the production process, including arbitration on wage levels.

Increasing state intervention, and with it a move towards much more formalised collective bargaining with trade unions, did not begin with

Figure 8: Profit, 1909-1917[520]

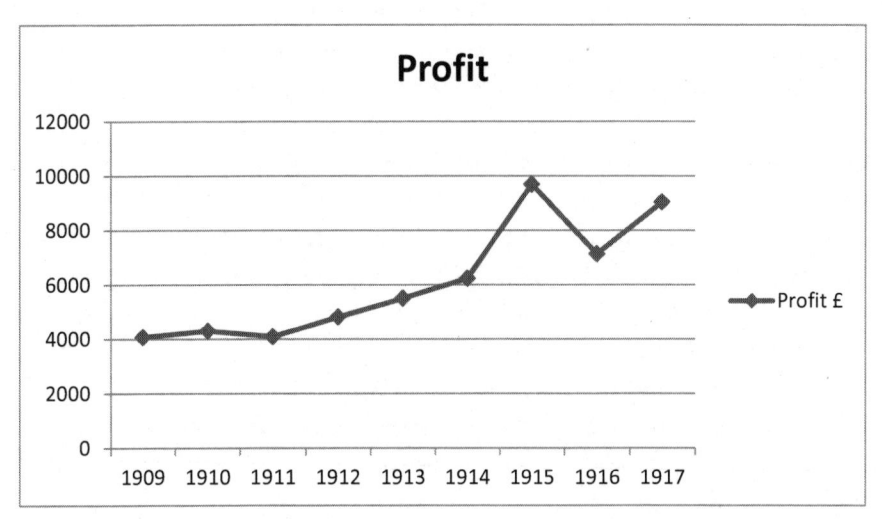

the war, however. Parliament introduced minimum wage levels in several sectors of industry where traditionally wages had been very low, including tailoring, with the passing of the Trade Boards Act of 1909. The relevant Trade Board for the tailoring and garment-making industry was established in December 1910 with its 49 members appointed by the Board of Trade, 22 to represent employers, 22 the unions and five to represent the wider public interest. The Trade Board after much negotiation between the two main sides agreed in August 1912 new minimum wages for the industry, which became mandatory six months later. The rates were calculated on an hourly basis, but represented in broad terms a minimum pay of 25s a week for men and 13s 6d for women.[521]

The creation of the Trade Board had much wider repercussions than this, however, in that it created a completely different climate for industrial relations. S.C. (Sam) Moore, the University Extension student who had been appointed the fustian society's Traveller in 1909 in replacement of Sam Greenwood, undertook a detailed study of the effect of the change in the whole of Hebden Bridge for a 1913 article for *The Economic Journal* and found that already after only a few months three things had happened. The first was that men's wages in the town, which had been notoriously low, had been increased by an average of 3s a week (women's wages, already above the threshold, had not been affected).

The second change was that both men and women had benefited from a major reduction in working hours which saw most Hebden Bridge mills move to a 52 hour week. (The Fustian Manufacturing Society participated in this general reduction in working time, although it may at this stage have moved to a 52½ standard week). This significant reduction might have been expected to have penalised piece-rate workers, including almost all the women machinists, but according to Moore this had not occurred. 'There is a general opinion that quite as much work has been done in the fifty-two hour week as in the fifty-eight ... As there has certainly been no outcry among the women about the matter, we may fairly conclude that their earnings have not been less,' he wrote.

The third change was in some ways even more profound: 'It has helped to create a new spirit among the men. The principle of combination as a means of improving wages and conditions of labour which had hitherto failed to grip more than a few individuals has now been suddenly adopted, and the men are joining the union in almost a mass movement,' Moore said. He added that the clothing operatives union the AUCO had seen the number of male members locally increase from 29 to over 300 in a single year.[522]

Moore's observation was to be echoed two years later by R.H. Tawney in a more comprehensive study of the effect of the Trade Board in the tailoring and garment-making sector. Tawney quotes the AUCO's General Secretary as saying 'The Act has had a most important educational effect. The notices posted in the factories rouse people. At Hebden Bridge the workers never before believed that it was possible they could get so much money. Now their interest is aroused and they are more ready to organise'. Tawney himself added the following observation: 'The psychological influence of the Trade Board system is, indeed, the most important of its results. Workers who were till recently convinced that agitation for higher wages was always futile and often dangerous have at last seen the advance for which they did not dare ask brought about by law and, now that the incredible has happened, have realised that there is no insuperable barrier in the way of better conditions.'[523]

The biggest changes in Hebden Bridge were at the other garment manufacturing mills – many of which had federated together in 1900 into a single Combine – rather than at the fustian society. But nevertheless relationships between workers and their management at the Nutclough were changing too, in quite a dramatic way.[524] We get a first inkling of what was ahead in an exchange of letters between eight Nutclough cutters (all male) and Sam Greenwood and the management committee in 1910. The workers wrote a long letter asking both for a rise in wages and for the adoption of a fixed wage list to replace the current individually negotiated wage system. 'We are given to understand that you are prepared to pay at least as high a rate of wages as any other firm in the trade in Hebden Bridge. This we contend you are not doing at present,' the workers wrote. 'During the last ten years the cost of living has gone up considerably whilst in our department the rate of wages has tended to go down.'

The workers' letter added another point. 'We have regularly an amount of short time which reduces our wages in average by 15%-20%, for the summer half year. No other large firm is so persistently bad in this respect and that ought to be taken into account in fixing our rate of wages.'

The fustian society's management committee was not convinced. 'We regard the wording of the application to say the least in rather bad taste,' the reply began. 'The Board are not at all satisfied with the quantity of work got thro as regards both the stock cutters and knife hands and they regard the application as altogether inopportune.' A wage list would mean all workers, whatever their standard of work, would receive the same pay and that, the management committee said, was not its policy.

The dispute carried on into late 1911 with the Nutclough workers asking their union's General Secretary Joseph Young to intervene on their behalf. It is not clear that Young managed to persuade the management committee to reconsider, but what is highly significant in this affair is the name of the person who was leading the dispute on behalf of his fellow cutters at the Nutclough: it was Sam Craven, Joseph Craven's son.[525]

The point about the cost of living in the original letter was a legitimate one. After a long period in the nineteenth century when workers' standards of living generally had improved, the first years of the twentieth century saw this trend halted and reversed: prices rose faster than wages. In the ten years prior to the outbreak of war, wages in general moved upwards by about 9 per cent, while retail food prices increased by around 12 per cent.[526] Partly as a consequence the years immediately before the war were a time of considerable industrial disturbance across the country, a period sometimes described as the 'great unrest'.

The fustian society took the decision in late 1911 that the rates of pay for its weavers were too low and a revised pay scale came in on 1 January 1912.[527] The dyers, whose union was the National Federation of Dyers and Finishers, promptly raised their own concerns. Their union leader Arthur Shaw wrote to the co-operative in February 1912 requesting among other things an across-the-board 1s a week increase. 'Trusting that the same good feelings which have existed between yourselves and employees will long continue,' Shaw concluded his letter. By early 1913 good feelings were in short supply, however. As part of a more general dispute in the area, the dyers at the Nutclough formally handed in strike notices to their management.

The fustian society had historically chosen to stand aside from employers' organisations locally, which included the Hebden Bridge and District Master Dyers Association. Instead of participating in local collective negotiations and signing up to the local agreements, the Nutclough management claimed that, as a co-operative, any disputes with employees should be arbitrated through the TUC/Co-operative Union Joint Committee, established almost three decades earlier in 1885 specifically to handle industrial disputes in co-operatives. The Joint Committee was clearly a good idea in theory, but in practice it had sometimes struggled to make its mark. It was slow-moving, with its members (at this point four from the TUC, four from the co-operative movement) summoned together when issues arose. Over the years it had managed to issue quasi-judicial rulings in some cases. In 1908, for example, it had instructed the CWS to reinstate an AUCO member at its Broughton tailoring works, a cut-and-dried case since the worker in question had been sacked for taking time off work specifically in order to meet the Joint Committee to present his case.[528] But in several other disputes it had found itself struggling to intervene or to make its rulings stick. Local union branches could sometimes challenge its legitimacy. Certainly Arthur Shaw appears to have been minded not to accept the Joint Committee machinery in this 1913 dispute. In the end the dispute seems to have been resolved by straightforward negotiation, and a memorandum of agreement among other things increasing dyers' and finishers' wages by between 1s and 2s a week was agreed on 23 February.[529]

The outbreak of war in August 1914 saw the flurry of letters from trade union officials to Leonard Stocks and Sam Greenwood temporarily come to a halt. But the lull lasted only until early 1915. In March, for example, Arthur Shaw was back in touch calling for further pay increases: 'Within the past six months all food-stuffs, coal and nearly every article required for domestic consumption has increased enormously in price'.[530]

He was right. Indeed the period of the First World War was to see a quite unprecedented increase in the prices of the everyday necessities of life for working-class families. There was an immediate increase in average retail prices straight after the war broke out. Taking July 1914 as the base month, the retail price index had increased from 100 to 144 by the end of December 1915. In December 1916 it was standing at 184. By December 1917 prices had effectively doubled in a little over three years, the index now standing at 205. [531]

Wages also increased during the war years, but at a much slower rate. War was not only bringing terrible suffering on the Western Front and in the other theatres of war, it was also bringing real hardship for those struggling to get by on the home front. The sense of patriotism there at the start of the war quickly disappeared; the government was aware that the industries it was relying on for the war effort were staffed by an increasingly restless and discontented workforce.[532]

The Fustian Manufacturing Society was doing business as never before, much of it work for army contracts. At the July 1915 members' meeting, Ainley was able to report 'the largest turnover the society had made in any half-year' with profits also 'very much larger than usual' (Figures 7,8). Although not giving details he mentioned that the Nutclough had been providing materials and making up and dyeing garments for both British troops and those of Britain's allies (there is a story told in the town that some of the garments may have ended up with the Russian army).[533] Some of the profit being made was salted away to be used to help pay for the new engine and more was put in reserves. 'The board felt that it would be wisest not to pay an increased dividend but to husband the resources of the society with a view to meeting any possible competition that might arise after the war,' Ainley went on.[534]

It is conceivable that the Nutclough may have been undertaking some of this work on a sub-contracting basis for CWS.[535] The CWS was certainly itself very heavily involved in army contracts. *Co-operative News* reported in early 1915 that the CWS was busy producing khaki suits. Apparently the Army had required about 2.5 million new khaki trousers, tunics, overcoats and caps in the six months after war broke out. Uniforms which lasted a year in peacetime were wearing out in 6-8 weeks under wartime conditions.[536]

The unprecedented levels of sales and profits at the Nutclough Mill did not compensate for the long shadow cast by the war. Leonard Stocks reported in October 1916 that approaching forty men from the co-operative had enlisted, of whom five had been killed.[537] Further deaths followed: Frank Mitchell, who had worked with Leonard Stocks in the Nutclough office, probably in the post Crossley Greenwood had once filled, had joined up in 1915 and was killed in May 1917. Leonard Stocks himself suffered the loss of his younger son William Henry Stocks, who was reported missing in action in March 1918, aged 24. He had tried to enlist several times but each time had been rejected because of poor eyesight; eventually he was accepted, serving in France, Greece and Palestine, where he died.[538]

Two of Joseph Greenwood's grandsons were to die as well. Percy, the son of Joseph's oldest son Virgil, enlisted in the Royal Army Military Corps and died in 1918 aged 26 whilst serving in East Africa, having contracted smallpox; he is buried in Mozambique.[539] Herbert Greenwood, son of Joseph's third son Harry, was reported missing in action in September 1915, aged 25. He had previously worked at the Nutclough Mill and had enlisted in January that year with two other workmates, Frank Sunderland and Edgar Helliwell. All three were to perish in the war.[540]

Back on the home front the fustian society's management committee had taken two steps to respond to the changing economic realities. During the months of February, March and April 1915 there had been a flurry of letters arriving at the Nutclough Mill office from the trade unions, not only from the National Society of Dyers and Finishers and the AUCO but also from the Todmorden Weavers' Association (as part of the Northern Counties Amalgamated Association of Weavers) and from the United Association of Power-Loom Overlookers, representing the small number of overlookers in the weaving shed. The management committee's first response, on 2 March, was to resolve to give a 5 per cent War Bonus to all its workers, backdated to the start of 1915. Six weeks later on 20 April the management committee considered the matter again and resolved to increase the War Bonus to 10 per cent. War Bonuses were at this stage intended as additional payments to be made only during the duration of the war.

The employees were called together the day after the April management committee meeting to be given the news. The Bonus payments meant that at this point the Nutclough workers were probably being better treated than other local workers, although the fustian society's committee made it clear that these Bonuses were to be set against any subsequent union-negotiated increases; the Society was not going any further.[541] Not all the unions were happy. Thomas Walmsley of the Overlookers wrote on 22 April, saying that his union did not agree with the War Bonus principles and wanted a permanent settlement. And anyway, he added for good measure, the Fustian Manufacturing Society's Bonus was 5 per cent below the CWS amount.[542]

Arthur Shaw of the Dyers' union was back in touch in October and November. The union had been successfully negotiating with the Hebden Bridge employers' association across-the-board increases for its members (3s for men, 2s for women, girls and boys, and 10 per cent for piecework), which meant – Shaw claimed – that the Nutclough's dyers and finishers, even with the 10 per cent bonus, were now worse off than their colleagues in other mills. Strike notices were handed in to the fustian society's management, as a way of focusing the management committee's attention on the matter. Sam Greenwood and Leonard Stocks offered to visit the union's office in Bradford to negotiate, but the union dug in. The management committee met in mid-November and agreed to pay the new rates to those employees who asked for it (some apparently chose to stick with the 10 per cent). Shaw wrote back on 17 November withdrawing the strike notices.[543]

It was to be the Nutclough members of the clothing operatives' union, newly amalgamated and renamed the United Garment Workers, who were to be the first to go one step further and actually withdraw their labour at the co-operative. They took part in the major Hebden Bridge-wide strike which broke out in early November 1916 and which was a highly significant local event, not least because the great majority of 2000-plus strikers were women. It was also a strike which saw Sam Craven, by this stage the local secretary of the union, in the thick of the action.

The women workers of Hebden Bridge were not only paid less than the men but had generally been overlooked in negotiations between employers and unions in the early period of the war. Old male attitudes died hard. However, the United Garment Workers Trade Union, when it was created through merger in 1915, had 13,000 women members as against 8,000 men[544] and had been actively using women organisers to strengthen its female membership. Negotiations between the union and the Hebden Bridge Wholesale Clothiers' Association began in the summer of 1916 but when on 6 October 1916 the employers advised the union that 'unless they were prepared to withdraw their applications with regard to women workers this Association were not prepared to make any offer or discuss the matter further,' the scene was set for a bitter dispute. As the union's full-time organiser Andrew Conley said, 'The masters refused to consider the women's case and as a union they could not betray their women members'.[545] The strike began on 3 November.

The fustian society was again in a somewhat anomalous position, negotiating separately from the masters' association. Sam Craven as branch secretary had written formally to the Society in late September when letters had gone to other local employers, and the co-operative had replied in early October. It pointed again to the 10 per cent War Bonus it was paying, but did offer to meet any better terms which might be agreed in the Hebden Bridge-wide negotiations. Attitudes hardened after strike notices were put in on 16 October, the co-operative telling the union that it would negotiate on the men's wages but would not consider any further increases to pieceworkers.[546] Piecework was, of course, the way that the vast majority of women in the mill were paid.

The reasoning behind this stance was set out later by the Society in a detailed negotiating statement where it claimed that the women machinists and finishers were already receiving good pay. 'At the time when this war bonus was rendered [1915], the Committee recognised even then that the piece workers in the clothing department were very highly paid, judged by the standard which obtained for women's work elsewhere in the district,' the statement reads. It goes on to suggest the average earnings of machinists had risen from 5.71d an hour in 1913 to 6.74d in 1916, with the twelve highest paid pieceworkers earning as much as 8.5d an hour. There was also a problem of pay differentials to consider with the women weavers who had come in to replace men in the weaving shed.[547]

The Society's decision not to look again at piece rates probably made it inevitable that the union would have to call out its members at the Nutclough Mill, even if the issues there were to an extent secondary to the main dispute being carried on in the town. 140 workers at the co-operative came out. Some of the workers in other parts of the mill contributed to the strike collections.[548]

Not everyone from the Nutclough Mill who was on strike was happy. The men in particular were not sure this was their dispute. Sam Craven received a letter from a fellow-cutter T.H. Needham on 30 November, which began 'Dear Craven, As workers of Hebden Bridge Fustian Society we very much regret and resent the actions of the Officials of the union in refusing the terms offered by the officials of the above Society. The majority of the workers are quite satisfied with the terms and conditions offered.' In the thick of a major dispute, Craven had no option but to slap him down: 'Dear Needham, I hear that you are thinking of holding a meeting of the Nutclough workers this morning. You could not do a more foolish thing in your own interest [underlined].' Craven went on to advise Needham that the Society's management committee were proposing to ask the Joint Board of Trade Unionists and Co-operators to arbitrate. 'If all is satisfactory we may be able to get a meeting of our members this week and allow Nutclough to start work immediately,' he added, in a more conciliatory manner.[549]

As both Needham's letter and Craven's reply ended up in the fustian society's files, it is likely that management was aware of Needham's initiative and was monitoring the union position. In the end, however, it was not to be the Joint Committee which undertook arbitration. By this stage, Whitehall and the War Office were taking a keen interest in what was happening at the Nutclough Mill. The War Office contracts department wrote to Sir George Askwith, the government's Chief Industrial Commissioner at the Board of Trade, complaining that the strike was at a factory 'engaged upon urgent War Office contracts and the holding up of the supply is a serious matter'. There was some initial confusion: Askwith thought the Nutclough Mill was run by the CWS and the CWS had to point out that their garment factory in Leeds was working normally. 'We ... would have been quite willing to have transferred to our factory at The Mint, Holbeck, Leeds, the manufacture of goods required by the Government, but fearing that by so doing our workers at Leeds would come out on strike at once.'[550]

Some confusion remained however. On 6 December a telegram was sent from the Board of Trade to Joseph Young, the United Garment Workers' General Secretary: 'Urgent requirements for the Army in France make it necessary that work at Co-operative Wholesale Factory (sic) Hebden Bridge should be resumed forthwith (stop) Have informed War Office that you are taking steps to this effect (stop) Will arrange for Arbitration on the points in dispute at this factory without delay.'[551]

Both the union and the fustian society were probably pleased at this stage to be able to see the strike called off and the issues taken to the government arbitrator. But there was a remaining problem. Sam Craven, as branch secretary, was fully engaged in leading the main strike in Hebden Bridge; in any case, what sort of signal would it send his members if he returned to work? Young telegrammed back: 'We are willing to advise workers to immediately resume work at Co-operative factory Hebden Bridge but management of factory threaten to victimise our Secretary Craven unless he resumes work being one their employees. This society requires Craven's services until conference on Tuesday can you take action.'[552]

For a few days this issue threatened to turn nasty. Leonard Stocks told the union on 7 December that Sam Craven had to resume work immediately. 'It is very necessary that all our cutting staff should be at work,' he wrote. Two days later he advised Sir George Askwith in London that since Craven had failed to return to work 'our Manager has taken steps to fill his position'. Askwith had to send another telegram: 'Am informed workers willing to resume immediately but that difficulty has arisen over man named Craven have suggested that this point can be raised before Independent Chairman ...'[553]

Sam Craven effectively had his way: the issue was resolved, but only on the following Tuesday, at the conciliation conference which had been called to arbitrate on the main Hebden Bridge dispute. The Nutclough's separate arbitration took place in mid-January, undertaken by one of Askwith's colleagues Charles Doughty who announced his judgment at the end of the month. It was a complex settlement, which reduced the 10 per cent War Bonus to 5 per cent but then added an increase in hourly pay of a halfpenny for adult women and a farthing for girls under 18, to be paid in addition to pre-war piece rates. Men's pay was also increased. The settlement was not well received by the workers, and in February Craven was back in touch with the fustian society management reporting on his members' dissatisfaction.[554] By this stage, however, the fustian society had decided that a change was necessary. The old ways of negotiating outside the local masters' associations and using the Joint Committee if necessary had not saved it from the 1916 strike. In future it would approach industrial relations as though it were just another employer: the Fustian Manufacturing Society joined the local employers' associations.

A symbolic rupture from the past had been made. Back in October the fustian society's management committee had tried to win over the union by suggesting that they shared common interests. 'We are all working men and have all the best interests of our employees at heart and as a matter of fact two thirds of us who are sitting round the table have got very near relatives among the employees who are out on strike so that it is quite obvious that all our sympathies are with our employees,' the letter had said. But it had gone on: 'At the same time the Board are custodians for the time being of the shareholders' interests'.

Sometimes, it seemed, the interests of labour and capital could not be easily reconciled.

CHAPTER 14

TAKEOVER

The usual half-yearly meeting of the Fustian Manufacturing Society took place on 26 January 1918, and Arthur Ainley as President had a very positive report to make to his members. For 1917, trade had increased by £49,829 over 1916 results, reaching the highest figure ever for turnover at £137,875. To an extent this was the result of wartime inflation but it also reflected, he said, the fact that all the different parts of the business had been very busy, much of it work directly or indirectly for the government.

Ainley went on:

> I may say in conclusion what I have said so often before, how proud I am to occupy the position of the President of this Society. I think I am right in saying that the feeling all through the works was never better than it is today. All through the year we have been very busy and I am sure everyone has done his or her best to bring about this splendid result.

Nevertheless, the management committee's proposal for the profits appears to have been a somewhat unusual one – to increase the interest payable to shareholders by a further 2½ per cent, up to 7½ per cent, while keeping the profit share to labour and on purchases as usual at 5 per cent. The reasoning may have been that sales to co-operative societies had been, because of the government orders, relatively small – and perhaps that the workers were now getting their bonuses through collective bargaining. However some workers at least did benefit from the extra interest. By this stage of its life £17,332 of the fustian society's total capital of £38,917 was held by employees, representing on average about £52 per person. This was, Ainley said, testimony of the faith which employees had in the stability of the business: 'I cannot help but feel that this is one of the sources of the continued success of the Society'.[555]

Immediately before the members' meeting started, the delegate from the CWS, T.E. Moorhouse, had sought out Ainley for a private word. The CWS, Moorhouse said, might be interested in acquiring the business. The term used was 'amalgamation'. What did Ainley and his colleagues think?

After the meeting was over and the audience dispersed, Arthur Ainley and several of the management committee talked further with Moorhouse on an informal basis and took him up to the Nutclough Mill to show him round the premises. The next Committee meeting was the following Tuesday when Ainley reported to his whole management committee: 'I gave them a very full report of what Mr Moorhouse had said to me on the Saturday. They discussed it quite impartially, every one of the Committee speaking either for or against the desirability of entering into negotiations with the CWS, and ultimately we came to a decision.' The motion agreed and minuted was as follows: 'That considering the very friendly relations which have existed for a long time between the two Societies, that we could do no less than enter into negotiations and that we should be prepared to send a Deputation to talk the matter over with them.'[556]

There were to be negotiations ahead, but from this point on there would be only one outcome.

The CWS in 1917 had a turnover of £57.7m, total capital and reserves of £15.2m, and over 22,800 employees.[557] Following its acquisition of Leicester Hosiery in 1903, it had continued – selectively – to acquire other independent co-operatives. More significant was its proposal in 1905 to take over the long-established co-operative flour mills, including the Sowerby Bridge and Halifax societies for which it offered £80,000 and £60,000 respectively. The shareholders of the relatively small Rochdale and Oldham Star mills accepted the offer but Halifax and Sowerby Bridge felt the money being proffered was too small. Halifax, for example, considered its assets worth £85,000 and wanted a further £15,000 for goodwill.[558]

Ten years later, in 1915, the CWS tried again, this time successfully, buying Sowerby Bridge, Halifax and the smaller Colne Valley flour societies for a total outlay of £124,000 – considerably less than had been on the table in 1905.[559] The move was controversial with some, according to one *Co-operative News* report: 'A delegate stated that he was passing the Sowerby Bridge mills with a friend and remarked that he supposed the CWS had bought them. 'No', said his friend, 'They've stown 'em.''[560] The Halifax shareholders had been the last to agree, asking for £85,000 against the CWS's initial offer of £40,000 before digging in on a non-negotiable £65,000. The CWS refused to go above £50,000. In June 1915 the sale went through – for £50,000.[561]

The CWS's most significant acquisition in this period, in partnership with the Scottish CWS, had been of the independent Co-operative Insurance Society (CIS) in 1912-13 for £120,000, a price which gave the CIS's shareholders over £3 for their £1 shares. The relationship between the CWS and the CIS had been a vexed one for some years with the CWS developing its own insurance operations separate from the CIS. There had been long discussions and sometimes very heated arguments between the CWS and CIS about the advantages of consolidating co-operative insurance, and the CIS directors finally bowed to the inevitable in late 1912: 'The forces arrayed against the separate existence of the Insurance Society had been too great, and they recognised ... in order to enable the movement to work in harmony for the Wholesale Society to take them over,' said the CIS Chairman Thomas Wood at the time.[562] Nevertheless, the takeover was nearly thwarted when CWS delegates heard that the proposed deal included a payment of £3,000 to the CIS's directors for loss of office, representing ten years' fees apiece. At a CWS meeting in December, a Warrington delegate suggested the amount should be reduced to £1,000; the Failsworth society went further and suggested two years' fees. The Sheffield and Eccleshall society delegate took an even stronger position: 'His society strongly objected to have a price put on co-operative positions in the form of money,' *Co-operative News* reported. 'He hoped that it would never be that democracy would have any other price put on than that of the honour of having been elected by their fellows.' In the end, the CIS directors received £600, representing two years' fees, for loss of office.[563]

A similar debate was to take place three years later in 1915, at what the local press called the 'stormy' final meeting of the Sowerby Bridge Flour Society. The proposal for the Flour Society's directors to be compensated with two years' fees was strongly criticised by the Ripponden society delegate who argued that the directors had already been well rewarded. The meeting pondered another option: why not perhaps share some of the windfall with the workers too?[564]

Not everyone, however, regretted the moves towards consolidation of the independent co-operative societies within the CWS. One of the Sowerby Bridge Flour Society's directors saw it as a step forward in the move towards the one national co-operative society which J.C. Gray had called for so passionately in 1906.[565]

Following the Hebden Bridge Fustian Manufacturing Society's management committee meeting on 29 January 1918, a first exploratory meeting was held between the Society and the CWS on 12 February when it was agreed to set up a small negotiating team from each side. Arthur Ainley, John Holt – a committee member, from Todmorden co-operative – and Leonard Stocks represented the fustian society; the CWS appointed four representatives, including Moorhouse. This committee met on 4 March and discussed six issues the fustian society had identified: the issue of the profit bonus to employees; the arrangements for employees' savings; the future of the manager, secretary and traveller; the position of foremen and workers; and the arrangements for appointing liquidators. The sixth item was the compensation to be paid to committee members for loss of office.

Most of these seemed to be issues which could be sorted out. The minutes of the meeting reported that 'a general undertaking shall be given by the CWS that the interests of the employés shall not suffer by their loss of Bonus'. Arrangements would be made for the CWS to provide an avenue for employees' savings. The meeting also agreed 'that we set aside a lump sum (the amount to be mutually agreed upon) as compensation for loss of office' for the committee men.

The 4 March meeting also discussed how the buildings and plant were to be valued. There was something of a problem here from the fustian society's point of view, in that the prudent approach to depreciation which had been followed meant that the total capital expenditure over the years of £59,077 now showed up on the balance sheet as an asset of only £19,920. Ironically this weakened the Society's bargaining position. Before the next joint meeting, held on 25 March, Leonard Stocks, at the management committee's request, prepared a negotiating memo for his committee, drawing on a valuation for tax purposes carried out in 1909 and a further valuation for insurance purposes undertaken in 1912. The higher of these valued the capital assets at £53,616, and it was this figure which the fustian society presented initially to the CWS. Stocks' memo, which has survived, suggests that the management committee had also considered the implications of being offered £48,000 or £45,000. In the event, after some bargaining, the 25 March negotiations ended with the fustian society announcing that its 'rock bottom' price was £48,000.[566]

The deal was struck a month later. Ainley reported the meeting with the CWS team as follows:

> We met them again on Monday, April 22nd. The chairman told us they had, since meeting us, gone carefully into the figures and made us a certain offer as against the offer we had left with them a month previously. We told them we would retire and consider it. We had a talk amongst ourselves in another room and decided we should tell them we could not possibly accept the sum mentioned, and asked them if they could not reconsider it and extend it. They agreed if we would retire again to consider and after a little while they sent for us again and I may say they had substantially increased their offer. They had got within speaking distance of what we ourselves had suggested.[567]

The offer was £42,000. The fustian society's negotiators decided to accept it.

Thereafter, things progressed quickly. On 30 April Ainley called the workforce together to explain developments. He gave them a lengthy account of the negotiations and explained how it was intended that the CWS would compensate them for the loss of the profit share to labour paid by the fustian society. The week's paid holiday recently introduced by the CWS was of itself equivalent of about half the usual 5 per cent profit bonus, Ainley said, while the CWS also ran a thrift fund for its employees, first introduced in 1904. This was an early type of superannuation scheme. Where employees contributed 2½ per cent of wages to the fund, the employer added its own contribution: a further 1¼ per cent for workers paid over 30s a week and 2½ per cent for those on lower wages. The fund could be taken by workers when they left employment, or at any time after ten years. 'These two things alone, the week's holiday and the Thrift Fund in our opinion will quite counter-balance any advantage which you may have derived from your bonus on labour,' Ainley said. He added that the CWS was also proposing to introduce a savings bond scheme, to replace the fustian society's share savings arrangement. 'I hope I have said sufficient to enable you to make up your minds to come to the meeting next Saturday week, and vote solidly for the recommendation,' Ainley concluded.[568]

The meeting he referred to was the special general meeting of members, which had been called for Saturday 11 May. Ainley again made the principal speech. He began, 'I suppose this is the most important meeting which has taken place in the history of the society for more than forty years,' before going on to pay tribute to the founders and early pioneers of the society, mentioning Joseph Greenwood by name. He described the move which the CWS had made from wholesaling into manufacturing, and he then summarised the negotiations which had gone on between the fustian society and the CWS over recent weeks. The proposed purchase price, he pointed out, valued the assets at £22,000 more than their current book value on the balance sheet. Add on the payment by the CWS for stock, to be made at valuation, and include also the co-operative's reserve fund of £17,000 and there would be at least £2 for each £1 share. He proposed the motion to accept the offer and to put the Fustian Manufacturing Society into voluntary liquidation.[569]

There was one significant speaker against: Joseph Greenwood. Eighty-four years old by this stage, Greenwood contributed his own story of the early days. He talked of Neale and the Christian Socialists, of the battle in the early days to defend the bonus to labour principle, of the fustian society's engagement with the Oxford University Extension scheme and the commitment which it had made more generally to its home town of Hebden Bridge. Would the CWS have such an interest? – he doubted it. And he concluded by criticising the deal struck: '£42,000 was not much to think of ... it was as cheap as chips'.[570]

Greenwood's speech was that of an old man, and his history lesson a tale of a time long gone. A significant number of the workers in the audience that day would not even have been alive in the nineteenth century or known Victoria as their queen. He would have been listened to politely, but his views could no longer command attention. Around 350 people were present, comprising about 170 workers, 120 delegates of co-operative societies and 50 individual shareholders. The vote when it came was overwhelming: only five hands went up against the takeover.[571]

Greenwood's intervention demands consideration, however. Was £42,000 a fair price or did the fustian society sell itself too cheaply? Certainly there was a gross inequality in negotiating power between the two parties, with all the expertise concentrated within the CWS. It is significant that the negotiations took place at the CWS's head office in Manchester, rather than in Hebden Bridge. It is also perhaps relevant that the fustian society allowed their three negotiators to meet with four CWS representatives, and with a CWS member as chairman of the committee. If you had to face either the CWS or the Fustian Manufacturing Society in a negotiating situation, you would opt every time not to be up against the CWS.

Greenwood had made the point that, with the level of profits which had been generated in recent years, the CWS would get back its outlay relatively quickly, in around six or seven years. It was a fair point. In terms of a return on investment, the CWS's £42,000 would be earning a far greater rate of return than was current at that time.

Perhaps we should conclude, therefore, that £42,000, even though it was well above the worth of the fustian society as shown on the balance sheet, was a little too much of a bargain for the CWS. But this is not really the main issue. The substantive question is whether the fustian society's directors were right to enter into negotiations. Could the Society have continued as an independent co-operative? Was there an alternative?

The twentieth century was to demonstrate that some of the other productive co-operatives from the nineteenth century could enjoy very long lives: Leicester's Equity Shoes, for example, was first established in 1886, traded throughout the twentieth century before finally succumbing in 2009. The CWS itself continued to operate the Nutclough works in Hebden Bridge for half a century.

Nevertheless, the fustian society's directors were very aware that the exceptional trading performances of the First World War years would not continue and that the post-war years could not be expected to be a period just of business-as-usual. Ainley made this point at the May special meeting:

> People are asking what is going to be the outcome of business after the war. In my judgment, the only logical outcome will be that large bodies of employers will be associated together in order to get production to the highest state of efficiency ... The country will have to do everything it possibly can to bring manufactures up to the highest state of efficiency in order to be able to compete with the other nations of the world.

He went on to describe how the German manufacturers in the dyeing business had achieved international domination of their industry by successfully amalgamating their businesses.

> We shall have to move somewhat in the same direction, I believe, and from the co-operative point of view I think we ought to direct our energies so far as we can to see that all the businesses that we can ... should be put into the hands of the CWS, because, after all, unlike most monopolies they are a body who are out in the consumer's interest.[572]

This argument was very much the CWS's, too. Twenty years earlier J.T.W. Mitchell's successor as chairman of the CWS, Thomas Tweddell, had written in the CWS magazine *The Wheatsheaf*, 'In all the principal trades and in many of the smaller ones the drift is irresistible in the direction of concentration. For good or ill, we have entered an era of big capitals, operating through gigantic factories ...'[573]

This is a legitimate argument to put forward. Ainley and his colleagues would also have been aware that fashions, and technologies, were changing. The dominance of fustian in working-class wardrobes could no longer be taken for granted. Other materials, including flannel and flannelette, were taking over.

The fustian society's committee would also have been aware that the CWS had become an increasingly dominant customer of the co-operative. Data produced, probably by Stocks as part of the information he pulled together for the negotiating team, showed that by 1916 over 90 per cent of the trade with co-operative societies had been invoiced through the CWS; the percentage of trade done directly for the CWS had also increased (Table 6).

Table 6
Trade undertaken directly or indirectly with the CWS, 1910-1916[574]

Year	Total co-op trade	Total trade with CWS	percentage of co-op trade invoiced through CWS
1910	£43,667	£5,094	60 per cent
1911	£48,494	£6,223	82.6 per cent
1912	£49,289	£5,853	85.4 per cent
1913	£55,494	£7,067	85.4 per cent
1914	£49,514	£7,634	89.3 per cent
1915	£58,348	£9,583	88.2 per cent
1916	£56,044	£10,546	90.1 per cent

There was a further point, rather less positive, to bear in mind. The CWS had demonstrated that it was prepared to bid for the fustian society; if it were now to be turned down, it could be presumed to feel free thereafter to enter directly into the fustian business itself. It could be a direct competitor. It was the dilemma faced at Leicester Hosiery fifteen years earlier.

A leading figure in the CWS Duncan McInnes had stated two years earlier that the CWS should increase its involvement in the manufacture of cloth.[575] Its ability to do so, had it chosen to operate independently from the Fustian Manufacturing Society, was demonstrated by the fact that less than a year after acquiring the Nutclough it bought the adjacent Hangingroyd Mill in Hebden Bridge from its private owners for £30,000.[576] This second purchase gave the CWS 521 looms to add to the 244 in the Nutclough's weaving shed.

The May members' meeting agreed that the transfer to the CWS would be made at the end of the ten-day August holiday shutdown. This meant that the takeover technically would take place on 3 August. The final meeting of the Hebden Bridge Fustian Manufacturing Co-operative Society Ltd before it entered voluntary liquidation was the usual half-yearly July meeting, held on 27 July 1918, and it was a reflective sort of affair. Ainley again made the main speech: 'I have tried honestly to do my duty to the Society ... I always put the interests of the Society first ... I hope to be forgiven for any unintentional offence which I may have given and I wish the Nutclough Works even greater success and prosperity in the future.' The main decision of the meeting was to agree to pay the directors and auditors the equivalent of two years' remuneration for their loss of office. Ainley had been getting £26 a year as President, the nine committee men £22 per year.[577]

Leonard Stocks and the local accountant Cressweller Crabtree were the liquidators. It was to be a slow and tiresome process, similar in many ways to the process undertaken by executors when an individual dies. There were endless letters to be written, the need to liquidate the fustian society's various investments, and the final tax liabilities (including the wartime Excess Profits Tax) worked out and paid. Stocks undertook the bulk of the work. It was a 'trying and somewhat enervating time' said the local paper later.[578] Eventually, in August 1919, all was ready for the winding-up meeting. The sums were done, and each shareholder received £2 15s 7d for their £1 share.

Before then there was, however, a sensitive issue for Stocks and Crabtree to resolve. It became clear in the Autumn of 1918 that the CWS had as part of the original negotiations put aside £1,000 which it intended to be shared equally between the ten members of the old management committee for loss of office.

Stocks was uncomfortable: 'We do not feel justified in so dealing with the amount (seeing the Directors of the Fustian Society have received an amount equal to two years' salary from the Fustian Society in respect of their office) until we have obtained the formal sanction of the members of the society,' he wrote in March 1919. The CWS, a little unhappy at the implications of this approach and preferring a quieter solution, responded: 'Our Directors expected that the directors of the Fustian Society would intimate to their members that they were to receive a sum from the Society [CWS] and would not make any claim on the funds of the [Fustian] Society'.

We have to assume that this problem was simply a misunderstanding but Stocks summoned his members to a special general meeting to discuss it. John Holt, from Todmorden, wrote to Stocks: 'There is one thing that should be pointed out to the Meeting if there is any quibbling about it, and that is that this £1,000 if not given to the old Directors will not come into the hands of the Liquidators to be dispersed to the shareholders'.[579] In the end, there was no quibbling. The meeting, held on 5 April, formally approved the extra payment.[580] The directors ended up with approaching seven years' compensation apiece for their loss of office.

CHAPTER 15

CONCLUSION

All stories require a proper ending, and there are some loose ends which are asking to be tied up.

Arthur Ainley was not to enjoy the extra CWS windfall voted through in April 1919. He died, still only in his mid-fifties, on 2 December 1918, having been suddenly taken ill. He was a victim of the terrible Spanish influenza pandemic which is estimated to have taken at least fifty million lives worldwide that year.[581]

Leonard Stocks' torrid time as the fustian society's liquidator completed a dismal period for him, for news of his son William's death in Palestine had come through right in the middle of the negotiations with the CWS. He was confirmed in his post (redefined as 'chief clerk and cashier') by the CWS following the takeover and worked at the Nutclough until early October 1924, when he was taken ill. He died a few days later, on 13 October, in a Manchester nursing home. 'Kindly and thoughtful in disposition, men such as he are rare nowadays,' wrote one of his friends to the local paper following his death.[582]

Sam Greenwood leaves our story almost as quietly as he entered it in 1909. He continued to manage the Nutclough Mill for six years after the takeover, retiring after 44 years' service at the end of 1926. There was probably an element of early retirement involved: Greenwood would only recently have turned sixty.[583]

S.C. (Sam) Moore appears to have lost his status as Traveller after the takeover and was reported in the local press in July 1918 as 'a commercial traveller, at present acting as a warehouseman'.[584] He continued to be active politically and among posts held was a Mytholmroyd urban district councillor. He was also the Labour representative on the local Military Service Tribunal assessing claims for conscientious objection during the war.[585]

Robert Halstead retired from the Co-operative Productive Federation in 1921 with a gratuity of £400 but no pension. He and his wife Martha (they had no children) moved from Leicester to Rochdale and then almost immediately to Bristol where Robert died in 1930, aged 72. He was buried there at Kingswood parish church.[586]

Crossley Greenwood did not stay long at Letchworth and seems to have returned to Hebden Bridge. He was forty when, in March 1911, he married Ada Arthur, originally from Wisbech, in Barnet and shortly afterwards the couple were recorded as living in North Finchley.[587] If family stories are to be believed, Crossley was occupied in the war in the procurement of horses for the military. By the end of the war, in December 1918, he was in Winnipeg, Canada, and working in the civil service ('My work here is awfully slow. I could do it all in half day each week, but there is no advancement,' he wrote to Leonard Stocks.)[588]

At the end of his life Crossley was still in touch with his niece Ethel Greenwood, the daughter of his brother William, by which time he was living on the south coast in Bournemouth. Ethel had kept the Greenwood name alive at the Nutclough Mill for all her working life, gaining a long-service award from the CWS in June 1960. Ethel sent her uncle a cheery postcard from Hebden Bridge in the summer of 1959; Crossley was to die in Bournemouth in December that year, aged 88.[589]

What of Joseph Greenwood himself? Joseph kept active in his retirement. He became a JP in 1910 and remained on the local urban district council until 1912.[590] With admirable chutzpah, or perhaps brass neck, he continued to put himself forward – successfully – for elections to the Co-operative Union's Central Board until 1920, when he was awarded the status of honorary member of the Board. He seems to have attended his last meeting of the North-West section in late 1920.[591]

At home, he spent time in his garden and greenhouse at the back of his house in Sandy Gate but he also frequented the billiards room at the Hebden Bridge Liberal Club. His prowess at billiards gained local renown; he won at least one competition when he was in his mid-eighties.[592]

Greenwood was widowed a second time in the autumn of 1915, when Ellen died.[593] He was to give his friends a final surprise, marrying for a third time in February 1920, when he was 86. His bride, also widowed, was, like his first wife another Sarah, Mrs Sarah Bancroft, and she was 77. They lived in companionship in Sandy Gate until Joseph's eventual death, aged almost 91, on 4 December 1924. 'The co-operative movement, and many other movements aiming at the betterment of humanity, have lost a 'Grand Old Man', whose life might be epitomised in one word – service,' said *Co-operative News*.[594]

Greenwood had looked after his money carefully and he died with a gross estate worth £9,475 and a net estate of £6,730. He was buried in the Baptist graveyard in Sandy Gate, Hebden Bridge, only a very short distance from J.C. Gray's grave. Gray, it will be remembered, had suffered ill health at the end of his life and had died in Manchester in 1912, with his body returned to his old home town of Hebden Bridge. A year later in January 1913 a fine marble monument subscribed to his memory by the co-operative movement had been formally unveiled at a ceremony in the graveyard.

'Whilst a memorial in cold marble may be something to look at, and a shrine for calling up memories of a distinguished comrade, let us seek rather to honour him by perpetuating his outlook,' *Co-operative News* said.[595] Joseph Greenwood's last resting place by contrast to Gray's is marked by a simple gravestone, but something similar could also be said of him.

***

So how then are we to assess the contribution made by Greenwood and his fellow co-operative pioneers of Hebden Bridge?

We can, like Greenwood himself at the 1918 special members' meeting which agreed the CWS takeover, have a sense of disappointment at the way the story of the Hebden Bridge Fustian Manufacturing Co-operative came to an end. There can be a feeling of anti-climax, perhaps, in the fact that the idealistic venture into 'self-employment' which Greenwood and his friends had originally launched had fizzled out in its final years with industrial relations difficulties and individual profit-taking.

An alternative moment to end this book would have been possible: we could have concluded the story, as we began it, with a celebratory event in the Hebden Bridge Co-operative Hall. We could have drawn a line on Saturday 17 April 1909, the day of Joseph Greenwood's retirement party. This was, by all accounts, quite an occasion. J.C. Gray and other old colleagues had turned up to applaud as Greenwood was presented with a 18-carat gold watch – one which, appropriately enough, had been made for him by the watchmaking co-operative society in Coventry. Greenwood had allowed himself a short reminiscence of the early days of the co-operative before the singing and dancing and partying had begun. Festivities had continued long into the Hebden Bridge night, with the last people leaving the Co-operative Hall just before midnight. Greenwood's retirement do was, the *Co-operative News* reported, one of the most enjoyable gatherings ever held in connection with the society.[596]

After 1909, without Joseph Greenwood at the helm, the fustian society inevitably moved into a new phase of its existence. But ending the story with Greenwood's retirement, tempting though it might be, is too easy an option. To get a full sense of the story of Greenwood and his co-operative, we do need to see what happened next. The legacy is part of the story too.

Nevertheless, an adequate appraisal of the Hebden Bridge Fustian Manufacturing Society should not be one that is unduly coloured by the events of the final few years. This was a business which, after all, operated successfully for 48 years, one which was both highly successful in commercial terms and strongly rooted in its community. Greenwood was right to hark back at that 1918 members' meeting to some of the highlights of the past – the battle to defend the workers' share of profits, or the University Extension work, for example.

Greenwood was on numerous occasions very clear about what had been his motivating factor – it was to build a business which gave the workers power over their working lives. More than that, it was to contribute to their general emancipation from the 'ceaseless toil' to which many had given their waking hours. 'The first object of the Hebden Bridge Society was the redemption of the working people,' he said on one occasion, adding, just in case there was any confusion on this point, 'and not simply to serve distributive societies'.[597]

But he also admitted on several occasions that what he and his colleagues had achieved at Hebden Bridge was, inevitably, less than perfect. 'They were conscious of many weak points in the constitution and working of their society; still they were trying honestly to work out the great problem of the reconciliation of capital and labour and they hoped that out of their imperfect society something better in the future might be evolved,' he said in 1887.[598]

As he described it to the Royal Commission on Labour five years later, there were different ways that productive co-operatives could be structured. The best, the 'higher form of co-operation', was this: 'Societies composed of working men employing themselves in their own industries and based on the principle of elevating the workers in each industry by the results of their own work; the workers subscribing all their own capital, managing their own affairs amongst themselves and taking all the profit to themselves either as dividend on their wages or on their capital'. But Greenwood had to admit to the Royal Commission that, at that stage, there were very few examples of co-operatives run in this way. Furthermore, this way of working might only prove to be achievable in a few limited industries, because of the difficulty of obtaining capital.[599]

The Fustian Manufacturing Society had not been able to achieve Greenwood's 'higher form' of co-operation. Along the way, it had necessarily found that it had to make compromises. E.O. Greening was inclined to blame the perfidiousness of the distributive societies, motivated by greed:

'The stores had been invited in as friends and allies of the workers; they had been allowed to alter the rules so as to give themselves the lion's share of the profits, they had become the practical masters of the concern,' he told *Co-operative News'* readers in 1881.[600] Greenwood would probably have made the point in a much more nuanced way, one which continued to see the distributive societies as forming part of a movement for social change and working-class betterment. But, as we have seen, his lifelong determination to defend the profit bonus to labour principle was to demonstrate that the fustian society was still run at a fundamental level for the workers' benefit.

Joseph Greenwood would have recognised today's workers' co-operatives as direct descendents of his own endeavour. The same impulse which led Greenwood and his fellow workers to attempt to create their own worker-run enterprise continues to be there today. The history from his time to ours is not a continuous one, however. A deep fissure with the past occurred during the twentieth century which meant that when a generation of co-operative activists began to develop a new wave of workers' co-operatives in Britain in the later decades of the last century, they did so without knowledge or understanding of the experiences of those in the early productive co-operatives.

This fracture is to be regretted and perhaps need not have happened. Hebden Bridge's Nutclough Mill had closed but several of the other nineteenth century productive co-operatives were still trading right through into the 1980s and beyond.

So, trying belatedly to rebuild the bridges back to that forgotten past, what lessons can we take from the experiences of co-operative manufacturing in Hebden Bridge? One concerns the way that the 1918 sale of the business took place. It is understandable that those who approved the co-operative's rules, drawn up with Edward Vansittart Neale's help in the early years of the venture, found it impossible to anticipate that, several decades in the future and in a new century, the co-operative would choose to distribute its accumulated assets and reserves in the way that it did. Effectively the fruits of 48 years' trading and careful husbandry of reserves were passed out to those who happened to be shareholders and employees (and in particular those who happened to be committee members) in the summer of 1918. Early sacrifices, by Greenwood and others, went to reward a later generation.

The issues of demutualisation, in its most brutal form through so-called carpet-bagging, have been live issues in recent decades in Britain and elsewhere and there is now much more understanding of the value of including asset locks in co-operative and not-for-profit legal rules. There still remains little discussion, however, of the broader implications of developing co-operative businesses through long periods of time and across several generations, and of the implicit contracts between the generations which this implies.

What assessment do we make of the provision in the rules which prevented employee members of the co-operative from being on the management committee? We have to guard against judging the past by today's standards, and while it can be superficially comforting to seek to find in past struggles our own preoccupations we should resist the temptation to assess the story of the Hebden Bridge Fustian Manufacturing Society simply through the prism of the workers' co-operative movement today. Nevertheless, there was at least one former employee of the Hebden Bridge fustian society who felt that the absence of workers from the management committee was a factor which contributed to the co-operative's eventual demise. Robert Halstead's assessment was offered at the time of Greenwood's death in 1924, in his generous obituary notice which was published in *Co-partnership* magazine.

Halstead was highly critical of the CWS takeover: 'Personal greed and dominating organisations beat him [Greenwood] and... largely destroyed his essential life's work.' But there were lessons which could be drawn: 'He was, perhaps, too much the Society, and when his large and dominant influence was taken from its oversight and management, the workers had not sufficiently acquired the habit of self-determination,' Halstead added.[601] It is hard to disagree with this assessment.

As this study has suggested, the way that the fustian society developed was towards what today we describe as the multi-stakeholder co-operative model. These hybrid models – where, for example, co-operative membership is shared between employees and the business's customers, or between employees and investors – are becoming increasingly a feature of the co-operative economy both in Britain and elsewhere. The Hebden Bridge experience would suggest, however, that this is a model to be adopted with some caution. Combining the interests of different groups of members may seem straightforward enough when a co-operative is drawing up its rulebook, but achieving a fair and genuinely co-operative reconciliation between potentially different interests in the context of a trading business can be challenging – or so at least E.O. Greening might have advised from what he had observed at the Nutclough Mill.

Those active in the workers' co-operative movement today are aware of the ambiguities which their organisations can face, as businesses with principles and objectives which may be antithetical to capitalism but which are nevertheless operating within the confines of the capitalist system.[602] The issues faced today are not, however, unique to our own time. One of the most intelligent analyses of the position of workers' co-operatives – although he called them productive co-operatives – is that offered in 1889 by the eminent economist Professor Alfred Marshall from Cambridge University. It may be appropriate to allow him the last word.

Marshall, who was a critical friend – but still a genuine friend – of the co-operative movement, was invited that year to give the Presidential address at the Co-operative Congress. Of all the numerous Presidential addresses which were given at Co-operative Congresses over the years, of differing degrees of quality and value, Marshall's is one which more than most deserves still to be read.

He began by suggesting that, in comparison with production, co-operative shopkeeping was a much more straightforward proposition:

> The system of co-operative retailing has such great inherent economies that it is likely to succeed if carried out with good faith and honesty and average good sense: the more business genius it has the better it will succeed but it can fairly well flourish without business genius.

But independent productive societies were altogether a more challenging proposition:

> There is no doubt that they labour under great difficulties. The management by working men of the businesses in which they are themselves employed is neither as efficient nor as free from friction as it would be if we social reformers had been able to arrange the world to our liking.

Idealism could bump up against the real world. Marshall continued:

> Managing a business is a very difficult matter. To carry on a great business, nothing is wanted except to organise it properly; but then that is just the difficulty. It is as easy as beating the big drum in an orchestral concert. Nothing more is needed than that you should do the right thing at the right time, but there are not many people who can do it.

Marshall went on to tackle one of Greenwood's key concerns, the issue of ensuring that a co-operative business is adequately capitalised:

> There is another difficulty. Nearly every kind of business requires every year a larger capital to carry it on; and the working man has seldom much

capital. It has been commonly said that in competition capital employs labour and pays it a fixed wage; but that in co-operation labour employs capital, and pays it a fixed rate of interest. But that is more easily said than done.

Marshall refined the argument:

In fact it is not true that under competition labour is hired by capital; it is hired by business ability in command of capital; and it is not true that in co-operation capital is hired by labour; it may be hired by the business ability that lives in the heads that the working men have on their shoulders; but if they have not much business ability, they will not get much capital, either of their own or of anyone else's; and if they get it, they will not keep it long; and it all comes back to that ...

What of the need for leadership? One of the facets of many workers' co-operative businesses (today, as much as in the past) which generally goes unremarked but deserves much greater discussion is the fact that – despite the collective and collaborative nature of the business form – their success is often closely linked up with one charismatic individual, or perhaps a handful of key people.

Marshall understood this too, and in the context of his time we can overlook the use of the masculine gender:

A productive society often owes whatever success it has almost entirely to a few men, perhaps to one man, of exceptional ability, fervent and strong in the co-operative faith. And then it is constantly at the mercy of cruel Death. He snaps the threads of a few lives, or perhaps of only one, and the society dwindles and decays, or is converted into a greedy joint-stock company; and so cherished hopes are once again disappointed and the proud boasts of confident co-operators are brought to naught.

And yet despite all these difficulties, Marshall said that he understood why so many of the most committed co-operators had such cherished hopes and warm affections towards productive co-operatives. It was because these co-operatives seemed 'to point more directly towards the true aims of the co-operative faith', he said. It was because 'they make the ordinary working man to get nearer to responsible work'.

In particular, it was because co-operative working offered an alternative to the wasteful way that work was conventionally organised: because co-operatives 'tend more directly to utilise *the* great waste product – the higher abilities that are latent among the working classes …'

Marshall offered a summation of his observations: 'Well then, productive co-operation is a very difficult thing, but it is worth doing'.[603]

Running the Nutclough Mill in Hebden Bridge as a co-operative undertaking was not always straightforward. But Joseph Greenwood would have agreed with Professor Marshall: it was worth doing.

AUTHOR'S AFTERWORD

The young Beatrice Potter, it seems, did not necessarily enjoy her research for the book *The Co-operative Movement in Great Britain*. 'A grind and no mistake! Six hours a day reading and note-taking from those endless volumes of the *Co-operative News*. A treadmill of disjointed facts, in themselves utterly uninteresting and appallingly dry ... A grim determination to finish with it makes me sit at the work longer than is good for body or mind,' she confided to her journal.[604]

I'm pleased to say that my experience hasn't been such an unhappy one, although I can confirm that there is certainly no shortage of material for researchers to go through in the pages of *Co-operative News*, (and I feel obliged to make the point that Potter only had twenty or so years' worth of editions to tackle – so what precisely *was* she complaining about?)

The effort feels worthwhile if only for those golden moments when the text leaps out from the page. I quoted early in this book the comment from a *Co-operative News* editorial that 'for a co-operator not to know Hebden Bridge is to argue himself unknown' although I did not at that point choose to attribute it to its author, who was E.O. Greening. I also did not go on to include the next few sentences in Greening's article:

> Just as by magical association of ideas we link Rochdale with successful co-operative distribution, we are coming to link Hebden Bridge with the idea of successful co-operative production. The story of Rochdale has been often told; the history of the Hebden Bridge Fustian Manufacturing Society equally deserves the attention of our co-operative historians. I do not pretend now to write it. I hope someone with sufficient time and adequate ability will yet perform the task.[605]

It is for others to assess my ability, but I do agree with Greening that the history of the Fustian Manufacturing Society deserves attention. It has simply taken more than a century and a quarter from the time Greening was writing to get the story into print.

Initially this seemed as though it was going to be little more than a booklet, a relatively quick canter through the outlines of the story of the life of Joseph Greenwood and of his mill at Nutclough. My worry was that the primary material would simply not be there after such a long period of time.

I need not have worried. Of course, it is enormously helpful that Greenwood wrote two accounts of the early decades of the fustian society, his *Story of the Formation* and his *Brief Sketch*. His series of articles for *Co-partnership* magazine which together comprise his *Reminiscences of Sixty Years Ago*, a retirement project he undertook immediately after stepping down as manager, are also a valuable starting point, as is his testimony before the Royal Commission on Labour in 1892.

But what became clear as my research developed was how much more material there is available, both to fill in some of the details of the fustian society's story and to put its development in the wider context of the co-operative movement of its time. Of course, there are gaps in the records which are to be regretted: the real jewel which is missing is the fustian society's minute book which, who knows, may yet be found to have survived. It is regrettable too that the fustian society's records held in the National Archives (stored most of the time in a salt mine in Cheshire) hold only the last two annual returns submitted to the Registrar of Friendly Societies; earlier returns and detailed accounts are missing, although the file does contain a helpful series of rule books as well as liquidation and share ownership records.

Against this we can set the remarkable good fortune which has seen two large archive boxes of material collected when the CWS finally closed its Hebden Bridge operation recently re-emerge from within the Co-operative Group's head office in Manchester. These boxes include both the correspondence between the fustian society and local trade unions before and during the First World War and detailed records about the CWS takeover and the liquidation process. These archive boxes, part of a much larger haul of archive material saved when the Co-operative Group was preparing to move to its new head office, provide the raw material for chapters 13 and 14.

These records – and so much other material which I have used in this book – are available to researchers through the National Co-operative Archive (part of the Co-operative Heritage Trust), located at Holyoake House in Manchester. My first thanks therefore must go to the archivist Gillian Lonergan and to Sophie Stewart (as well as to their erstwhile colleague Adam Shaw) for their enormous help during my period of research. Stephen Yeo, chair at time of writing of the Co-operative Heritage Trust, has gone out of his way to help me, and I very much appreciate his insights and suggestions. My thanks too to Mervyn Wilson, recently retired Principal of the Co-operative College, to Linda Shaw, to Jennifer Mabbott (Manager, Rochdale Pioneers Museum), and to Rachael Vorberg-Rugh.

In Hebden Bridge, I have had great help and support from two professional historians with a deep knowledge of the Lancashire textile industry and its trade unions, Terry Wyke and Alan Fowler. There are a host of people to thank who are associated with the extremely active Hebden Bridge Local History Society: Frank Woolrych and Ann Kilbey (Pennine Horizons Digital Archive) for their help with the images for this book; Dr Nigel Smith, archivist; Justine Wyatt, who first encouraged me to take an interest in Joseph Greenwood; Diana Monahan; Barbara Atack and many others. John Rhodes, David Fletcher, Mike Barrett, Peter Thomas and Tony Boughton have also offered their help in different ways.

I am grateful to Charles Gould, director-general of the International Co-operative Alliance and to the ICA's Jan Schiettecatte for facilitating my visit to the ICA archives, and to the librarians and archivists at the Modern Records Centre (Warwick), the Hull History Centre, Cambridge University Library, West Yorkshire Archives Service (Halifax), the British Library, the Working Class Movement Library (Salford), the National Archives, the Hebden Bridge and Halifax reference libraries, the London School of Economics library, the Bodleian Library and The Queen's College Oxford library. At Merlin Press, my thanks to Tony Zurbrugg and Adrian Howe.

I also acknowledge with thanks the help from Joseph Greenwood's great-great granddaughter Irene Kirk and her husband Phil and great-grandson Jim Wilkinson and his wife Eleta.

A particular thank you is needed to Jane Scullion, for her support and encouragement during the writing of this book.

As authors always say at this point, any errors or omissions are mine alone. I fear that mistakes may have crept into this account, but I hope others will now want to take a closer interest both in the fustian society and the wider story of the early productive co-operatives and will be able both to identify any errors and take forward my efforts. My research notes, which include a significant number of photocopies and transcriptions, will in due course be placed in the Hebden Bridge Local History Society archive and may be accessed by contacting the archivist.

BIBLIOGRAPHY AND SOURCES

Archive collections
National Co-operative Archives, Manchester.
Letters of E.O. Greening.
Letters of George Jacob Holyoake (3611).
Mytholmroyd Co-operative Society.
CWS Minute Book numbers 88-9, 91-2, (1916-1920) [minute book 90 is currently missing].
CWS Balance sheets, selected years.
Co-operative Group, archive boxes C64 and C65 (HB Fustian Society archives).

International Co-operative Alliance (Vilvoorde, near Brussels).
Archive box 4024249 (ICA minute books and documents 1892-1910).

National Archives, Kew.
FS17/23 (HB Fustian Society).
LAB 2/187/IC478/1917/Parts1and2 (1916 strike, HB Fustian Society).
ED 27/8916 (Joseph Greenwood Trust).
16/941/H202 no 1874 (HBICS v HB Cotton & Commercial).
LAB 83/1327, 2/1024/IC446/1917/PartsI-III (Industrial arbitration, Hebden Bridge).

Hebden Bridge Local History Archive.
IND/13 (Eaves dispute).
LMG 24-30 (Goldthorp papers).
HBLSS 1/1 (Minute book, Hebden Bridge Literary and Scientific Society, 1905-1913).
CJ/21 (sale of HBICS, 1968).
MIN/1 (Minute book, Hebden Bridge Mechanics' Institute).
GJ A MISC HB4 (HBICS almanac 1880).
WEA/281-b (Research notes for *Pennine Valley*).
Pennine Heritage collection (lecture notes 1914).

West Yorkshire Archive Service, Calderdale.
TU:39 (HB Ind Co-operative Society archive).
TU:90 (AUCO archive).
TU:70 (Cragg Vale Co-operative Society, Mytholmroyd Co-operative Society).
TU:36 (Todmorden Weavers' Association archive).
DW:1221, SU/D:71 (Purchase of Nutclough estate).
BIP/HB:7, 18, 82, 109, 119, 121, 123, 193, 266, 268, 289, 306, 481, 498, 579, 631, 681 (architects' plans, works at Nutclough Mill and estate).
WYC:1356/18/1 (conveyance, J Greenwood to son).

Oxford University archives.
CE3/18; CE3/21/1-2; CE3/22/4; CE3/20; CE3/28/1-31; CE3/52/5; CE3/315/42 (Oxford University Extension).
CE3/45/120, 121, 122A, 124, 125, 126 (Correspondence).
CE3/35; CE3/37/10-13, 15-16 (Summer Meetings).

Cambridge University archives.
(archives of the Board of Extra-Mural Studies)
15/2, 3, 5, 6; 13/1; 2/16; 43/8 (University Extension and Summer Meetings)

Modern Records Centre, Warwick.
MSS310/1/2/1-2, 5-7; 310/1/4/1; 310/1/5/1 (Labour Association minute books)

Hull History Centre.
DCF/1-2, 5 (CPF minute book).
DLB/1/97, /101; DLB2/50 (Dictionary of Labour Biography: JC Gray, J Greenwood, R Halstead).

Privately held.
Abstract of the Title of the Trustees of the Will of Joseph Greenwood deceased to land and premises in Sandy Gate Hebden Bridge in the County of York.

Census records 1841-1911

Births, deaths and marriages records; wills and probate records

Newspapers and journals

Agricultural Economist
The Commonwealth, A Social Magazine
Co-operative News [CN]
The Co-operative Official
Cotton Factory Times
Halifax Courier
Halifax Guardian
Hebden Bridge Times (1882-1930) [HBT]
Huddersfield Chronicle and West Yorkshire Advertiser
Labour Co-partnership; Co-partnership
Leeds Mercury
The Morning Post
Oxford University Extension Gazette
The Producer (CWS)
Todmorden and District News
Todmorden and Hebden Bridge Weekly Advertiser
University Extension Journal
The Wheatsheaf
Yorkshire Factory Times

Year books and annuals etc

Co-operative Congress Reports (1869-1921)
Co-operative Directory (1887, 1893, 1900, 1905)
Co-operative Productive Federation Report and Balance Sheet (1909-)
Co-operative Productive Federation Year Book (1897-1899);Co-operators' Year Book (from 1900)
Co-operative Wholesale Societies Annual; CWS People's Year Book (from 1919)
International Co-operative Alliance Congress reports (1895, 1896, 1897, 1900, 1902, 1904)
Women's Co-operative Guild annual reports

Primary sources

Published by Hebden Bridge Fustian Manufacturing Co-operative Society
Report of Coming-of-age celebrations of the Hebden Bridge Fustian Co-operative Society Ltd Sep 23rd and 26th 1891 (reprinted in booklet form from the Co-operative News, Todmorden and district News, Todmorden Advertiser), Hebden Bridge: Hebden Bridge Fustian Manufacturing Co-operative Society, 1891.
The Industrial Commonwealth at Hebden Bridge, [reprinted from *Yorkshire Factory Times*, Mar 5 and Mar 12 1897], Manchester: Co-operative Printing Society, 1897 [Hebden Bridge Local History archive, ref IND/17].

Rules, Sep 1870; amended rules July 1872, Jan./Feb. 1873; amended rules Jan./Feb. 1877; amended rules Feb. 1882; amended rules July 1884; amended rules Jan. 1890; amended rules 1908.

Writings by Joseph Greenwood
Greenwood, 'Henry', 'Hebden Bridge Manufacturing Society', in *Proceedings of the Co-operative Congress 1872*, Manchester, 1872 (It is assumed that this attribution to a 'Henry' Greenwood is erroneous; the paper is in the style of Joseph Greenwood and no Henry Greenwood was present at the Co-operative Congress that year).
Greenwood, Joseph, *A Brief Sketch of Twenty-one Years' Work in Co-operative Production*, Hebden Bridge: The Hebden Bridge Fustian Manufacturing Society, 1891; revised edition, *A Brief Sketch of Twenty-six Years' Work in Co-operative Production*, Hebden Bridge: The Hebden Bridge Fustian Manufacturing Society, n.d. [1897].
—, 'Co-operative Production', in *Co-operative News*, vol. X, no. 49 (6 Dec. 1879), pp. 791-3.
—, 'Education in Co-operation', in *Co-operative News*, vol. VI, no. 25 (29 May 1875), pp. 292-3.
—, 'The Fustian Society and its Relations with Distributive Societies', in *Co-operative News*, vol. IV, no. 10 (7 Mar. 1874), pp. 110-11.
—, 'The Place of the Labourer in Co-operation', in *Proceedings of the Co-operative Congress 1877*, Manchester, 1877.
—, 'Reminiscences of Sixty Years Ago', in *Co-Partnership*, vol. 15 (1909) Sep. 1909, Oct. 1909, Nov. 1909, Dec. 1909; vol. 16 (1910) Jan. 1910, Feb. 1910, Mar. 1910, Apr. 1910, June 1910, July 1910, Sep. 1910, Oct. 1910, Nov. 1910, Dec. 1910; vol. 17

(1911) Jan. 1911, Feb. 1911, Mar. 1911, Apr. 1911, May 1911, June 1911, July 1911, Aug. 1911. Also reprinted in *Hebden Bridge Times,* 1909-1911.
—, *The Story of the Formation of the Hebden Bridge Fustian Manufacturing Society Ltd,* Manchester: Central Co-operative Board, 1888.

Writings by J.C. Gray
Allan, John and Gray, J.C., *The Co-operative Union: Its necessity and its advantages,* Manchester: Co-operative Union Ltd, 1892.
Gray, J.C., 'Association in Production', in *Co-operative News,* vol. XVI, no. 1 (3 Jan. 1885), pp. 4-5.
—, 'Co-operation and the Poor', in *The Co-operative Wholesale Societies Annual,* 1902.

—, *Co-operation as a Factor in the Education of the Citizen,* Manchester: Co-operative Union Ltd, 1891.
—, *Co-operative Production, A Paper,* Manchester: Co-operative Union Ltd, 1886.
—, *Co-operative Production in Great Britain,*(reprinted from the 'Age of Steel', Jan. 1887), Manchester: Central Co-operative Board, 1887.
—, *Co-operation versus Competition, A Paper read at the Conferences of the Calderdale and Huddersfield District Associations, held in Hebden Bridge on January 21st 1888 and at Huddersfield on February 18th 1888,* Manchester: Central Co-operative Board, 1888.
—, 'The Educational Scheme of the Co-operative Union and the New Code issued by the Educational Department of the Government for Evening Continuation Schools', in Allan, John and Gray, J.C., *The Necessity for Educational Funds; Educational Scheme and the New Code,* Manchester: Co-operative Newspaper Society, n.d.
—, 'The Loyalty of Distributive Societies to Productive Societies', in *Co-operative News,* vol. XII, no. 12 (19 Mar. 1881), pp. 183-4.

Writings by Robert Halstead
Halstead, Robert, *Co-operative Production viewed in the Light of some first Principles,* London: Labour Association, 1898.
—, 'Co-partnership in Store and Works; in *Co-operators' Year Book 1907,* Leicester: Co-operative Productive Federation, 1907.
—, 'Practical Co-operation', in *Economic Review,* vol. VIII, Oct. 1898, pp. 446-62.
—, 'Some Co-operative Reminiscences', in *The Co-operative Official,* vol. III., no 31 (Oct. 1922), pp. 179-80; no. 32 (Nov. 1922), pp. 203-4.
—, 'Some Thoughts of a Workman concerning the Plea for a Living Wage', in *Economic Review,* vol. V, July 1895, pp. 350-69.
—, 'The Stress of Competition from the Workman's Point of View', in *Economic Review,* vol. IV, Jan. 1894, pp. 43-59.
—, *Variation of Wages in some Labour Co-partnership Workshops* (paper read before the Economic Section of the British Association, Sep. 10 1900), London: The Labour Association, n.d.
—, 'Working men and University Extension', in *Oxford University Extension*

Gazette, vol. III, no. 32 (May 1893), pp. 108-10.
Writings by other Hebden Bridge Fustian Society participants
Greenwood, William, 'Fifty Years of British Industry from the Workman's Point of View' in *Economic Review*, vol. X, July 1900, pp. 323-32.
Moore, S.C., *Evolution of Industry in Sowerby Division*, Sowerby Division Conference of Youth, 1913.
—, 'The Industrial Evolution of a Manufacturing Village', in *The Economic Journal*, vol. 21, no. 84 (Dec. 1911), pp. 613-24.
—, 'The Trades Board Act at Work', in *The Economic Journal*, vol. 23, no. 91 (Sep. 1913), pp. 443-7.

Secondary sources

Books: The co-operative movement
Acland, Arthur H. Dyke and Jones, Benjamin, *Working Men Co-operators*, London: Cassell, 1884 rev. 1893.
Aves, Ernest, *Co-operative Industry*, London: Methuen, 1907.
Backstrom, Philip N., *Christian Socialism and Cooperation in Victorian England*, London: Croom Helm, 1974.
Birchall, Johnston, *Co-op, The People's Business*, Manchester: Manchester University Press, 1994.
—, *The International Co-operative Movement*, Manchester: Manchester University Press, 1997
Blandford, Thomas, *Co-operative Workshops in Great Britain*, London: The Labour Association, 1898.
Blaszak, Barbara J., *The Matriarchs of England's Cooperative Movement*, Westport: Greenwood Press, 2000.
Board of Trade, Profit-Sharing and Co-partnership (Labour Department), [George Stapylton Barnes] *Report on profit-sharing and labour co-partnership in the United Kingdom*, Cd.6496, London, 1912.
Board of Trade (Profit-Sharing) (Labour Department) *Report by Mr D. F. Schloss on Profit-Sharing*, C.7458, London, 1894.
Board of Trade (Labour Department), *Report on Workmen's Co-operative Societies in the United Kingdom*, Cd.698, London, 1901.
Board of Trade [J. Lowry Whittle], *Report to the Board of Trade on Profit-Sharing*, C. 6267, London, 1891.
Bonner, Arnold, *British Co-operation*, Manchester: Co-operative Union Ltd, 1961.
Carr-Saunders A.M. et al, *Consumers' Co-operation in Great Britain*, London: George Allen and Unwin, 1938, rev. ed. 1940.
Cattell, Charles C., *Co-operative Production*, Birmingham: G.H. Reddalls, 1874.
Cole, G.D.H., *A Century of Co-operation*, Manchester: Co-operative Union Ltd, 1944.
Co-operative Productive Federation, *Historical sketches of our productive societies*, London: Co-operative Productive Federation, 1893.
Crimes, Tom, *Edward Owen Greening*, Manchester: Co-operative Union Ltd, 1923.
Fairbairn, Brett, *The Meaning of Rochdale: The Rochdale Pioneers and the Co-*

operative Principles, Saskatoon: Centre for the Study of Co-operatives, University of Saskatchewan, 1994.

Fay, C.R., *Co-operation at Home and Abroad*, London: P.S. King & Son, 1908.

Flanagan, Desmond, *A Centenary Story of the Co-operative Union*, Manchester: Co-operative Union Ltd, 1969.

Gaffin, Jean and Thoms, David, *Caring and Sharing: The Centenary History of the Co-operative Women's Guild*, Manchester: Co-operative Union Ltd, 1983.

Gide, Charles, *The International Co-operative Alliance*, London: International Co-operative Alliance, n.d. [c. 1914-18].

Gregory, N.H. *A Century's Progress 1848-1948, The story of a hundred years of co-operation in Hebden Bridge*, Hebden Bridge, 1948.

Grey, Albert Henry George [Earl], *What Co-operation will do for the People*, London: The Labour Association, 1898.

Gurney, Sybella, *Sixty Years of Co-operation*, London: The Labour Association, 1897.

Harwood, H.W., *100 Years of Co-operation, the Midgley Story*, Midgley, n.d. [1961?].

Holyoake, George Jacob, *The History of Co-operation*, 1875 and 1879, complete edition London: T. Fisher Unwin, 1906.

—, *The History of Co-operation in Halifax and of some other institutions around it*, London: London Book Store, 1867.

—, *Self-help by the People, The history of Co-operation in Rochdale*, London: Holyoake & Co, first ed. 1857, seventh ed. 1872.

Hughes, Thomas and Neale, E.V., *Foundations: A study in the Ethics and Economics of the Co-operative Movement*, prepared at the request of the Co-operative Congress held at Gloucester in April 1879, Manchester: Co-operative Union Ltd, 1916.

Jones, Benjamin, *Co-operative Production, vol. I and vol. II*, Oxford: Clarendon Press, 1894.

Krasheninnikov, A.I., *The International Co-operative Movement, Past, Present, Future*, Moscow, 1988.

Llewelyn Davies, Margaret (ed.), *Life as We have Known it*, London: The Hogarth Press, 1931.

—, *The Women's Co-operative Guild 1883-1904*, Kirkby Lonsdale: Women's Co-operative Guild, 1904.

Lloyd, Henry Demarest, *Labor Copartnership*, London/New York: Harper and Brothers, 1898.

Ludlow, J.M. and Jones, Lloyd, *Progress of the Working Class 1832-1867*, London: Alexander Strahan, 1867.

Magnanie, Lawrence, 'An Event in the Culture of Co-operation: national co-operative festivals at Crystal Palace' in Yeo, Stephen (ed.), *New Views of Co-operation*, London/New York: Routledge, 1988.

Marx, Karl, *Instructions for the Delegates of the Provisional General Council*, The International Workingmen's Association, 1866 [downloaded Apr. 2015 from www.marxists.org].

Ministry of Labour (Intelligence and Statistics Department), *Profit-sharing and Labour Co-partnership, Report on Profit-sharing and labour co-partnership in the United Kingdom*, London: HMSO, 1920.

Mytholmroyd Industrial Society, *Jubilee 1861-1911, Short History*, Mytholmroyd: Mytholmroyd Industrial Society, 1911.
Neale, E. Vansittart, *The Principles, Objects and Methods of the Labour Association*, London: The Labour Association, 1897.
Potter, Beatrice, *The Co-operative Movement in Great Britain*, 1891, second ed. London: Swan Sonnenschein, 1904.
Pratt, Hodgson, *The Marriage of Labour and Capital*, London: The Labour Association, 1896.
Redfern, Percy, *The new History of the C.W.S.*, London: J.M. Dent/C.W.S. 1938.
—, *The Story of the C.W.S., The Jubilee History of the Co-operative Wholesale Society 1863-1913*, Manchester: Co-operative Wholesale Society, n.d. [1913].
Rhodes, Rita, *The International Co-operative Alliance During War and Peace, 1910-1950*, International Co-operative Alliance, 1995.
Royal Commission on Labour, *Minutes of Evidence taken before the Royal Commission on Labour (sitting as a whole), Representatives of Co-operative Societies, and of Various Movements, and of Public Officials*, C.7063-I, London: HMSO, 1893 (bound as Parliamentary Papers, Reports of Commissioners, Inspectors and others, 24, part I, session 1893-1894, vol. XXXIX.I).
Royal Commission on Labour, *Appendix of the Minutes of Evidence taken before the Royal Commission on Labour (sitting as a whole)*, C.7063-III.A, London: HMSO, 1894 (bound as Parliamentary Papers, Reports of Commissioners, Inspectors and others, 24, part I, session 1893-1894, vol. XXXIX.I).
Smith-Gordon, Lionel and O'Brien, Cruise, *Co-operation in Many Lands, vol. 1*, Manchester: Co-operative Union Ltd, 1919.
Thornes, Robin, 'The origins of the Co-operative Movement in Huddersfield: the Life and Times of the 1st Huddersfield Co-operative Trading Association' in Haigh, E.A. Hilary (ed.), *Huddersfield, A Most Handsome Town*, Huddersfield: Kirklees Cultural Services, 1992.
Vivian, Henry, *Partnership of Capital and Labour as a Solution of the Conflict between Them*, London: The Labour Association, 1898.
—, *What Co-operative Production is Doing*, London: The Labour Association, 1897.
Watkins, W.P., *The International Co-operative Alliance, 1895-1970*, London: International Co-operative Alliance, 1970.
—, *The International Co-operative Movement, Its Growth, Structures and Future Possibilities*, Manchester: Co-operative Union Ltd, 1967, revised ed. n.d.
Webb, Catherine (ed.), *Industrial Co-operation*, Manchester: Co-operative Union Ltd, first ed. 1904; eighth ed. 1919.
—, *The Machinery of the Co-operative Movement*, Manchester: Co-operative Union, 1896.
—, *The Woman with the Basket*, Manchester: Women's Co-operative Guild, 1927.
Wilson, John F. et al, *Building Co-operation, A Business History of The Co-operative Group, 1863-2013*, Oxford: Oxford University Press, 2013.
Yeo, Stephen, 'Cooperative Associations', in Bottomore, Tom (ed), *A Dictionary of Marxist Thought*, Oxford: Blackwell, 1983, second rev. ed. 1991.
—, *Who was J.T.W. Mitchell?* Manchester: CWS Member Services, 1995.

Books: Adult education and university extension

Goldman, Lawrence, *Dons and Workers, Oxford and Adult Education since 1850*, Oxford: Clarendon Press, 1995.
Harrison, J.F.C., *Learning and Living 1790-1960, A study in the history of the English adult education movement*, London: Routledge, 1961.
Jennings, Bernard, *Albert Mansbridge*, Leeds: University of Leeds, 2002.
—, *Knowledge is Power: A short history of the W.E.A. 1903-78*, Hull: University of Hull, 1979.
Jepson, N.A., *The Beginnings of English University Adult Education*, London: Michael Joseph, 1973.
Mackinder, H.J. and Sadler, M.E., *University Extension Past, Present, and Future*, (3rd edition of University Extension: Has it a Future?) London: Cassell, 1891.
Mansbridge, Albert, *An adventure in Working-class education*, London: Longmans, 1920.
Royal Commission on Secondary Education, vol. IV, Minutes of Evidence, C. 7862-111, London: HMSO, 1895.
Simon, Brian, *Education and the Labour Movement 1870-1920*, London: Lawrence and Wishart, London 1974.
Traice, W.H.J., *Hand-book of Mechanics' Institutions with Priced Catalogue of Books suitable for Libraries*, Leeds: Longman, Brown & Co, 1856.
Tylecote, Mabel, *The Mechanics Institutes of Lancashire and Yorkshire Before 1851*, Manchester : Manchester University Press, 1957.

Books: The textile industry

Board of Trade, *Report of an enquiry by the Board of Trade into the earnings and hours of labour of workpeople of the United Kingdom: textile trades in 1906*, Cd.4545, London, 1906 .
Bowker, B., *Lancashire Under the Hammer*, London: The Hogarth Press, 1928.
Fowler, Alan, 'The Impact of the First World War on the Lancashire cotton industry and its workers', in Wrigley, Chris (ed.), *The First World War and the International Economy*, Cheltenham: E Elgar Pub, 2000.
—, *Lancashire Cotton Operatives and Work, 1900-1950*, Aldershot: Ashgate, 2003.
Fowler, Alan and Wyke, Terry (eds.), *The Barefoot Aristocrats, A history of the Amalgamated Association of Operative Cotton Spinners*, Littleborough: George Kelsall, 1987.
Giles, Colum and Goodall, Ian H., *Yorkshire Textile Mills*, Royal Commission on the Historical Monuments of England and West Yorkshire Archaeology Service, London: HMSO, 1992.
Goldthorp, Leslie, 'The Fustian Weavers' Strike at Hebden Bridge, 1906-1908', in *Hebden Bridge Literary and Scientific Society Local History Section Booklets vol. 3*, Hebden Bridge: Hebden Bridge Literary and Scientific Society Local History Section, 1982.
Henderson, Hubert D., *The Cotton Control Board*, Oxford, 1922.
Holt, William, *I Haven't Unpacked*, London: George G. Harrap & Co, 1939.
Hopwood, Edwin, *A History of the Lancashire Cotton Industry and the Amalgamated Weavers' Association*, Manchester: Amalgamated Weavers' Association, 1969.

Liddington, Jill and Norris, Jill, *One Hand Tied Behind Us*, 1978, revised edition London: Rivers Oram, 2000.
Poole, B.W., *The Clothing Trades Industry*, Pitman and Sons, 1920.
Stewart, Margaret and Hunter, Leslie, *The Needle is Threaded*, London: Heinemann/ Newman Neame (National Union of Tailors and Garment Workers), 1964.
Tawney, R.H., *The Establishment of Minimum Rates in the Tailoring Industry under the Trade Boards Act of 1909*, London: Bell, 1915.
Timmins, Geoffrey, *The Last Shift, The Decline of Handloom Weaving in Nineteenth-century Lancashire*, Manchester: Manchester University Press, 1993.
Todmorden Weavers' Association, *Jubilee 1880-1930: Fifty Years Progress*, Todmorden: Todmorden Weavers' Association, 1930.
Wood, George Henry, *The History of Wages in the Cotton Trade during the past Hundred Years*, London/Manchester: Sherratt and Hughes, 1910.
Wyatt, Justine (coordinator), *Fustianopolis, Hebden Bridge: The Growth of a Textile Town*, Hebden Bridge: Hebden Bridge Alternative Technology Centre, 2011.
Wyatt, Justine (coordinator), *The Mills of the Hebden Valley*, Hebden Bridge: Hebden Bridge Alternative Technology Centre, 2011.

Books: others

Barker, Paul, *Hebden Bridge, A sense of belonging*, London: Frances Lincoln, 2012.
Bowley, Arthur L., *Prices and Wages in the United Kingdom 1914-1920*, Oxford, 1921.
Brittain, Vera, *Testament of Youth*, London: Victor Gollancz, 1933.
Campbell, Richardson, *Rechabite History: A record of the origin, rise and progress of the Independent Order of Rechabites*, Salford: Salford Unity, 1911.
Croft, Linda, *John Fielden's Todmorden*, Todmorden: Tygerfoot Press, 1994.
Harrison, Brian, *Drink and the Victorians, The Temperance question in England 1815-1872*, London: Faber and Faber, 1971.
Hartley, W.C.E., *Banking in Yorkshire*, Clapham (N Yorkshire): Dalesman Books, 1975.
Industrial Remuneration Conference: the Report of the Proceedings and Papers read in Prince's Hall, Piccadilly under the presidency of the Right Hon Sir Charles W Dilke Bart., MP, on the 28th, 29th and 30th January 1885.
Jennings, Bernard (ed.), *Pennine Valley, A history of upper Calderdale*, Hebden Bridge WEA Local History Group, Otley: Smith Settle, 1992.
Jeuda, Basil, *The Churnet Valley Railway*, Lydney: Lightmoor Press, 1999.
Liddington, Jill, *Rebel Girls*, London: Virago, 2006.
Lockhart, J.G., *Cosmo Gordon Lang*, London: Hodder and Stoughton, 1949.
Mellor, Sam (ed.), *Biographies, Sketches, and Rhymes, by the Calder Valley Poets*, Halifax: Edward Mortimer, 1916.
Pelling, Henry, *Origins of the Labour Party*, Oxford: Clarendon Press, 1965.
Purdom, C.B., *The Garden City*, London: J.M. Dent & Sons, 1913.
Ruskin, John, *The Crown of Wild Olive*, London: Smith, Elder & Co, 1866.
Spencer, Colin, *A Century of Change*, Hebden Bridge: Hebden Bridge Literary and Scientific Society (Local History Section), 1999.
—, *The History of Hebden Bridge*, Hebden Bridge: Hebden Bridge Literary and

Scientific Society, 1991.
Thompson, E.P., *The Making of the English Working Class*, London: Victor Gollancz, 1963.
Webb, Beatrice, *My Apprenticeship*, London: Longmans, Green & Co, 1926.
Wilson, Benjamin, *The Struggles of an Old Chartist*, Halifax, 1887.

Journal and magazine articles, papers

Bellamy, Joyce, 'Gray, Jesse Clement', in Bellamy, Joyce M. and Saville, John, *Dictionary of Labour Biography, volume I*, London: Macmillan, 1972.
Bing, H.F., 'Greenwood, Joseph', in Bellamy, Joyce M. and Saville, John, *Dictionary of Labour Biography, volume I*, London: Macmillan, 1972.
Blake, Barnett, 'The Mechanics' Institutes of Yorkshire' in *Transactions of the National Association for the Promotion of Social Science*, 1859, pp. 835-40
Blaszak, Barbara J., 'The Women's Co-operative Guild, 1883-1921', in *International Social Science Review*, vol. 61, no. 2 (Spring 1986), pp. 76-86.
Cameron, Julia Margaret, 'Hughes, Thomas', in *Oxford Dictionary of National Biography*, Oxford: Oxford University Press, 2004-2014.
Davis, John, 'Webb [née Potter] (Martha) Beatrice' in *Oxford Dictionary of National Biography*, Oxford: Oxford University Press, 2004-2014.
Day, Mrs, *Women on Management Committees*, Women's Co-operative Guild, paper read at the annual meeting, Plymouth, July 1899.
de Peuter, Greig and Dyer-Witheford, Nick, 'Commons and Cooperatives' in *Affinities: A Journal of Radical Theory, Culture and Action*, vol. 4, no.1, Summer 2010, pp. 30-56.
Denholm, Anthony F., 'Robinson, George Frederick Samuel, first marquess of Ripon', in *Oxford Dictionary of National Biography*, Oxford: Oxford University Press, 2004-2014.
Gide, Charles, 'Has Co-operation introduced a new Principle into Economics?', in *The Economic Journal*, vol. 8, no. 32 (Dec. 1898), pp. 490-511.
Greenwood, George Hall, *The English Fustian Manufacturing Co Ltd*, 1969 [downloaded Apr. 2015 from www.fustianopolis.co.uk].
Gurney, Peter, 'A Higher State of Civilisation and Happiness: Internationalism in the British Co-operative Movement c.1869-1918' in van Holthoon, Fritz and van der Linden, Marcel (eds.), *Internationalism in the European Labour Movement, 1830-1940*, Leiden: E.J. Brill, 1988.
—, 'The Middle-Class Embrace: Language, Representation and the Contest over Co-operative Forms in Britain c. 1860-1914', in *Victorian Studies*, vol. 37, no. 2 (Winter 1994), pp. 253-86.
Hills, Sally and Thomas, Ryland, 'The UK recession in context – what do three centuries of data tell us?' in *Bank of England Quarterly Bulletin*, 2010, quarter 4, pp. 277-91.
Holton, Sandra Stanley, 'Craigen, Jessie Hannah' in *Oxford Dictionary of National Biography*, Oxford: Oxford University Press, 2004-2014.
Howard, Robert, *A History of the Typhus of Heptonstall Slack which Prevailed during the winter of 1843-1844*, n.d. .
Huffman, Wallace R. and Lothian, James T., 'The Gold Standard and the

Transmission of Business Cycles, 1833-1932' in Bordo, Michael D. and Schwartz, Anna J., *A Retrospective on the Classical Gold Standard*, Chicago, 1984.
Jennings, Bernard, 'Halstead, Robert', in Bellamy, Joyce M. and Saville, John, *Dictionary of Labour Biography, volume II*, London: Macmillan, 1974.
Jones, Benjamin, 'Co-operation and Profit-sharing', in *The Economic Journal*, vol. 2, no. 8 (Dec. 1892), pp. 616-28.
Jossa, Bruno, 'Marx, Marxism and the cooperative movement' in *Cambridge Journal of Economics*, 29, (2005), pp. 3-18.
Lee, Matthew, 'Jones, (Patrick) Lloyd' in *Oxford Dictionary of National Biography*, Oxford: Oxford University Press, 2004-2014.
—, 'Neale, Edward Vansittart', in *Oxford Dictionary of National Biography*, Oxford: Oxford University Press, 2004-2014.
Marriott, Stuart, 'Oxford and working-class adult education: A foundation myth re-examined' in *History of Education: Journal of the History of Education Society*, 12:4, (1983), pp. 285-99.
—, 'Shaw, (George William) Hudson', in *Oxford Dictionary of National Biography*, Oxford: Oxford University Press, 2004-2014.
Miller, Carmen, 'Grey, Albert Henry George', in *Oxford Dictionary of National Biography*, Oxford: Oxford University Press, 2004-2014.
Neale, E.V., *The Economic Aspect of Co-operation*, paper originally read at Derby Congress, 1884.
Ockwell, Anne, 'Acland, Sir Arthur Herbert Dyke', in *Oxford Dictionary of National Biography*, Oxford: Oxford University Press, 2004-2014.
Pottle, Mark, 'Vivian, Henry Harvey', in *Oxford Dictionary of National Biography*, Oxford: Oxford University Press, 2004-2014.
Price, L.L., 'Profit-Sharing and Cooperative Production' in *The Economic Journal*, vol. 2, no. 7 (Sep. 1892), pp. 442-62.
Purvis, Martin, 'Acland [née Cunningham], Alice Sophia', in *Oxford Dictionary of National Biography*, Oxford: Oxford University Press, 2004-2014.
Rowbotham, Sheila, 'Travellers in a strange country: responses of working class students to the University Extension Movement 1873-1910', in *History Workshop*, no. 12 (Autumn 1981), pp. 62-95.
Rowe, J.W.F., 'Wages in the Cotton Industry, 1914-1920' in *The Economic Review*, vol. 34, no. 134 (June 1924), pp. 200-10.
Royle, Edward, 'Holyoake, George Jacob', in *Oxford Dictionary of National Biography*, Oxford: Oxford University Press, 2004-2014.
—, 'Mechanics' Institutes and the Working Classes, 1840-1860', in *The Historical Journal*, vol. 14, no. 2 (June 1971), pp. 305-21.
Saville, John, 'Greening, Edward Owen', in *Oxford Dictionary of National Biography*, Oxford: Oxford University Press, 2004-2014.
Scott, Gillian, 'Webb, Catherine', in *Oxford Dictionary of National Biography*, Oxford: Oxford University Press, 2004-2014.
Singleton, John, 'The cotton industry and the British war effort, 1914-1918' in *Economic History Review*, vol. XLVII, no. 3 (1994), pp. 601-18.
Sires, Ronald V., 'The Beginnings of British Legislation for Old-Age Pensions', in *The Journal of Economic History*, vol. 14, no. 3 (Summer 1954), pp. 229-53.

Toms, Steven, 'Producer co-operatives and economic efficiency: evidence from the nineteenth century cotton textile industry', in *Business History*, vol. 54, no. 6, Oct. 2012, pp. 855-82.

Vorberg-Rugh, Rachael, 'Employers *and* workers: conflicting identities over women's wages in the co-operative movement, 1906-18', in Black, Lawrence and Robertson, Nicole, *Consumerism and the Co-operative movement in Modern British History*, Manchester: Manchester University Press, 2009.

Webb, Sidney and Beatrice, 'The Draft of the First Report of the Committee of the Fabian Research Department, The Control of Industry ('Can the Organisation of Industry be based exclusively on Associations of Producers?')' in *New Statesman (Special Supplement on Co-operative Production and Profit-Sharing)*, vol. II, no. 45 (Sat. 14 Feb. 1914).

—, 'The Draft of the Second Report of the Committee of the Fabian Research Department, The Control of Industry ('Can the Organisation of Industry be based on Voluntary Associations of Consumers, such as those of the Co-operative Societies?')' *New Statesman (Special Supplement on the Co-operative Movement)*, vol. III, no. 6 (Sat. 30 May 1914).

Wilkinson, Alan, 'Lang, (William) Cosmo Gordon' in *Oxford Dictionary of National Biography*, Oxford: Oxford University Press, 2004-2014.

Williams, Aneurin, 'The International Co-Operative Alliance and its Congress', in *The Economic Journal*, vol. 5, no. 19 (Sep. 1895), pp. 456-60.

Theses and unpublished works

Boughton, Tony, *The culture of working-class co-operation in Hebden Bridge, 1860-1890*, undergraduate dissertation, Oxford Brookes University, 2013.

Butler, John H., *The origins and development of the retail co-operative movement in Yorkshire during the nineteenth century*, PhD thesis, University of York, 1986.

Greenwood, Tom, *The Origins and Development of the Clothing Industry in Hebden Bridge*, Ruskin College Labour Studies Diploma, 1982.

Hebden Royd Town Council, *Hebden Bridge and District Roll of Honour 1914-1919*, 2014.

Jones, Derek C., *The Economics of British Producer Cooperatives*, thesis, Cornell University, 1974.

Thomas, Peter, *The Origins and Early Ideals of the Workers' Educational Association of Hebden Bridge, West Riding of Yorkshire*, University of Leeds thesis, 1974.

Thornes, R.C.N., *The Early Development of the Co-operative Movement in West Yorkshire, 1827-1863*, PhD thesis, University of Sussex, 1984.

Personal interviews

Jim Wilkinson (great-grandson, Joseph Greenwood).
Irene Kirk (great great-granddaughter, Joseph Greenwood).

Notes

Abbreviations used: *CN: Co-operative News*; HBLHS: Hebden Bridge Local History Society; *HBT: Hebden Bridge Times*; WYAS: West Yorkshire Archive Service

1. *Report of Coming-of-age celebrations of the Hebden Bridge Fustian Co-operative Society Ltd*, 23 & 26 Sep. 1891, p.12.
2. Joseph Greenwood, *A Brief Sketch of Twenty-six Years' Work in Co-operative Production*, n.d. [1897], p. 27.
3. Joseph Greenwood, *A Brief Sketch of Twenty-six Years' Work*, pp. 24-7.
4. *Report of Coming-of-age celebrations*, p. 51.
5. *CN* 9 July 1881 (see also author's afterword).
6. *CN* 19 Dec. 1903.
7. *Report of Coming-of-age celebrations*, p. 33.
8. Parallel to it is Mitchell Street, named after the Co-operative Wholesale Society's J.T.W. Mitchell.
9. *Report of Coming-of-age celebrations*, pp. 24, 31.
10. *CN* 11 June 1892.
11. *Report of Coming-of-age celebrations*, p. 39.
12. Quoted in G.D.H. Cole, *A Century of Co-operation*, 1944, p. 75.
13. E.V. Neale, 'The Economic Aspect of Co-operation', paper originally read at Derby Congress 1884, p. 5.
14. *CN* 19 March 1881.
15. Paul Barker, *Hebden Bridge*, 2012, p.190.
16. Bernard Jennings (ed), *Pennine Valley*, 1992, p. 191; Paul Barker, *Hebden Bridge*, p. 20.
17. Joseph Greenwood, *A Brief Sketch of Twenty-one Years' Work in Co-operative Production*, 1891, p. 5; Joseph Greenwood, *The story of the formation of the Hebden Bridge Fustian Manufacturing Society*, 1888, p. 6.
18. The surname is variously spelled in census and newspaper records.
19. *Todmorden and District News*, 24 June 1870.
20. Joseph Greenwood, *The story of the formation*, p. 6.
21. Royal Commission on Labour, Minutes of Evidence taken before the Royal Commission on Labour, Representatives of Co-operative Societies and of Various Movement and of Public Officials, C.7063-1, 1893, p. 63.
22. Henry Demarest Lloyd, *Labor Copartnership*, 1898, p. 172.
23. *Todmorden and District News*, 24 June 1870; Census returns for 1861 (Hebden Bridge), 1841 (Salford).
24. E.P. Thompson, *The Making of the English Working Class*, 1963, pp. 316, 321 (Penguin edition).
25. Robert Howard, surgeon, *A History of the Typhus of Heptonstall Slack which prevailed during the Winter of 1843-1844*, pp. 2-3.
26. E.P. Thompson, *The Making of the English Working Class*, p. 297.
27. William Cobbett, *Political Register*, 20 June 1832, quoted in E.P. Thompson, *The Making of the English Working Class*, p. 314.
28. Joseph Greenwood, 'Reminiscences of Sixty Years Ago', *Co-partnership*, vol.15

(1909), Sep. 1909, p. 131.
29 Joseph Greenwood, 'Reminiscences of Sixty Years Ago', *Co-partnership*, vol. 15 (1909), Sep. 1909, p. 131.
30 Joseph Greenwood, 'Reminiscences of Sixty Years Ago', *Co-partnership*, vol. 16 (1910), Feb. 1910, p. 23.
31 Joseph Greenwood, 'Reminiscences of Sixty Years Ago', *Co-partnership*, vol. 15 (1909), Nov. 1909, p. 165.
32 S.C. Moore, *The Industrial Evolution of a Manufacturing Village*, 1911, passim; Bernard Jennings (ed), *Pennine Valley*, p. 109.
33 Linda Croft, *John Fielden's Todmorden*, 1994, pp. 57-78.
34 Joseph Greenwood, 'Reminiscences of Sixty Years Ago', *Co-partnership*, vol. 15 (1909), Dec. 1909, p. 181; Industrial Remuneration Conference; the Report of the Proceedings and Papers 1885, p. 488.
35 Joseph Greenwood, 'Reminiscences of Sixty Years Ago', *Co-partnership*, vol. 16 (1910), July 1910, p. 103.
36 N.H. Gregory, *A Century's Progress 1848-1948, The story of a hundred years of co-operation in Hebden Bridge*, 1948, p. 5.
37 N.H. Gregory, *A Century's Progress 1848-1948*, p. 4.
38 Joseph Greenwood, 'Reminiscences of Sixty Years Ago', *Co-partnership*, vol. 16 (1910), June 1910, p. 87; July 1910, p. 103.
39 Basil Jeuda, *The Churnet Valley Railway*, 1999.
40 Joseph Greenwood, 'Reminiscences of Sixty Years Ago', *Co-partnership*, vol. 16 (1910), Dec. 1910, p. 182.
41 HBLHS archive, ref MIN1, minute book, minutes 2 May 1856.
42 Joseph Greenwood, 'Reminiscences of Sixty Years Ago', *Co-partnership*, vol. 16 (1910), Dec. 1910, p.182.
43 HBLHS archive, ref MIN1, minute book, various entries including 26 May 1855, 5 Jan. 1857.
44 HBLHS archive, ref MIN1, minute book, minutes 1 June 1859.
45 *Todmorden and Hebden-Bridge Weekly Advertiser*, 20 Sep. 1862, 29 Nov. 1862.
46 HBLHS archive, ref MIN1, minute book, various entries including 4 Dec.1861, 8 Jan. 1862, 15 Jan. 1862, 1 July 1863, 1 June 1864.
47 Joseph Greenwood, 'Reminiscences of Sixty Years Ago', *Co-partnership*, vol. 17 (1911), Aug. 1911, p. 120.
48 Joseph Greenwood, 'Reminiscences of Sixty Years Ago', *Co-partnership*, vol. 17 (1911), May 1911, p. 69.
49 N.H. Gregory, *A Century's Progress 1848-1948*, pp. 16-18; *CN* 27 July 1872.
50 *HBT* 15 May 1903.
51 National Archives, 16/941/H202.
52 *The Co-operator and Anti-Vaccinator*, 30 July 1870, 6 Aug. 1870, 13 Aug. 1870, 20 Aug. 1870.
53 Joseph Greenwood, *The story of the formation*, p. 5.
54 *CN* 19 Nov. 1881.
55 *Todmorden and District News*, 22 July 1870.
56 Royal Commission on Labour, Minutes of Evidence, p. 63.
57 Royal Commission on Labour, Minutes of Evidence, pp. 63-4; Joseph

Greenwood, *A Brief Sketch of Twenty-one Years' Work*, p. 6.
58 'Henry Greenwood' [assumed error for Joseph Greenwood], *Hebden Bridge Manufacturing Society*, Co-operative Congress 1872 report, pp.112-13; Joseph Greenwood, *The story of the formation*, pp. 7-10.
59 Joseph Greenwood, *The story of the formation*, passim; Royal Commission on Labour, Minutes of Evidence, pp. 63-4.
60 'Henry Greenwood', *Hebden Bridge Manufacturing Society*, Co-operative Congress 1872 report, pp. 112-13.
61 Joseph Greenwood, *The story of the formation*, p. 10.
62 Joseph Greenwood, *The story of the formation*, p. 8.
63 'Henry Greenwood', *Hebden Bridge Manufacturing Society*, Co-operative Congress 1872 report, pp.112-13.
64 *Todmorden and District News*, 14 Oct. 1870.
65 Benjamin Jones, *Co-operative Production*, 1894, p. 333.
66 *CN* 23 Mar. 1872, 27 July 1872.
67 N.H. Gregory, *A Century's Progress 1848-1948*, p. 17.
68 This was the Derdale Cotton Company; *Todmorden and District News*, 12 Nov. 1869.
69 'Henry Greenwood', *Hebden Bridge Manufacturing Society*, Co-operative Congress 1872 report, pp. 112-13.
70 Joseph Greenwood, *A Brief Sketch of Twenty-one Years' Work*, p. 7, pp. 24-7.
71 Joseph Greenwood, *A Brief Sketch of Twenty-one Years' Work*, p. 7.
72 Joseph Greenwood, *A Brief Sketch of Twenty-one Years' Work*, pp. 24-7.
73 Joseph Greenwood, *The story of the formation*, p. 12.
74 Matthew Lee, 'Jones, (Patrick) Lloyd', *Oxford Dictionary of National Biography*.
75 Co-operative Congress 1872 report, pp. 16ff; Joseph Greenwood, *The story of the formation*, p. 12; *CN* 8 Apr. 1876.
76 Joseph Greenwood, *A Brief Sketch of Twenty-one Years' Work*, pp. 24-7.
77 *CN* 19 Nov. 1887.
78 Henry Demarest Lloyd, *Labor Co-partnership*, 1898, pp. 170-1.
79 Joseph Greenwood, *A Brief Sketch of Twenty-one Years' Work*, pp. 8, 27.
80 Percy Redfern, *The Story of the CWS*, n.d., pp. 66-7.
81 Royal Commission on Labour, Minutes of Evidence, pp. 64, 69.
82 Joyce Bellamy, 'Gray, Jesse Clement', in Joyce M. Bellamy and John Saville, *Dictionary of Labour Biography*, vol. I, 1972, pp. 134-6.
83 National Archives, ref FS 17/23.
84 Recent History of the Hebden Bridge Fustian Manufacturing Society, *Co-operators' Year Book*, 1917.
85 Co-operative Congress 1895 report, p. 3.
86 *CN* 12 Feb. 1881.
87 *CN* 3 Jan. 1885.
88 Joseph Greenwood, *A Brief Sketch of Twenty-one Years' Work*, pp. 24-7.
89 *CN* 15 Jan. 1876, *Todmorden and District News*, 14 Jan. 1876; Joseph Greenwood, *The Story of the formation*, pp. 19-20.
90 *CN* 22 Jan. 1876.
91 *CN* 29 Jan. 1876.

92 Joseph Greenwood, *A Brief Sketch of Twenty-one Years' Work*, pp. 24-5.
93 Three centuries of data, downloaded from www.bankofengland.co.uk Apr. 2015; bank rate changes, downloaded from tinyurl.com/bpaav8h [accessed Apr. 2015].
94 *HBT* 5 Aug. 1887; *CN* 26 May 1888.
95 *CN* 12 Feb. 1881.
96 *HBT* 3 Aug. 1888.
97 Joseph Greenwood, *A Brief Sketch of Twenty-one Years' Work*, pp. 26-7.
98 Joseph Greenwood, *The story of the formation*, pp. 12-13.
99 Joseph Greenwood, *A Brief Sketch of Twenty-one Years' Work*, p. 24.
100 National Archives, ref FS 17/23, Rules of Hebden Bridge Fustian Manufacturing Co-operative Society, by resolution of a Special General Meeting held 22nd day of February 1873.
101 Joseph Greenwood, *A Brief Sketch of Twenty-one Years' Work*, pp. 26-7.
102 G.D.H. Cole, *A Century of Co-operation*, p. 90.
103 Quoted in Benjamin Jones, *Co-operative Production*, p. 263.
104 Benjamin Shaw, *The Huddersfield Chronicle and West Yorkshire Advertiser*, 8 July 1895.
105 *CN* 24 May 1873, 22 Nov. 1873.
106 *Todmorden & Hebden Bridge Weekly Advertiser*, 10 Oct. 1863.
107 John Saville, 'Greening, Edward Owen', *Oxford Dictionary of National Biography*; Benjamin Jones, *Co-operative Production*, pp. 444-6; *Report of Coming-of-age celebrations*, pp. 44-5.
108 *CN* 28 Feb. 1874.
109 *CN* 3 July 1875.
110 *CN* 25 Mar. 1876.
111 *CN* 18 Mar. 1876.
112 Co-operative Congress 1876 report, pp. 48ff, 51.
113 *CN* 29 May 1880.
114 *HBT* July 30 1884.
115 *CN* July 16 1881.
116 Joseph Greenwood, *A Brief Sketch of Twenty-six Years' Work*, pp. 24-5, data analysis by author.
117 Joseph Greenwood, *A Brief Sketch of Twenty-six Years' Work*, pp. 24-27, data analysis by author.
118 Co-operative Congress 1874 report, p. 28.
119 J.C. Gray, *Co-operative Production in Great Britain*, reprinted from the 'Age of Steel', Jan. 1887, p. 12.
120 Co-partnership, vol. 1 (1894-1895), p. 92.
121 J.C. Gray, 'Co-operative Production', A Paper read at the Congress held at Plymouth, Whitsuntide, 1886, p. 10.
122 Joseph Greenwood, *A Brief Sketch of Twenty-one Years' Work*, p. 10.
123 *HBT* 4 Dec. 1896.
124 *Co-operators' Year Book 1910*, pp. 124-8; *HBT*, 10 Sep. 1909.
125 *Co-operators' Year Book 1910*, p. 127.
126 *Co-partnership*, vol. 15 (1909), Oct. 1909, p. 150. The obituary was contributed

by Joseph Greenwood's son Crossley.
127 Joseph Greenwood, *A Brief Sketch of Twenty-one Years' Work*, pp. 24-7.
128 *CN* 10 Aug. 1878.
129 *Todmorden and District News*, 16 Nov. 1877, 25 July 1879, 1 Aug. 1879.
130 Sally Hills and Ryland Thomas, 'The UK recession in context – what do three centuries of data tell us?' *Bank of England Quarterly Bulletin* [2010, quarter 4], p. 283.
131 *Todmorden and District News*, 21 Mar. 1879; Joseph Greenwood, *A Brief Sketch of Twenty-one Years' Work*, pp. 24-7.
132 *Co-operators Yearbook 1910*, p. 127.
133 Joseph Greenwood, *The Story of the Formation*, p. 7 (Greenwood wrote 'Braybrook').
134 National Archives, ref FS 17/23.
135 Beatrice Potter, *The Co-operative Movement in Great Britain*, 1891, p. 148.
136 Royal Commission on Labour, Minutes of Evidence, pp. 67-9.
137 Joseph Greenwood, 'The Place of the Labourer in Co-operation', Co-operative Congress 1887 report pp. 66-8, and *CN* 16 June 1877.
138 Beatrice Potter, *The Co-operative Movement in Great Britain*, p. 148.
139 Royal Commission on Labour, Minutes of Evidence, p. 70.
140 Board of Trade, Profit-Sharing and Co-partnership (Labour Department), *Report on Profit-Sharing and Labour Co-partnership in the United Kingdom*, 1912, p. 85.
141 Ministry of Labour (Intelligence and Statistics Department) Profit-sharing and Labour co-partnership, *Report on profit-sharing and labour co-partnership in the United Kingdom*, HMSO 1920, pp. 134 ff.
142 *CN* 3 Feb. 1894.
143 National Co-operative Archive, Mytholmroyd co-operative society, minute book.
144 National Co-operative Archive, Mytholmroyd co-operative society, minute book, minutes 8 Aug. 1878.
145 Statement of accounts for the half-year ending June 30th 1892, included as Appendix XXII. Royal Commission on Labour, Appendix of the Minutes of Evidence taken before the Royal Commission on Labour, C.7063-III.A, 1894.
146 National Co-operative Archive, archive box C64, uncatalogued paper.
147 *CN* 12 Feb. 1881.
148 Statement of accounts for the half-year ending June 30th 1892, included as Appendix XXII. Royal Commission on Labour, Appendix of the Minutes of Evidence.
149 National Co-operative Archive, archive box C64, uncatalogued papers.
150 Royal Commission on Labour, Minutes of Evidence, p. 69.
151 Joseph Greenwood, *A Brief Sketch of Twenty-one Years' Work*, p. 12.
152 *CN* 14 Sep. 1878, 19 Oct. 1878, 9 Nov. 1878, 21 Dec. 1878.
153 *CN* 8 Mar. 1879, 15 Mar. 1879.
154 Co-operative Congress reports: 1873 p. 64; 1874 p. 65; 1875 p. 60. *CN* May 1878.
155 *CN* 10 June 1882, 23 June 1883, 23 July 1894.

156 *CN* 8 Mar. 1879, 15 Mar. 1879.
157 *CN* 19 Mar. 1881.
158 *CN* 27 Sep. 1879.
159 Royal Commission on Labour, Minutes of Evidence, p. 69.
160 Joseph Greenwood, *A Brief Sketch of Twenty-six Years' Work*, pp. 24-7.
161 Joseph Greenwood, *A Brief Sketch of Twenty-six Years' Work*, pp. 24-7.
162 Joseph Greenwood, *A Brief Sketch of Twenty-one Years' Work*, p. 13.
163 WYAS, architects' plans ref BIP/HB119, /HB121, /HB123.
164 *HBT* 1 Aug. 1883.
165 WYAS, architects' plans ref BIP/HB193, /HB18.
166 *CN* 5 Aug. 1882.
167 Joseph Greenwood, *A Brief Sketch of Twenty-one Years' Work*, pp. 17-18.
168 WYAS, architects' plans ref BIP/HB266, /HB268, /HB289.
169 Statement of accounts for the half-year ending June 30th 1892, included as Appendix XXII. Royal Commission on Labour, Appendix of the Minutes of Evidence.
170 WYAS, architects' plans ref BIP/HB306; *CN* 3 Feb. 1912; *HBT* 26 Jan. 1912.
171 Joseph Greenwood, *The story of the formation*, p. 19.
172 Royal Commission on Labour, Minutes of Evidence, p. 64.
173 National Co-operative Archive, Mytholmroyd co-operative society minute book, minutes for 19 June 1879.
174 *CN* 12 Feb. 1881.
175 *CN* 8 Oct. 1881, 8 Apr. 1882.
176 Joseph Greenwood, *A Brief Sketch of Twenty-one Years' Work*, pp. 24-5.
177 *CN* 15 Apr. 1882.
178 *HBT* 3 Aug. 1888.
179 *CN* 2 Feb. 1889.
180 *CN* 3 Aug. 1889.
181 Joseph Greenwood, *A Brief Sketch of Twenty-one Years' Work*, p. 17.
182 *CN* 21 Dec. 1889.
183 *CN* 1 Feb. 1890.
184 *CN* 15 Sep. 1883, 29 Sep. 1883.
185 *CN* 22 Dec. 1883.
186 Beatrice Webb, *My Apprenticeship*, 1926, p. 361.
187 *CN* 2 Mar. 1912.
188 Oxford University archives file CE 3/45/120, letter from J.C. Gray, 20 Mar. 1900.
189 Beatrice Webb, *My Apprenticeship*, p. 362.
190 Co-operative Congress 1906 report, pp. 36ff.
191 *CN* 26 Jan. 1884; *HBT* 16 Jan. 1884.
192 *HBT* 17 Oct. 1924.
193 *Todmorden and District News*, 18 Jan. 1878.
194 *Todmorden and District News*, 28 Oct. 1881.
195 Evidence on the sons' occupations from census records.
196 *Todmorden and District News*, 29 Aug. 1879.
197 Co-operative Directory 1893; *HBT* 1 Aug. 1902; *Co-partnership*, vol. 11 (1905),

Jan. 1905, pp. 4-6.
198 Henry Demarest Lloyd, *Labor Copartnership*, p. 185.
199 *Todmorden and District News*, 14 Jan. 1876.
200 Joseph Greenwood, *The story of the formation*, p. 15.
201 *CN* 16 Jan.1892.
202 Barbara Blaszak, *The Matriarchs of England's Cooperative Movement*, 2000, p. 72.
203 *CN* 5 June 1897.
204 Co-operative Congress 1897 report, p. 48.
205 Jean Gaffin and David Thoms, *Caring and Sharing*, 1983, passim.
206 *CN* 6 Oct. 1883. Co-operative News gives the date of the first meeting as 17 September, Martha Helliwell (*CN* 8 Mar. 1884) says the meeting was on 19 September and this, a Wednesday evening, seems more likely.
207 Co-operative Congress 1883 report.
208 Census records 1881, 1891, 1901, 1911 (1911 living in Pendleon).
209 *CN* 26 May 1883.
210 *CN* 10 Feb. 1883.
211 *CN* 17 Feb. 1883, quoted in Jean Gaffin and David Thoms, *Caring and Sharing* p. 3.
212 Jean Gaffin and David Thoms, *Caring and Sharing* pp. 3-5, p. 266; Martin Purvis, 'Acland [née Cunningham] Alice Sophia', *Oxford Dictionary of National Biography*.
213 *HBT* 28 Dec. 1882, 10 Jan. 1883; Anne Ockwell, 'Acland, Sir Arthur Herbert Dyke', *Oxford Dictionary of National Biography*.
214 *CN* 14 Apr. 1883.
215 *CN* 20 Oct. 1883.
216 *CN* 22 Dec. 1883.
217 *CN* 8 Mar. 1884, also quoted in Margaret Llewelyn Davies, *The Women's Co-operative Guild 1883-1904*, 1904.
218 Jean Gaffin and David Thoms, *Caring and Sharing*, p. 5.
219 *CN* 12 July 1884.
220 *CN* 19 July 1884.
221 *CN* 19 July 1884.
222 *CN* 16 Aug. 1884.
223 *CN* 5 Dec. 1885.
224 *CN* 11 June 1887.
225 *CN* 6 Nov. 1897.
226 *CN* 13 Aug. 1892.
227 Fourteenth annual report of the Women's Co-operative Guild, April 1896-April 1897.
228 National Co-operative Archive, archive box C64 (the statement prepared by Fustian Society board at the time of the 1916 dispute mentions women weavers at the mill).
229 S.C. Moore, *The Industrial Evolution of a Manufacturing Village*, passim; Tom Greenwood, 'Origins and Development of the Clothing Industry in Hebden Bridge' (thesis), p. 27. Tom Greenwood suggests that 3,000 people were

employed in the clothing industry in 1914, of whom 2,600 were women.
230 'The Industrial Commonwealth at Hebden Bridge', reprinted from the *Yorkshire Factory Times*, 5 and 12 March 1897, p. 11.
231 Ministry of Labour (Intelligence and Statistics Department) *Profit-sharing and Labour co-partnership*, 1920, pp. 141ff.
232 Robert Halstead, Some Thoughts of a Workman concerning the plea for a living wage, in *Economic Review*, vol. V, July 1895, p. 358.
233 The Industrial Commonwealth at Hebden Bridge, p. 11.
234 George Greenwood, *The English Fustian Manufacturing Co*, 1969 [Accessed from www.fustianopolis.co.uk Jan. 2015].
235 *CN* 11 Jan. 1896; *HBT* 3 Jan. 1896, 10 Jan. 1896.
236 *Report of Coming-of-age celebrations*, pp. 17, 54.
237 Oxford University archive CE3/28/3.
238 *HBT* 12 Oct. 1888.
239 *Oxford University Extension Gazette*, Special Summer Meeting Number (8 Aug. 1890) p. 8; no. 22, July 1892 p. 116.
240 Joseph Greenwood, *A Brief Sketch of Twenty-one Years' Work*, p. 13.
241 *CN* 10 June 1882.
242 *CN* 29 May 1875.
243 *CN* 5 Aug. 1882.
244 *HBT* 28 Dec. 1882, 10 Jan. 1883.
245 *CN* 17 Mar. 1883.
246 N.A. Jepson, T*he Beginnings of English University Adult Education*, 1973, pp. 85-6.
247 Oxford University archive CE3/28/1.
248 Oxford University archive CE3/28/2.
249 Oxford University archive CE3/28/2.
250 Oxford University archive CE3/28/3 ; *CN* 27 July 1889.
251 Oxford University archive CE3/28/3.
252 Census returns 1881, 1891.
253 *CN* 30 Mar. 1889.
254 *CN* 30 Mar. 1889.
255 *HBT* 8 Mar. 1889, Oxford University archive CE3/18.
256 N.A. Jepson, *The Beginnings of English University Adult Education*, p. 278.
257 J.G. Lockhart, *Cosmo Gordon Lang*, 1949, p. 47.
258 Beatrice Webb, *My Apprenticeship*, p. 158.
259 Beatrice Webb, *My Apprenticeship*, p. 359.
260 Quoted in J.G. Lockhart, *Cosmo Gordon Lang*, pp. 47ff.
261 Oxford University archive CE3/28/5, CE3/28/7, CE3/28/9 .
262 Robert Halstead, 'Some Co-operative Reminiscences', *The Co-operative Official*, vol. III., no. 31 (Oct. 1922), p. 179.
263 Bernard Jennings, 'Halstead, Robert' in Joyce M. Bellamy and John Saville, *Dictionary of Labour Biography*, vol. II, 1974, pp. 154-9; *HBT* 17 Oct. 1930; *CN* 18 Oct. 1930; Robert Halstead, 'Some Co-operative Reminiscences', *The Co-operative Official*, vol. III., no. 31 (Oct. 1922), p. 180.
264 Fourteenth annual report of the Women's Co-operative Guild April

1896-April 1897; Sixteenth annual report of the Women's Co-operative Guild April 1998-April 1899.
265 *CN* 18 Oct. 1930.
266 William Holt, *I Haven't Unpacked*, 1939 (p. 45, paperback edition); Alan Fowler, *Lancashire Cotton Operatives and Work, 1900-1950*, 2003, p. 119.
267 John Ruskin, *The Crown of Wild Olive*, (1909 edition) p. 42.
268 Quoted in J.G. Lockhart, *Cosmo Gordon Lang*, pp. 47ff.
269 Oxford University archives CE3/28/7. CE3/28/9, CE3/28/16, CE3/28/19, CE3/28/22; CE3/52/5.
270 *Oxford University Extension Gazette*, no. 32, May 1893, pp. 108-10.
271 Oxford University Extension Gazette, no. 31, Apr. 1893, p. 96.
272 Vera Brittain, *Testament of Youth*, 1933, pp. 63-4.
273 *University Extension Journal*, vol. IV, no. 28, Oct. 1898, pp. 9-10.
274 *CN* 17 Aug. 1889.
275 Oxford University archive CE3/35; *CN* 14 Sep. 1889.
276 *Oxford University Extension Gazette*, Special Summer Meeting Number (8 Aug. 1890), p. 8; no 31, Apr 1893, p. 96.
277 *Oxford University Extension Gazette*, vol. 1, no 1, (Oct 1890), p. 11.
278 Peter Thomas, 'The Origins and Early Ideals of the Workers' Educational Association of Hebden Bridge' (thesis), p. 19; Co-operative Congress 1894 report, p. 89.
279 *HBT* 4 Mar. 1885.
280 Bernard Jennings (ed), *Pennine Valley*, p. 184; *HBT* 18 Dec. 1925.
281 Oxford University archive CE3/45/126: letter from Halstead to J.A.R. Marriot, 22 June 1899.
282 Sam Mellor (ed), *Biographies, Sketches, and Rhymes, by the Calder Valley Poets*, 1916, p. 109; Labour Co-partnership, vol. 6 (1900), July 1900, p. 122.
283 *CN* 12 Mar. 1904.
284 Oxford University archive CE3/37/15, Archives of the Board of Extra-Mural Studies, University of Cambridge, 15/4; marriage record; *CN* 21 Sep. 1907.
285 *CN* 2 Sep. 1899, 7 Oct. 1899.
286 Oxford University archive CE3/37/10.
287 Archives of the Board of Extra-Mural Studies, University of Cambridge, 13/1 (letter book) p. 261.
288 H.J. Mackinder and M.E. Sadler, *University Extension Past, Present, and Future*, 1891, p. 82; *Labour Co-partnership*, vol. 1 (1894-5), p. 143.
289 *The Industrial Commonwealth at Hebden Bridge*, p. 12.
290 Labour Co-partnership, vol. 5 (1899), June 1899, p. 101.
291 *HBT* 24 May 1893.
292 *CN* 1 May 1897; *University Extension Journal*, vol. II, no. 17, May 1897.
293 Royal Commission on Secondary Education, vol. IV, Minutes of Evidence, 1895, pp. 396-417; Robert Halstead, 'Some Co-operative Reminiscences', *The Co-operative Official*, vol. III., no. 32 (Nov. 1922), p. 204.
294 *CN* 12 June 1897.
295 Oxford University archive CE3/45/126.
296 Oxford University archive CE3/45/120, CE3/45/126.

297 John H. Butler, 'The origins and development of the retail co-operative movement in Yorkshire during the nineteenth century' (thesis), p. 289.
298 Sources: (until 1895) Joseph Greenwood, *A Brief Sketch of Twenty-six Years' Work*, pp. 24-7; (from 1896) data in Co-operative Congress reports.
299 Oxford University archive CE3/21/1, CE3/28/16, CE3/28/19, CE3/28/22, CE3/28/24, CE3/28/26.
300 Co-operative Congress report 1899, p. 91; Peter Thomas, 'The Origins and Early Ideals of the Workers' Educational Association of Hebden Bridge,' p. 27.
301 Oxford University archive, CE3/21/1, CE3/28/28, /30,/31.
302 *CN* 16 June 1900.
303 *CN* 15 May 1897, 6 Aug. 1898.
304 *CN* 19 Aug. 1899.
305 University Extension Journal, April 1903, p. 100; Bernard Jennings, *Albert Mansbridge*, 2002, pp. 21-3.
306 Brian Simon, *Education and the Labour Movement 1879-1920*, 1974, p. 306.
307 Quoted in Albert Mansbridge, *An Adventure in Working-class Education*, 1920, p. 12.
308 *Labour Co-partnership*, vol. 9 (1903), Oct. 1903, p. 154.
309 Oxford University archive CE3/45/126.
310 *CN* 17 Jan. 1885.
311 Oxford University archive CE3/45/126.
312 Modern Records Centre Warwick MSS 310/1/2/5, Labour Association minute book 1896-1901, minutes 19 Sep. 1898.
313 Modern Records Centre Warwick MSS 310/1/2/5, Labour Association minute book 1896-1901, minutes 19 Mar. 1900.
314 Hull History Centre, DCF/1: CPF minute book 1896-1901, minutes 21 Sep. 1900.
315 Bernard Jennings, 'Halstead, Robert', *Dictionary of Labour Biography*, vol. II, pp. 154-9.
316 G.D.H. Cole, *A Century of Co-operation*, p. 204.
317 *CN*, 11 July 1891.
318 Ministry of Labour (Intelligence and Statistics Department) Profit-sharing and Labour co-partnership, 1920, pp. 128-9.
319 Robert Halstead, 'Profit-sharing and Distributive Co-operation,' *Labour Co-partnership*, vol. 5 (1899), Jan 1899, p. 3; R[obert] Halstead, 'Co-partnership in Store and Works', *Co-operators' Year Book 1907*, pp. 113-17.
320 G.D.H. Cole, *A Century of Co-operation*, p. 170.
321 Benjamin Jones, *Co-operative Production*, p. 219.
322 Co-operative Congress report 1879, pp. 38, 39, 41.
323 Percy Redfern, *The Story of the C.W.S.*, pp. 419-20.
324 Benjamin Jones, *Co-operative Production*, pp. 446-58.
325 *CN* 15 June 1878.
326 Benjamin Jones, *Co-operative Production*, pp. 358-63.
327 *CN* 30 June 1883.
328 *HBT* 14 Jan. 1885.
329 J.C. Gray, 'Co-operative Production', A Paper read at the Congress held at

Plymouth, Whitsuntide, 1886, pp. 5-9.
330 J.C. Gray, 'Co-operative Production', a Paper read at a Conference at Derby on Saturday October 23rd 1886, pp. 14-16.
331 *CN* 1 June 1889.
332 J.C. Gray, 'The Future of Productive Co-operation: Isolation or Federation?' presented at the Birmingham district conference, 1890 (*CN* 28 June 1890); Co-operative Congress 1886 report, p. 80.
333 *CN* 11 June 1887.
334 Quoted in Philip N. Backstrom, *Christian Socialism and Co-operation in Victorian England*, 1974, p. 177.
335 National Co-operative Archive, E.O. Greening collection, 13 Dec. 1881 (ref 16.12).
336 Modern Records Centre Warwick MSS 310/1/2/1, Labour Association minute book 1884-1887, minutes 24 Sep. 1885.
337 Modern Records Centre Warwick MSS 310/1/2/1, Labour Association minute book 1884-1887, minutes 4 Oct. 1887.
338 Modern Records Centre Warwick MSS 310/1/2/2, Labour Association minute book 1887-1889, minutes 25 Oct. 1887.
339 *CN* 22 Oct. 1887.
340 Modern Records Centre Warwick MSS 310/1/2/2, Labour Association minute book 1887-1889, minutes 25 Oct. 1887.
341 Co-operative Congress 1888 report.
342 *CN* 18 May 1889.
343 *CN* 20 June 1891.
344 Co-operative Congress 1892 report, p. 6.
345 Beatrice Potter, *The Co-operative Movement in Great Britain*, pp. 147, 155, 157.
346 Beatrice Potter, *The Co-operative Movement in Great Britain*, pp. 134, 144
347 *Morning Post*, 17 Aug. 1891.
348 L.L. Price, 'Profit-sharing and Cooperative Production', *The Economic Journal*, vol. 2, no. 7 (Sep. 1892) pp. 445-6.
349 Benjamin Jones, *Co-operative Production*, p. 249.
350 *CN* 27 May 1893.
351 Robert Halstead, 'Co-operative production viewed in the light of some first principles', 1898, pp. 3-7.
352 *CN* 22 Oct. 1887.
353 *CN* Congress supplement (31 May 1890); *CN* 8 Sep. 1894.
354 *CN* 15 June 1895.
355 *CN* 18 Jan. 1896.
356 Modern Records Centre Warwick MSS 310/1/2/5, Labour Association minute book 1896-1901, minutes 23 Aug. 1895 reported in 1896 minute book.
357 *HBT* 28 May 1897; Modern Records Centre Warwick MSS 310/1/2/5, Labour Association minute book 1896-1901, minutes 26 May 1897; *Labour Co-partnership*, vol. 3 (1897), June 1897, p. 101.
358 *Labour Co-partnership*, vol. 3 (1897), Aug. 1897, p. 142.
359 *CN* 29 Mar. 1896.

360 Co-operative Congress report 1893, p. 28.
361 *CPF Yearbook 1898.*
362 Hull History Centre, DCF/1, CPF minutes 1896-1901, minutes Feb. 1897.
363 Hull History Centre, DCF/2, CPF minutes 1901-1907, minutes 5 Nov. 1904.
364 Hull History Centre, DCF/2, CPF minutes 1901-1907, minutes 4 June 1906, 2 Aug. 1906.
365 *CN* 18 Oct. 1830; Bernard Jennings, 'Halstead, Robert', *Dictionary of Labour Biography*, vol. II, p. 158.
366 *CN* 14 Sep. 1901, 21 Sep. 1901.
367 *HBT* 24 Jan. 1913.
368 *HBT* 10 Nov. 1893, *CN* 11 Nov. 1893, 16 Dec. 1893.
369 Quoted in Bruno Jossa, Marx, 'Marxism and the cooperative movement', *Cambridge Journal of Economics* 2005, 29, pp. 3 ff; for a more comprehensive assessment of Marx's views on productive co-operation see Stephen Yeo, 'Cooperative Associations' in Tom Bottomore (ed), *A Dictionary of Marxist Thought*, second rev. ed. 1991, pp. 111-12.
370 Friedrich Engels, letter of 18 Jan. 1893, quoted in Henry Pelling, *The Origins of the Labour Party 1880-1900*, 1965, p. 123.
371 *HBT* 29 May 1896; *Yorkshire Factory Times*, 29 May 1896.
372 Jesse Gray, *Co-operation v Competition*, 1888, p. 8.
373 *CN* 3 Apr. 1886; International Co-operative Alliance, *Report of the First International Co-operative Congress*, p. 111.
374 Co-operative Congress 1895 report, p. 3.
375 *Labour Co-partnership*, vol. 1 (1894-5), p. 162.
376 *CN* 25 July 1903.
377 *Labour Co-partnership*, vol. 5 (1899), Feb 1899, pp. 20 ff.
378 *The Commonwealth*, a Social Magazine, vol. IV, 1899, no. 1 p. 3 ; no. 3, pp. 75-6.
379 Labour Co-partnership, vol. 2 (1896), July 1896, pp. 124-5.
380 Sidney and Beatrice Webb, the Draft of the First Report of the Committee of the Fabian Research Department, 'The Control of Industry' ('Can the Organisation of Industry be based exclusively on Associations of Producers?'), *New Statesman* Special Supplement on Co-operative Production and Profit-Sharing, Sat Feb. 14 1914 (vol. II, no. 45).
381 Quoted in Benjamin Jones, *Co-operative Production*, p. 23.
382 *CN* 3 Apr. 1886.
383 *CN* 7 May 1898; *Oxford Dictionary of National Biography*.
384 *CN* 7 May 1898.
385 Earl Grey, *What Co-operation will do for the People*, 1898, pp. 4-5, 8.
386 *Co-operators' Year Book 1903*, p. 143.
387 *Agricultural Economist*, vol. XLII (1909), Aug. 1909, p. 224; Lawrence Magnanie, 'An event in the culture of co-operation: national co-operative festivals at Crystal Palace', in Stephen Yeo (ed), *New Views of Co-operation*, 1988, pp. 174-86.
388 Introductory Information, Records of the Involvement and Participation Association, Modern Records Centre, University of Warwick.

389 *CN* 3 June 1882.
390 Royal Commission on Labour, Minutes of Evidence, p. 62.
391 Joseph Greenwood, 'The Place of the Labourer in Co-operation', Co-operative Congress 1877 report, p. 67.
392 George Jacob Holyoake, Inaugural Address delivered at the Nineteenth annual Co-operative Congress, Co-operative Congress 1887 report, p. 4.
393 Greenwood's home town would have been 'Ebden Brig' for most local people at this time.
394 *CN* 18 Oct. 1930.
395 Beatrice Potter, *The Co-operative Movement in Great Britain*, p. 170.
396 See for example Stephen Yeo, *Who was J.T.W. Mitchell?*, 1995, pp. 22-6, 47-51.
397 *Todmorden Advertiser and Hebden Bridge Newsletter*, 22 Mar 1894.
398 *HBT* 10 Sep. 1909; for the issue of class, see also Sheila Rowbotham, *Travellers in a Strange Country*, 1981, passim.
399 Alliance Cooperative Internationale, Deuxième Congres, tenu au Musée social, du 28 au 31 Octobre 1896, *Compte Rendu Officiel*; *CN* Nov. 21 1896, 28 Nov. 1896.
400 W.P. Watkins, *The International Co-operative Alliance 1895-1970*, 1970, p. 15; Co-operative Congress 1869 report.
401 W.P. Watkins, *The International Co-operative Alliance 1895-1970*, pp. 20-22; Johnston Birchall, *The International Co-operative Movement*, 1997, pp. 38-40.
402 ICA archives, box 4024249 padded archive envelope; Minute book ICA Committees, June 1892- 14 Aug. 1895, and 24 Nov. 1898-25 May 1904; W.P. Watkins, *The International Co-operative Alliance 1895-1970*, p. 24.
403 ICA archives box 4024249, padded archive envelope.
404 ICA archives, box 4024249 Minute book ICA Committees, June 1892-14 Aug 1895, and 24 Nov. 1898-25 May 1904.
405 ICA archives, box 4024249 Minute book ICA Committees, June 1892-14 Aug 1895, and 24 Nov. 1898-25 May 1904.
406 ICA archives, box 4024249 Minute book, 19-22 Aug. 1895 Provisional Central Ctte, 14 Nov. 1895-17 Mar. 1897, Executive Bureau and Profit sharing committee, minutes 22 Aug. 1895.
407 International Co-operative Alliance, *Report of the First International Co-operative Congress*, 1895, p. 200.
408 International Co-operative Alliance, *Report of the Proceedings of the Second Congress*, 1896, p. 117.
409 International Co-operative Alliance, *Report of the First International Co-operative Congress*, 1895, p. 67; Joseph Greenwood, *A Brief Sketch of Twenty-six Years' Work*, pp. 24-5.
410 International Co-operative Alliance, *Report of the Proceedings of the Second Congress*, 1896, pp. 37-40; ICA archives, box 4024249 supplement to Rough minute book ICA Executive Sub-Ctte, 17 Nov. 1895-20 Oct. 1897.
411 ICA archives, box 4024249, Minute book, 19-22 Aug. 1895 Provisional Central Ctte; 14 Nov. 1895-17 Mar. 1897, Executive Bureau and Profit sharing committee, minutes 12 Dec. 1895.
412 International Co-operative Alliance, *Report of the Proceedings of the Fourth*

Congress (1900), p. 37; International Co-operative Alliance, *Report of Proceedings at the Fifth Congress* (1902), p. 20.
413 ICA archives, box 4024249 Minute book, 19-22 Aug. 1895 Provisional Central Ctte; 14 Nov. 1895-17 Mar. 1897, Executive Bureau and Profit sharing committee.
414 ICA archives, box 4024249, Minute book ICA Executive Bureau, 17 Mar. 1897-24 Nov. 1898.
415 *HBT* 18 Sep. 1896; Co-operative Congress reports for 1897-1914.
416 International Co-operative Alliance, *Report of the Proceedings of the Third Congress* (1897), pp. 132ff.
417 International Co-operative Alliance, *Report of the Proceedings of the Fourth Congress* (1900).
418 International Co-operative Alliance, *Report of Proceedings at the Fifth Congress* (1902), p. 272.
419 G.J. Holyoake, *The History of Co-operation*, 1906 edition, p. 658.
420 Charles Gide, *The International Co-operative Alliance*, n.d., p. 5.
421 International Co-operative Alliance, *Report of Proceedings at the Fifth Congress* (1902), passim.
422 *CN* 9 Aug. 1902, *HBT* 1 Aug. 1902; International Co-operative Alliance, *Report of Proceedings at the Fifth Congress* (1902), pp. 427-32.
423 *CN* 9 Aug. 1902; *HBT* 1 Aug. 1902; International Co-operative Alliance, *Report of Proceedings at the Fifth Congress* (1902), pp. 427-32.
424 *Co-operators Year Book 1906*.
425 Hebden Bridge Local History Archive, Pennine Heritage collection, Lecture Notes circa 1914.
426 *Labour Co-partnership*, vol. 4 (1898), Dec. 1898, p. 191.
427 *CN* 20 June 1874.
428 Edwin Hopwood, *A History of the Lancashire Cotton Industry and the Amalgamated Weavers' Association*, 1969, pp. 68ff; Alan Fowler, *Lancashire Cotton Operatives and Work, 1900-1950*, pp. 148ff.
429 *Co-partnership*, vol. 16 (1910), Sep. 1910, p. 140; Hebden Bridge Local History Archive, Pennine Heritage collection, Lecture Notes circa 1914.
430 Joseph Greenwood, *A Brief Sketch of Twenty-six Years' Work*, pp. 30-31.
431 Women and Labour Co-Partnership, *Co-partnership*, vol. 14 (1908), July 1908, pp. 106-7.
432 The Industrial Commonwealth at Hebden Bridge, p. 11.
433 Robert Halstead, 'The Stress of Competition from the Workman's Point of View', *Economic Review*, vol. IV, Jan. 1894, pp. 46-8.
434 *Co-operators' Year Book 1915*, pp. 129-34.
435 Comprehensive information on hours worked at different times in the Nutclough's history is not readily available. Colin Spencer, *The History of Hebden Bridge* (1991), includes the following extract which is given as being taken from the *HBT* for 22 March 1894: 'Nutclough Fustian Society will commence working 56 hours per week after Easter, instead of 59 hours as hitherto, half an hour being taken off at night'. However, the *HBT* was not published on 22 March that year and the quoted reference has not been

traced. Other information on hours worked is included in the Co-operative Directory for 1893 and 1905, and Co-operative Congress reports for 1901 and 1902; see also Robert Halstead, Variation on Wages in some Labour Co-partnership Workshops (paper read before the Economic Section of the British Association, 10 Sep.1900), passim.
436 Robert Halstead, 'Variation on Wages in some Labour Co-partnership Workshops', passim.
437 Ministry of Labour (Intelligence and Statistics Department) *Profit-sharing and Labour co-partnership*, 1920, p. 143.
438 Royal Commission on Labour, Minutes of Evidence, p. 65; *CN* 25 Dec. 1886.
439 Average Wages of Workpeople since the Time of Entering the Employment of Hebden Bridge Fustian Manufacturing Society, included as Appendix XLIV, Royal Commission on Labour, Appendix of the Minutes of Evidence.
440 The Industrial Commonwealth at Hebden Bridge, p. 12.
441 Robert Halstead, 'Variation of Wages in some Labour Co-partnership Workshops', passim.
442 Royal Commission on Labour, Minutes of Evidence, p. 69.
443 Edwin Hopwood, *A History of the Lancashire Cotton Industry and the Amalgamated Weavers' Association*, pp. 37ff.
444 Edwin Hopwood, *A History of the Lancashire Cotton Industry and the Amalgamated Weavers' Association*, pp. 56ff ; Alan Fowler, *Lancashire Cotton Operatives and Work, 1900-1950*, pp. 23ff.
445 Co-operative Congress 1874 report, p. 59.
446 Royal Commission on Labour, Minutes of Evidence, p. 66.
447 *Cotton Factory Times* 22 July 1898, 5 Aug. 1898, 12 Aug. 1898, 19 Aug. 1898, 26 Aug. 1898, 2 Sep. 1898, 9 Sep. 1898, 16 Sep. 1898.
448 *Cotton Factory Times*, 7 Oct. 1898; Todmorden Weavers' Association, Jubilee 1880-1930 Fifty Years Progress, p.13; *CN* 25 Mar. 1899.
449 *Labour Co-partnership*, vol. 5 (1899), Jan. 1899, p. 9.
450 *Cotton Factory Times*, 9 Dec. 1898.
451 WYAS, TU:36/34, Todmorden Weavers Association minute book 1899-1902, inter alia see minutes for 14 Feb. 1900, 12 Mar. 1900, 11 Sep. 1900, 31 Oct. 1901, 14 Nov. 1901, 19 Nov. 1901, 28 Nov. 1901, 20 Feb. 1902.
452 The AUCO was also sometimes referred to as the Amalgamated Union of Clothing Operatives.
453 Alan Fowler, *Lancashire Cotton Operatives and Work, 1900-1950*, pp. 50ff.
454 *HBT* 7 Apr. 1899; *Oxford Dictionary of National Biography*.
455 WYAS, TU:90/1, AUCO contributions book; Margaret Stewart and Leslie Hunter, *The Needle is Threaded*, 1964, pp. 119-20.
456 Data here and in the following paragraphs in this chapter are from statistics included in the Co-operative Congress reports, published annually.
457 Source: data in Co-operative Congress reports, 1896-1909. This data set cannot be directly compared with the data set used for Figure 2, although differences between the two sets for the year 1895 (where both data sets are available) suggest relatively minor differences.
458 Source: data in Co-operative Congress reports, 1896-1909.

459 Source: data in Co-operative Congress reports, 1896-1909, *CN* and *HBT* reports for relevant years.
460 National Co-operative Archive, archive box C65, Rules of the Hebden Bridge Fustian Manufacturing Co-operative Society Limited 1908.
461 *HBT* 2 Feb. 1900, 3 Aug. 1900.
462 *CN* 1 Feb. 1890, Feb 1897, 5 Aug. 1893; *HBT* 7 Aug. 1897.
463 *CN* 5 Aug. 1893, 4 Aug. 1894, 3 Aug. 1895, 6 Feb. 1897; Labour Co-partnership, vol. 4 (1898), Mar. 1898, p. 36.
464 *CN* 4 Aug. 1894; 6 Feb. 1897; *HBT* 7 Aug. 1897.
465 Co-operative Congress 1903 report, p, 105; *CN* 24 Jan. 1903.
466 *CN* 2 Feb. 1895; 9 Apr. 1898; 6 Aug. 1898.
467 *CN* 2 Feb. 1889, 4 Feb. 1893; *HBT* 31 July 1903, 4 Aug. 1899, 3 Aug. 1906.
468 *CN* 4 July 1903; 2 Apr. 1904.
469 Modern Records Centre Warwick MSS 310/1/2/6, Labour Co-partnership Association minute book 1901-1906, minutes 29 June 1903.
470 Modern Records Centre Warwick MSS 310/1/2/6, Labour Co-partnership Association minute book 1900-1906, minutes 5 Aug. 1903, 9 Apr. 1904; Labour Co-partnership, vol. 10 (1904), Mar. 1904, p. 44.
471 *CN* 11 May 1901; Co-operators' Year Book 1902.
472 *Agricultural Economist*, vol. XXXVI (1903), no 397, 1 Jan. 1903.
473 National Co-operative Archive, E.O. Greening collection, 23 Oct. 1902 (ref. 17.44s), 5 Nov. 1902 (ref. 17.47), 18 Nov. 1902 (ref. 17.50).
474 National Co-operative Archive, E.O. Greening collection, 29 Nov. 1902 (ref 17.52).
475 *Agricultural Economist*, vol. XXXVI (1903), no. 399, Mar. 1904.
476 *CN* 3 Jan. 1903.
477 *CN* 15 June 1907.
478 Hull History Centre DCF/2, paper from Aneurin Williams, enclosed in Co-operative Productive Federation minute book 1901-1907, minutes 21 Mar. 1903.
479 *HBT* 15 May 1903.
480 Conveyance between William Sutcliffe of Sandal House, Heptonstall and Joseph Greenwood of Nutclough, 6 Oct. 1902 (privately held by owners of 1 Sandy Gate, Hebden Bridge).
481 *HBT* 31 July 1896.
482 *HBT* 2 Feb. 1906.
483 *HBT* 6 Dec. 1918.
484 HBLHS archive ref. HBLSS GEN MIN 1M, Hebden Bridge Literary and Scientific Society First Minute Book 4 Dec. 1905-11 Oct. 1913.
485 Modern Records Centre Warwick MSS 310/1/2/6, Labour Co-partnership Association minute book 1900-1906, minutes 6 Mar. 1906.
486 Aneurin Williams, 'Co-operation in Housing and Town-Building', in Co-operative Congress 1907 report, pp. 379ff.
487 International Co-operative Alliance, *Report of Proceedings at the Fifth Congress* (1902), p. 314.
488 Aneurin Williams, 'Co-operation in Housing and Town-Building', in Co-

operative Congress 1907 report, pp. 379ff.
489 *CN* 22 Apr. 1905.
490 Aneurin Williams, 'Co-operation in Housing and Town-Building', in Co-operative Congress 1907 report, pp. 379ff ; C.B. Purdom, *The Garden City*, 1913, pp. 268-9.
491 C.B. Purdom, *The Garden City*, p. 58.
492 *Co-partnership*, vol. 13 (1907), Jan. 1907, p. 11.
493 *Co-partnership*, vol. 13 (1907), Dec. 1907, p. 187.
494 *CN* 20 July 1907.
495 WYAS, ref. TU:36/445, Todmorden and district weavers, reports and balance sheets, quarterly meeting October 1907; January 1908.
496 *HBT* 1 Feb. 1907; Leslie M. Goldthorp, *The Fustian Weavers' Strike at Hebden Bridge 1906-1908*, 1982, pp. 10-11.
497 *HBT* 18 Nov. 1910.
498 *Co-partnership*, vol. 13 (1907), Aug. 1907, p. 120; *Co-partnership*, vol. 14 (1908), Feb. 1908, pp. 19-20.
499 Co-operative Congress 1896 report (data tables); Co-operative Congress 1897 report (data tables); *HBT* 31 Jan. 1896.
500 Co-partnership, vol. 15 (1909), Feb. 1909, p. 30; Labour Co-partnership, vol. 2 (1896), Oct. 1896 p. 217.
501 National Co-operative Archive, E.O. Greening collection, 16 Sep. 1907 (ref. 17.84a).
502 *CN* 9 May 1908; *HBT* 18 Nov. 1910.
503 *CN* 1 Aug. 1908.
504 *HBT* 18 Nov. 1910.
505 Joseph Greenwood, Reminiscences of Sixty Years Ago, *Co-partnership*, vol. 17 (1911), May 1911, p. 69.
506 *Agricultural Economist*, vol. XLII (1909), Oct. 1909, p. 280.
507 Joseph Greenwood, In memoriam – Joseph Craven, in Co-operators' Yearbook 1910.
508 Joseph Greenwood, In memoriam – Joseph Craven, in Co-operators' Yearbook 1910.
509 *CN* 2 Jan. 1909; *HBT* 25 Dec. 1908.
510 Modern Records Centre Warwick MSS 310/1/2/7, Labour Co-partnership Association minute book 1906-1913, minutes 6 May 1909.
511 *CN* 20 Mar. 1909.
512 Sam Greenwood's younger brother was given the name Greenwood Greenwood.
513 The Producer, Dec. 1926, pp. 53-4.
514 Oxford University archive CE3/28/3; *The Producer*, Dec. 1926, pp. 53-4.
515 *HBT* 23 Apr. 1909.
516 National Co-operative Archive, archive box C64, uncatalogued paper.
517 WYAS, architects' plans ref BIP/HB:579, /HB:631.
518 *HBT* 21 Apr. 1916; *Co-partnership*, vol. 22 (1916), May 1916, p. 56.
519 Source: data in Co-operative Congress reports, 1910-1918.
520 Source: data in Co-operative Congress reports, 1910-1918.

521 R.H. Tawney, *The Establishment of Minimum Rates in the Tailoring Industry under the Trade Boards Act of 1909*, 1915, pp. 24ff.
522 S.C. Moore, The Trades Board Act at Work. *The Economic Journal*, vol. 23, no. 91 (Sep. 1913) pp. 442-7.
523 R.H. Tawney, *The Establishment of Minimum Rates in the Tailoring Industry under the Trade Boards Act of 1909*, pp. 93, 91.
524 Much of the material in this chapter is based on correspondence between unions and the Fustian Society which has survived and is in the National Co-operative Archive, archive box C64 (uncatalogued).
525 National Co-operative Archive, archive box C64, letters n.d., 6 Dec. 1910, 1 Nov. 1911, 3 Nov. 1911, 6 Nov. 1911.
526 Arthur L. Bowley, *Prices and Wages in the United Kingdom 1914-1920*, 1921, p. 87.
527 *CN* 10 Feb. 1912.
528 *CN* 12 Sep. 1908, 19 Sep. 1908.
529 National Co-operative Archive, archive box C64, letters 28 Feb. 1912, 25 Jan. 1913, n.d. reply, 15 Feb. 1913, 16 Feb. 1913, 26 Feb. 1913, 24 Apr. 1913, 1 May 1913; Memorandum of Agreement, 23 Feb. 1913.
530 National Co-operative Archive, archive box C64, letter 18 Mar. 1915.
531 Arthur L. Bowley, *Prices and Wages in the United Kingdom 1914-1920*, p. 35.
532 Arthur L. Bowley, *Prices and Wages in the United Kingdom 1914-1920*, p. 96.
533 Private communication to author. There is also a local story that some clothing ultimately found its way to enemy armies: no evidence has been found to back up this allegation.
534 *CN* 31 July 1915.
535 National Archives, LAB 2/187/IC478/1917/Parts1and2, letter from William Gibson, CWS, 30 Nov. 1916.
536 *CN* 13 Feb. 1915.
537 *Halifax Courier*, 14 Oct. 1916.
538 Hebden Royd Town Council, *Hebden Bridge and District Roll of Honour*.
539 http://www.briercliffesociety.co.uk/Soldiers/William%20Percy%20 Greenwood.htm [Accessed Apr. 2015].
540 Hebden Royd Town Council, *Hebden Bridge and District Roll of Honour*.
541 National Co-operative Archive, archive box C64, text of speech [by A Ainley?] to workforce, n.d. [late 1916]; Hebden Bridge Fustian Manufacturing Society {A Ainley?] submission to arbitration, n.d. [late 1916].
542 National Co-operative Archive, archive box C64, letter 22 Apr. 1915.
543 National Co-operative Archive, archive box C64, letters 4 Oct. 1915; 3, 9, 11, 12 & 17 Nov. 1915.
544 M Stewart and L Hunter, *The Needle is Threaded*, p. 172.
545 *HBT* 10 Nov. 1916.
546 National Co-operative Archive, archive box C64, letter 25 Oct. 1916.
547 National Co-operative Archive, archive box C64, Hebden Bridge Fustian Manufacturing Society [A Ainley?] submission to arbitration, n.d. [late 1916].
548 National Co-operative Archive, archive box C64, letter 28 Nov. 1916, union flyer 2 Dec. 1916.

549 National Co-operative Archive, archive box C64, letters 30 Nov. 1916, n.d.
550 National Archives, LAB 2/187/IC478/1917/Parts1and 2, letters dated 24 Nov. 1916, 28 Nov. 1916.
551 National Archives, LAB 2/187/IC478/1917/Parts1and2, telegram dated 6 Dec. 1916.
552 National Co-operative Archive, archive box C64, letters 7 Dec. 1916, 9 Dec. 1916.
553 National Archives, LAB 2/187/IC478/1917/Parts1and 2, telegram dated 8 Dec. 1916.
554 National Co-operative Archive, archive box C64, arbitration award, letters from S. Craven 15 Feb. 1917, n.d. [Feb. 1917]; the arbitration award is also in the National Archives file LAB 2/187/IC478/1917/Parts1 and 2.
555 *HBT* 2 Feb. 1918.
556 National Co-operative Archive, archive box C64: unattributed [A. Ainley] speech to workforce [n.d., made on April 30 1918].
557 Percy Redfern, *The new history of the C.W.S.*, 1938, pp. 532-3, 541.
558 *CN* 7 Oct. 1905; G.D.H. Cole, *A Century of Co-operation*, p. 258.
559 Percy Redfern, *The new history of the C.W.S.*, p. 171.
560 *CN* 19 June 1915.
561 *CN* 8 May 1915, 22 May 1915, 5 June 1915.
562 *CN* 25 Jan. 1913.
563 Percy Redfern, *The Story of the C.W.S.*, pp. 333-46; *CN* 21 Dec. 1912.
564 *HBT* 11 June 1915.
565 Co-operative Congress 1916 report, p. 437.
566 National Co-operative Archive, archive box C64, miscellaneous uncatalogued papers.
567 National Co-operative Archive, archive box C64: [A. Ainley] speech to workforce.
568 National Co-operative Archive, archive box C64: [A. Ainley] speech to workforce.
569 National Co-operative Archive, archive box C64: unatttributed [A. Ainley] speech to members' meeting made on 11 May 1918.
570 *HBT* 17 May 1918.
571 *HBT* 17 May 1918.
572 National Co-operative Archive, archive box C64: [A. Ainley] speech to members' meeting.
573 The Wheatsheaf, vol. II, no. 8 (Feb. 1898), p. 114, quoted in Stephen Yeo, *Who was J.T.W. Mitchell?* p. 53.
574 Source: National Co-operative Archive, archive box C64, uncatalogued paper.
575 *CN* 25 Mar. 1916.
576 National Co-operative Archive, CWS Minute Book, 25 Oct 1918–17 July 1919, minutes 2 May 1919; The Producer magazine, 17 Mar. 1919.
577 *HBT* 2 Aug. 1918; National Co-operative Archive, archive box C64.
578 *HBT* 17 Oct. 1924.
579 National Co-operative Archive, archive box C64, letters dated 6, 8, 17 Mar. 1919.

580 WYAS, ref TU:70/7: Cragg Vale co-operative society minute book, minutes 27 Mar. 1919; ref TU: 70/12: Mytholmroyd co-operative society minute book, minutes 24 Mar. 1919.
581 *HBT* 6 Dec. 1918.
582 *HBT* 17 Oct. 1924.
583 National Co-operative Archive, archive box C65, chairman's speech at the retirement of Sam Greenwood and Jas Wm Blackburn, CWS paper dated 192x; *The Producer*, Dec. 1926, pp. 53-4.
584 *Halifax Guardian*, 13 July 1918.
585 Information from John Rhodes.
586 Bernard Jennings, 'Halstead, Robert' in *Dictionary of Labour Biography*, vol. II, pp. 154-9; *HBT* 17 Oct. 1930; *CN* 18 Oct. 1930.
587 1910 rates record for Hebden Bridge shows a Crossley Greenwood living as an owner-occupier in Sackville Street; 1911 census; marriage record 11 March 1911 in Barnet.
588 National Co-operative Archive, archive box C64, letter 20 Dec. 1918.
589 National Co-operative Archive, archive box C65, photo of award presentation for Ethel Greenwood; family research undertaken by Irene Kirk.
590 *HBT* 19 Aug. 1910.
591 Co-operative Congress reports until 1921.
592 *Halifax Guardian*, 26 Feb. 1916; *Halifax Daily Courier*, 5 Dec. 1924.
593 *Halifax Courier*, 9 Oct. 1915.
594 *CN* 13 Dec. 1924.
595 *CN* 2 Mar. 1912, 18 Jan. 1913; *HBT* 1 Mar. 1912, 24 Jan. 1913.
596 *CN* 24 Apr. 1909.
597 *CN* 14 July 1888.
598 *CN* 22 Oct. 1887.
599 Royal Commission on Labour, Minutes of Evidence, p. 68.
600 *CN* 16 July 1881.
601 *Co-partnership*, vol. 31 (1924), Feb. 1924, p. 18.
602 See for example Greig de Peuter and Nick Dyer-Witheford, *Commons and Co-operatives*, 2010.
603 *CN* 15 June 1889.
604 Beatrice Webb, *My Apprenticeship*, p. 357.
605 *CN* 9 July 1881.

INDEX

Accidents, industrial 71
Accrington 33, 158
Acland, Alice 76-77, 85
Acland, Arthur H.D. 76-77, 85
Agnetapark 133-134
Agricultural and Horticultural Association 41-42, 59, 123, 133
Ainley, Arthur 57, 158, 167-68, 173, 179-86, 188
Alcester 132
Amalgamated Union of Clothiers' Operatives (AUCO) 148-49, 170-72, 174 (see also United Garment Workers)
Amalgamated Weavers Association 161, 174
American Civil War 21, 41
Anseele, Edward 135-36
Askwith, Sir George 176-77

Bacup 17, 27, 88
Balfour, Gerald 53, 56, 145
Baptists 18, 32, 70
Barber, Reginald 165
Batley 104, 107
Belfast co-operative society 103
Belloc, Hilaire 84, 99
Birchcliffe Baptist Chapel 18, 32, 95, 158
Birmingham co-operative society 103
'Black Monday' 122
Blackburn 145
Blackshawhead co-operative society 57
Blandford, Thomas 116, 131, 134
Blatchford, Robert 119
Bolton 145
bonus to labour – see profit-sharing

Bournville 160
Brabrook, E.W. 51
Bradbury, John 57
Bradford Cabinet-makers co-operative 154
Bridge End co-operative society (Todmorden) 56
Brighouse co-operative society 57
Bright, John 49
Bristol 103, 189
Brittain, Vera 92-93
Brown, W. Henry 90
Brownfield Guild Pottery 154
Burnley 71, 102, 145, 154
Burnley Self-help Manufacturing Society 154
Bury 23, 102, 146-48

Calder Valley Poets' Society 93
Calderdale Co-operative Association 33, 57, 77, 93, 154-55, 167
Calderdale Co-operative Clog Sundries 162-63
Cambridge University 85; Summer Meetings 94 (see also University extension movement)
Capital and labour, relation between 40, 106-107, 113, 121-22, 124-25, 130, 178, 193-95
Capital, access to 26, 28-29, 66-69, 115-16, 194-95
Carlyle, Thomas 86
Central Board, Co-operative Union 6, 9, 60-62, 74-75, 77, 108, 189; North-Western section 60-61, 75
Central Co-operative Agency 4
Chambrun, le Comte de 128

Chartism 7, 16-18
Chester-le-Street 59
Christian Socialists 4, 5, 24, 29, 37, 38, 77, 103, 108, 110, 120, 122, 129, 183
Churnet Valley railway construction 19
Clarion 119
class conflict and harmony 121-22, 123-27
Cobbett, William 14
Cobden, Richard 49
Colden Cotton Company 23, 49
Conley, Andrew 175
Cooper, William 40
Co-operative College, proposal for 87
Co-operative Congress 7, 23-24, 27, 29, 33, 43, 46, 53, 60-61, 70, 76, 79, 84-85, 87, 91, 96-97, 101, 103-104, 106, 108, 109-10, 112-13, 120, 125, 129, 130-31, 134, 160, 166, 196
co-operative distribution 6, 26-27, 62, 103, 123, 191-92, 194 (see also individual societies)
co-operative dividend 7, 29, 39, 43, 79
co-operative exhibitions of goods 33, 59-60, 62, 117, 123
Co-operative Group 71, 198
co-operative housing 5, 7, 65, 135, 159-61
Co-operative Insurance Company (Co-operative Insurance Society) 6, 180-81
co-operative loan funds 115-16
co-operative production 2, 4, 5, 6-9, 23-24, 38, 40-41, 46, 54-55, 59, 74, 97, 105-107, 110, 115, 118-19, 121, 126, 132, 141, 145, 154-55, 157, 184-85, 191-96 (see also individual societies)
Co-operative Productive Federation 9, 100, 102-103, 114-17, 142, 154, 155, 157, 161, 188-89
Co-operative Union 3, 5, 7, 24, 32, 43, 60-61, 69, 95-96, 106, 114, 116, 121, 123, 130-131, 135, 145, 159; and education 95-97, 99, 153, 154 (see also Central Board)

Co-operative Wholesale Society 6, 30-31, 40, 44, 62, 65, 66, 75, 85, 99, 105-106, 123, 126, 130, 198; manufacturing operations 8, 41, 59, 102-107, 136, 172, 173, 174, 176; banking 6, 31; attitude to profit-sharing 8, 35, 41-42, 103-104, 108-109, 110-14, 116-17; acquisitions of co-operatives 155-57, 180-81; takeover of Hebden Bridge fustian society 9, 179-87, 190, 193
Co-operatives UK 3, 71
co-partnership 111-17, 120-22, 130, 134-35, 141-42, 155-57
Co-partnership Tenants' Housing Council 161
Cotton Famine 21, 41, 130
cotton spinning 16
Coventry Watchmakers' co-operative 6, 59, 78, 107, 190
Cowdenbeath co-operative society 154
Crabtree, Cressweller 186-87
Crabtree, Henry 93
Cragg Vale co-operative society 56, 57, 158, 159
Craigen, Jessie 24
Craven, Emily 82
Craven, Hannah 88
Craven, Joseph 48-51, 58, 76, 78, 82, 84-85, 87, 92, 114-16, 126, 130, 134-36, 140, 149, 157-58, 163-64
Craven, Sam 82, 87, 149, 171, 175-77
Crystal Palace – see National Co-operative Festival

Dawson, John 68
de Boyve, Eduoard 129-30
Delft 133-34
demutualisation 192-93
Derby 103, 106
Doughty, Charles 177-78
Dunfermline 59

Ealing Tenants co-operative 160
Eaves Bottom Self-Help society 161-64
Eccles 59

electricity 59-60
Engels, F. 119
Equity Shoes 184

Fabian Society 3, 120-21
Familistère, le 155
Farn, J.C. 23
Faure, Félix (President of France) 128
Fielden, John 14
Fielding, Samuel 93, 159
flour societies, co-operative 59, 106, 107, 180-81 (see also Sowerby Bridge Flour Society, Halifax Flour Society)
France, co-operation in 4, 5, 128-30, 132, 135
fraud in co-operatives, measures against 53-54
fustian cutting 15, 137
fustian dyeing 16, 138
fustian trade 1, 16

garden cities 135, 159-62
Garden City Tenants 159-60
garment making 28, 80-82, 137
Gide, Charles 135
Godin, J.-B. A. 155
governance, co-operative 51-58, 74-75
Gray, J.C. 5, 7, 10, 31-32, 58, 62, 65, 67, 74, 84, 87, 96, 113-17, 118, 119, 148, 190; on purpose of productive co-operation 7; on distribution of profits 46-47, 67; moves to Co-operative Union 69-70, 71; call for national society 70-71, 107, 181; call for restructuring of production 106-109; and international co-operation 131-36; final illness and death 70-71, 190
Greening, E.O. 41-42, 43, 44, 59, 60, 102, 103, 105, 108-109, 123, 130-34, 156, 163-64, 191-93, 197
Greenwood, Abraham 6, 17, 40, 42, 67, 78, 85, 105
Greenwood, Crossley 27, 71-72, 86, 87, 93, 154-55, 158-61, 167, 173, 189
Greenwood, Ellen 134, 189

Greenwood, Ethel 189
Greenwood, Fred 22, 71
Greenwood, Harry 22, 71, 173
Greenwood, Herbert 173
Greenwood, Joseph 1-2, 7, 64, 71, 73, 77-78, 80, 139, 142-45, 158, 196, 198; birth and childhood 12-15; religious affiliation 18; and temperance 18; early work 18-19; and Mechanics' Institute 19-21, 85; first attempt at co-operative 22, 54; establishment of Hebden Bridge fustian society 11-12, 26-29, 31-32, 34-38, 43-44, 47; and Joseph Craven 48-51, 164; and co-operative governance 51-58; expansion into weaving 65-66; and reward to capital 67-68; views on co-operative production 2, 62-63, 120, 190-92; engagement in co-operative movement 9, 24-25, 60-62, 76, 102, 104, 155-56, 161, 189; as local councillor and JP 72, 189; and university extension 84-85, 88, 90, 96; and other productive co-operatives 105; and co-partnership 108-109, 114, 123-25; and socialism and trade unionism 120, 146-48; and social class 125-27; and international co-operation 128-36; and Eaves Bottom initiative 162-64; accident 164; retirement 164-65, 167, 174, 189-92; views on CWS takeover 183-84
Greenwood, Lloyd 30, 71
Greenwood, Percy 173
Greenwood, Sam 166-70, 172, 174, 188
Greenwood, Sarah (first wife of Joseph Greenwood) 20, 27, 71, 88, 130
Greenwood, Sarah (third wife of Joseph Greenwood) 189
Greenwood, Virgil 21, 71, 173
Greenwood, William (father of Joseph Greenwood) 12, 15
Greenwood, William (son of Joseph Greenwood) 21, 71, 189
Grey, Albert (Earl), 122-23, 125

INDEX

Halifax 41, 71
Halifax co-operative society 30, 57, 67, 105, 139
Halifax Flour Society 180-81
Halstead, Robert 10, 89-94, 95-100, 101-103, 112-17, 120-21, 125-26, 141-42, 144-45, 147-48, 153, 154, 155-56, 161, 167, 188-89, 193
Hampstead Garden Suburb 160
hand loom weavers 12-13
Hardie, Keir 119, 123
Hartley, John 17, 18, 23-24, 28, 32, 35, 37, 48, 56, 60, 76, 78, 84, 105, 157, 166
Hebden Bridge 1, 9, 106, 119, 146-49, 161-62, 175-78; local economy 9, 15-16, 81, 169-70; weavers' strike 161-64; 1916 strike 175-78
Hebden Bridge branch, Women's Co-operative Guild – see Women's Co-operative Guild
Hebden Bridge Cotton and Commercial Company 22-23, 28, 50
Hebden Bridge Fustian Manufacturing Co-operative: origins 11-12, 23-25; early years 26-29; and capital 26, 28, 35-39, 66-69, 74, 151-53, 183; purchase of Nutclough Mill 30-31; growth 32-33, 63-65; rules revisions 38-39, 45, 64, 66, 67; membership 38-39, 63-64, 73-74, 140; wage levels 43-44, 142-45; profit-sharing 9, 34-39, 43-45, 47, 74, 151-52, 183; Craven joins management committee 48-50; trading difficulties 50-51, 150-53; governance and management 51-58, 110, 126, 140-41, 157-58, 191-93 ; introduction of weaving 65-66; coming of age celebrations 1-7, 83; women workers 73-82; engine naming event 109; as co-operative exemplar 115, 117, 123; international trade 132-33; working conditions 137-43; trade unionism 146-49, 169-72, 174-78; charitable and other donations 153- 54; retirement of Joseph Greenwood 164-65, 166; Sam Greenwood as manager 166-72; First World War 172-78, 179; sale to CWS 9, 179-87, 190; concluding remarks 190-93, 196
Hebden Bridge Industrial Co-operative Society 17-18, 22, 23, 27, 28, 42, 50, 56, 57, 75, 80, 98, 157, 163
Hebden Bridge Literary and Scientific Society 159
Hebden Bridge Local Board 72
Hebden Bridge Mechanics' Institute 19-21, 85, 93
Hebden Bridge Urban District Council 72
Heckmondwike 104, 107
Helliwell, Martha 75-79
Helliwell, Shackleton 75-76, 78
Heptonstall 13, 14, 16, 18, 48-49
Heptonstall co-operative society 48, 56, 57, 159, 163
Hicks-Beech, Sir Michael 124
Holt, John 181, 187
Holyoake, George Jacob 3-4, 5, 7, 30, 71, 104, 108-109, 110-11, 113, 123, 125, 128-29, 131, 135, 156
Horsburgh. E.L.S. 83-84, 91, 99
hours of work 142, 170
Howard, Ebenezer 135, 160
Howard, Robert 13-14
Huddersfield 6, 22, 40-41, 80-81, 103, 114, 120, 131, 134, 142
Hudson Shaw, G.W. 83-84, 86-87, 89, 91, 100
Hughes, Thomas 3, 4, 35, 37, 43, 65, 77, 103, 108, 109, 114, 120, 122, 126, 138

Independent Labour Party 119-20
Industrial and Provident Societies Act 22, 31, 51
Inskip, William 148
International Co-operative Alliance 3, 9-10, 128-36, 137-39, 154; 1895 Congress 129, 131-32; 1896 Congress 128-29, 132; 1897 Congress 133-34; 1900 Congress 134, 135; 1902 Congress 134-36, 137-39

Jackson, Henry 35
Jones, Ernest 16
Jones, Lloyd 29-30, 35, 42, 102, 103-105, 108, 146

Kettering 97, 123, 155
Killeen, Daniel 11-12, 24
Kings Lynn 102
Kingsley, Charles 4, 24

Labour Association (Labour Co-partnership Association) 46, 101-103, 108, 110-11, 114-16, 122, 123-25, 147, 154-55, 157-60, 164-65
Labour Party 94, 188
Lancashire & Yorkshire flannel co-operative 59, 105
Lang, Cosmo Gordon 3, 84, 86, 87, 88, 89, 90, 125-26
Lawrenson, Mary 75, 76, 79
Leeds 149, 176
Leeds co-operative society 68-69
Leek 59, 107
Leicester 41, 59, 97, 100, 102, 103, 104-105, 107, 123, 154, 155, 160, 161, 184, 188
Leicester Hosiery 155-57, 180, 186
Letchworth Garden City 159-61, 189
Littleborough 59, 105
Livesey, Joseph 18
Llewelyn Davies, Margaret 76, 96
Lomax, George 19
Luddenden and district co-operative society 56
Luddendenfoot co-operative society 56, 57

Macclesfield 132, 154
Machin, J.S. 68
Mackinder, H.J. 84, 89
Macrosty, Henry 120-21
Maddison, Fred 99, 156
Mann, James 18
Mann, Tom 118-19
Mansbridge, Albert 99-100, 116
married women and work 81
Marriott, J.A.R. 97, 101-102

Marshall, Alfred 52, 194-96
Martyn, Caroline 119, 123
Marx, Karl 118
Maurice, F.D. 4
Mazzini, Guiseppe 114
McInnes, Duncan 186
Midgehole 11, 22
Midgley co-operative society 56, 57
Mills, James 147-48
mining disasters 153
Mitchell, Frank 173
Mitchell, J.T.W. 40, 85, 105, 108, 110, 111-12, 113, 114, 185
Mitchell, Thomas 17
Molesworth, Rev. W. Nassau 24
Mondragon 107
Moore, Samuel C. 94, 95, 159, 169, 188
Moorhouse, T.E. 179-81
Morgan, Thomas 57
Moss, John 18, 19, 21
multi-stakeholder co-operatives 39, 42-43, 193
Mundella, A.J. 54-55
Mytholm 16
Mytholmroyd 12, 19, 42, 71, 102, 158, 162, 188
Mytholmroyd co-operative society 27, 55, 56, 57, 93
Mytholmroyd Manufacturing society 162

National Co-operative Festival 123, 130-31, 167
National Society of Dyers and Finishers 148, 171-72, 174-75
Neale, Edward Vansittart 4-5, 7, 24, 29, 35, 37-38, 41-42, 46, 60, 65, 67, 69-70, 77, 85, 87, 102, 103, 104, 106, 107, 108-109, 111, 114, 120, 122, 130-31, 139, 159, 183, 192
Needham, T.H. 176
Newark 154
Newbottle co-operative society 154
Newell, George 155
Non-conformism 18, 49 (see also Baptists, Wesleyans)
Northern Star 16-17

Norwich 102, 110
Nottingham 103
Nowell, William 94-95, 159
Nutclough Mill purchase 30-31 (see also Hebden Bridge Fustian Manufacturing Co-operative)
Nuttall, William 105-106, 110

O'Connor, Feargus 16-17
Oldham 22, 84, 91, 97, 160, 180
Ouseburn Engine Works 105
Owen, Robert 153
Owenism and co-operation 3, 24
Oxford University 76, 83-100, 101, 125, 184; Summer Meetings 92-95

Paisley 59, 107
Pankhurst, Emmeline 162
Pecket Well co-operative society 56
Peterborough 102
Peterloo massacre 12
Pickles, George Herbert 87, 94, 140
Pickles, Thomas 57, 87, 140
Plug Riots 16
Plymouth 70, 103, 106, 140
Portsea Island 103
Potter, Beatrice (Beatrice Webb) 3, 52, 54, 69, 70, 88, 110-11, 121, 125-26, 140, 197
profit-sharing 2, 8-9, 23, 40-47, 103-104, 108-109, 111-13, 120-22, 128, 131-32; at Hebden Bridge fustian society 34-39, 151-52, 183, 191 (see also co-partnership)

Rechabites, Order of 18, 49, 93
Reddish, Sarah 75
Reform Act 1884 86
Ripon, Marquess of (George Robinson) 5, 7, 97, 109, 122, 128
River Pollution Prevention Act 138
Robert, Charles 130
Rochdale 49, 130, 145, 180, 188, 197
Rochdale Equitable Pioneers 3-4, 6-7, 17, 24, 40, 49, 129, 136
Royal Commission on Hand-Loom Weavers 14

Royal Commission on Labour 12, 31, 52-54, 56, 58, 125, 142-46, 191, 198
Royal Commission on Secondary Education 96
Rushworth, Jemima 94-95
Ruskin College 93, 94
Ruskin, John 6, 24, 80, 90

Sadler, Michael 86, 87, 97, 102
St Helens 154
Scarborough 102
Scottish Co-operative Wholesale Society 8, 30, 65, 103, 109, 114, 117, 180
Sevenoaks Tenants 160
Shaw, Arthur 171, 174
Shaw, George Bernard 161
Sheffield 59
Shillito, John 44
Shufflebotham, Charles 6, 78
Shufflebotham, Miss 78
silk mills 17, 18
sizing of cloth 139
Smith, George 67
Smith, Joseph 69
Social Democratic Federation 122
socialism 118-22
Society for Promoting Working Men's Associations 4
Sowden, Rev Canon 83
Sowerby Bridge 84
Sowerby Bridge co-operative society 57
Sowerby Bridge Flour Society 49-50, 59, 60, 163, 180-81
Speak, John 57, 76
Stocks, Leonard 71, 86, 88, 130, 134-35, 147-48, 154, 166-67, 172-73, 174, 177, 181-82, 186-87, 188, 189
Stocks, Mary 88
strikes 104-105, 146-48, 153, 161-64, 175-78
Sunderland co-operative, Coronation Street initiative 94
Sutcliffe, Adam 57
Sutcliffe, Marianne 79

Talbot, Rev Edward 92
Tawney, R.H. 170
Taylor, Sedley 108
temperance movement 18-19, 49, 93
Tenant Co-operators 159-60
Thomson, George 6, 80-81, 134, 142
Todmorden 16, 17, 28, 41, 84, 89, 91, 94, 139, 146, 162
Todmorden Co-operative Society 17, 56, 57, 67, 76, 91, 98, 181
Todmorden Weavers' Association 145, 148, 161, 174
Toothill, John 57
Toynbee, Arnold 84-85, 87, 91
Trade Boards Act 169-70
trade unions 21, 118, 145-49, 161-64, 169-72, 174-78
TUC 146
TUC/Co-operative Union Joint Committee 146, 148, 172, 176, 177
Tweddell, Thomas 185

United Association of Power-Loom Overlookers 148, 174
United Garment Workers union 175-78
University extension movement 83-100, 101, 153, 154, 167, 169, 184, 191

van Marken, J.C. 133-34
Vivian, Henry 101-102, 116, 131, 134, 155-56, 159-60, 163

Wainstalls co-operative society 56
Walmsley, Thomas 174
Walsall 132
Walsden 89, 162
Walsden co-operative society 56
War, First World 172-78
Watts, John 108
Webb, Beatrice – see Potter, Beatrice
Webb, Catherine 74
Webb, Sidney 3, 121
Wesleyans 18
Whiley, Henry 42
Whittaker, Thomas 18
Wigan 154
Williams, Aneurin 133, 157, 160
Wilson, Mona 149
Wolff, Henry 131, 134
women and co-operative governance 74-75
women workers 28, 31, 73-82, 121, 137, 141, 149, 175-78
Women's Co-operative Guild 10, 75-76, 78-79, 80-81, 89, 94, 137; Hebden Bridge branch 75-81
Women's Trade Union League 149
Wood, Thomas 181
Woodhouse Mills 6, 80-81, 134, 142
Woolwich 97, 103
workers' co-operatives 10, 56, 192-93 (see also co-operative production)
Workers' Educational Association 10, 100, 116
working-class education 10, 19, 83-100, 114
working-class joint-stocks 22-23, 37, 38

York 103
Young, Joseph 171, 177